Structural Transformation and Rural Change Revisited

D1342272

Structural Transformation and Rural Change Revisited

Challenges for Late Developing Countries in a Globalizing World

Bruno Losch
Sandrine Fréguin-Gresh
Eric Thomas White

A copublication of the Agence Française de Développement and the World Bank

Cover photo: Bruno Losch. A street in Ségou, Mali. *Cover design:* Debra Naylor, Naylor Design, Inc.

Library of Congress Cataloging-in-Publication Data
Losch, Bruno.
    Structural transformation and rural change revisited : challenges for late developing countries in a globalizing world / by Bruno Losch, Sandrine Fréguin-Gresh, and Eric Thomas White.
        p. cm.
    Includes bibliographical references and index.
    ISBN 978-0-8213-9512-7 — ISBN 978-0-8213-9513-4 (electronic)
    1. Agriculture—Economic aspects—Developing countries.   2. Rural development—Developing countries.   3. Economic development—Developing countries.   4. Developing countries—Economic conditions.   I. Fréguin-Gresh, Sandrine, 1977–   II. White, Eric Thomas, 1981–   III. Title.
    HD1417.L67 2012
    338.1091724—dc23
                                                                                          2012011116

Africa Development Forum Series

The **Africa Development Forum series** was created in 2009 to focus on issues of significant relevance to Sub-Saharan Africa's social and economic development. Its aim is both to record the state of the art on a specific topic and to contribute to ongoing local, regional, and global policy debates. It is designed specifically to provide practitioners, scholars, and students with the most up-to-date research results while highlighting the promise, challenges, and opportunities that exist on the continent.

The series is sponsored by the Agence Française de Développement and the World Bank. The manuscripts chosen for publication represent the highest quality in each institution's and have been selected for their relevance to the development agenda. Working together with a shared sense of mission and interdisciplinary purpose, the two institutions are committed to a common search for new insights and new ways of analyzing the development realities of the Sub-Saharan Africa region.

Advisory Committee Members

Agence Française de Développement
Pierre Jacquet, Chief Economist
Robert Peccoud, Director of Research

World Bank
Shantayanan Devarajan, Chief Economist, Africa Region
Celéstin Monga, Senior Adviser, Development Economics and Africa Region
Santiago Pombo-Bejarano, Editor-in-Chief, Office of the Publisher

Sub-Saharan Africa

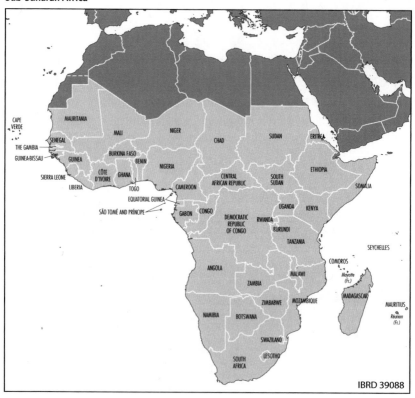

CAPE VERDE

MAURITANIA

THE GAMBIA
SENEGAL
GUINEA-BISSAU
GUINEA
SIERRA LEONE
LIBERIA

MALI

BURKINA FASO
BENIN
CÔTE D'IVOIRE
GHANA
TOGO

NIGER

NIGERIA

CHAD

CAMEROON

EQUATORIAL GUINEA
SÃO TOMÉ AND PRÍNCIPE
GABON
CONGO

CENTRAL AFRICAN REPUBLIC

DEMOCRATIC REPUBLIC OF CONGO

SUDAN

SOUTH SUDAN

UGANDA
RWANDA
BURUNDI

ERITREA

ETHIOPIA

SOMALIA

KENYA

TANZANIA

ANGOLA

ZAMBIA

ZIMBABWE

NAMIBIA
BOTSWANA

MALAWI

MOZAMBIQUE

SWAZILAND
LESOTHO

SOUTH AFRICA

COMOROS
Mayotte (Fr.)

MADAGASCAR

SEYCHELLES

MAURITIUS
Réunion (Fr.)

IBRD 39088

Titles in the Africa Development Forum Series

Africa's Infrastructure: A Time for Transformation (2010) edited by Vivien Foster and Cecilia Briceño-Garmendia

Gender Disparities in Africa's Labor Market (2010) edited by Jorge Saba Arbache, Alexandre Kolev, and Ewa Filipiak

Challenges for African Agriculture (2010) edited by Jean-Claude Deveze

Contemporary Migration to South Africa: A Regional Development Issue (2011) edited by Aurelia Segatti and Loren Landau

Light Manufacturing in Africa: Targeted Policies to Enhance Private Investment and Create Jobs (2012) by Hinh T. Dinh, Vincent Palmade, Vandana Chandra, and Frances Cossar

Empowering Women: Legal Rights and Economic Opportunities in Africa (2012) by Mary Hallward-Driemeier and Tazeen Hasan

Informal Sector in Francophone Africa: Firm Size, Productivity, and Institutions (2012) by Nancy Benjamin and Ahmadou Aly Mbaye

Financing Africa's Cities: The Imperative of Local Investment (2012) by Thierry Paulais

RURALSTRUC

The RuralStruc Program on the **Structural Dimensions of Liberalization in Agriculture and Rural Development** is a joint initiative of the World Bank, the French Cooperation (French Development Agency, Ministry of Agriculture and Fisheries, Ministry of Foreign, Agricultural Research Centre for International Development—CIRAD) and the International Fund for Agricultural Development. It is managed by the World Bank.

With a duration of five years (2006–2010), its objective was to analyze the processes of liberalization and economic integration and their impacts on agriculture and the rural sector of developing countries. It also aimed to illustrate the situation of rural economies in terms of income, diversification, and overall transformation. The results obtained make it possible to improve the dialogue between national and international partners and to provide orientations for the agricultural and rural policy debates.

The program adopted a comparative approach across seven countries—Mexico, Nicaragua, Morocco, Senegal, Mali, Kenya and Madagascar—which correspond to different stages of the processes of economic and demographic transition. The Program's work was conducted with teams of national experts and researchers. Two phases were implemented: a first phase providing an overview of each country's dynamics (2006–2007), and a second phase comprising sectoral and regional case studies, supported by rural household surveys (2007–2010).

http://www.worldbank.org/afr/ruralstruc

AGENCE FRANÇAISE
DE DÉVELOPPEMENT

IFAD

Liberté • Égalité • Fraternité
RÉPUBLIQUE FRANÇAISE
MINISTÈRE
DE L'AGRICULTURE
ET DE LA PÊCHE

Liberté • Égalité • Fraternité
RÉPUBLIQUE FRANÇAISE
MINISTÈRE
DES
AFFAIRES ÉTRANGÈRES

cirad
AGRICULTURAL RESEARCH
FOR DEVELOPMENT

Contents

For editorial reasons, detailed annexes are not provided in this book.
See the appendix posted at http://www.worldbank.org/afr/ruralstruc

Boxes

Figures

Tables

Foreword

Following a long dormancy, structural issues are again ascendant in development economics. After enjoying prominence in the aftermath of the Second World War, structural economics was largely banished from the Washington Consensus that emerged in the 1980s. Now, however, a new development thought is arising that takes a more nuanced view. It acknowledges the important role of markets yet maintains the need for tailored approaches to development that allow a more active role for the state, and that are more reflective of economic realities—what I referred to as *New Structural Economics.*

Structural Transformation and Rural Change Revisited—Challenges for Late Developing Countries in a Globalizing World is an extremely thorough and important contribution to this renewal of structural economics. It significantly improves our understanding of rural economies and structural transformation, and it could not be more timely.

The book is based on the results of the RuralStruc program, implemented through a strong collaborative framework in seven countries and coordinated by Bruno Losch. Launched in 2006 at a time when the international dialogue on agricultural policy had become trapped in trade issues, and was therefore missing the broader perspective of rural change, the program foresaw the need to reinvest in structural issues. Its results add value to the *World Development Report 2008,* which served as a first reminder of agriculture's role for development. They revive an old paradigm to offer a new perspective, one that challenges much current thinking on rural development, notably for countries at the first stages of their structural transformation.

Relying on a methodology that articulated microdata collection with a macrostructural perspective, the program conducted extensive fieldwork to investigate livelihood strategies of rural households, and married the results with a thorough understanding of structural change. The book highlights recurring patterns of diversification and specialization along the process of structural transformation. Further, reconnecting with a broader vision, it emphasizes the difficulties faced by late developers, whose economies offer few alternatives for households to diversify. This is particularly the case for Sub-Saharan Africa, where a still incipient economic transition and the ongoing demographic transition result in a quickly growing labor force, leading to dramatic challenges for the youth of the continent.

Based on their assessment, the authors draw a series of policy lessons. They rightly point out the importance of states rebuilding their internal capacities to design comprehensive development strategies. These capacities are critical to addressing major constraints, defining priorities, and ensuring adequate sequencing. Above all, they show that for Sub-Saharan Africa, in the coming two decades, a strong reinvestment in agriculture (in addition to seizing opportunities for the development of manufacturing and services) will be the major policy tool for progressively raising income, mitigating risks, and fostering innovation and rural demand, which constitutes the main engine for rural diversification—a major step for structural transformation. The authors also stress the role of the state in provisioning public goods, in adequately and carefully designing incentives, and in using the leverage offered by the development of small towns as a critical mechanism for rural change. These are all sensible and useful reminders for the donor community, governments, and local stakeholders, and represent an important contribution to the role of agriculture for development.

Justin Yifu Lin
Senior Vice President and Chief Economist
The World Bank

Acknowledgments

This book is dedicated to the memory of Jacques Faye (1946–2010), rural sociologist and founding member of IPAR (Initiative Prospective Agricole et Rurale, Sénégal)

This book is one of the many outputs of the World Bank's Program on the "Structural Dimensions of Liberalization on Agriculture and Rural Development" (RuralStruc). During the four-year implementation of RuralStruc's two phases, and a fifth year dedicated to producing a synthesis document and beginning to disseminate results, the program collaborated closely with numerous experts and researchers in its seven participating countries.

RuralStruc's activities were implemented under the guidance of Bruno Losch (TTL, World Bank, and CIRAD). The fieldwork was developed with the support of a coordination team that included Bruno Losch, as well as Sandrine Fréguin-Gresh and Thierry Giordano (French Ministry of Foreign and European Affairs), respectively based at the University of Pretoria (Postgraduate School of Agriculture and Rural Development) and the Development Bank of Southern Africa.

The program was initiated with the full support of John McIntire, sector director of ESSD Africa. The peer reviewers of the program's objectives and design were Louise Cord and Robert Schneider (World Bank) and Camilla Toulmin (IIED). The program's development was enhanced by guidance from Karen Brooks, sector manager (AFTAR), and Stephen Mink, senior adviser (AFTSN), who was involved in every step of the process. Shanta Devarajan, chief economist for the Africa region, and Justin Yifu Lin, Senior Vice President and Chief Economist, provided strong support to the dissemination of results.

The final report of the program on which this book is based was prepared by Bruno Losch, Sandrine Fréguin-Gresh, and Eric Thomas White (World Bank), with substantial contributions from Thierry Giordano and Jean-François

Bélières (CIRAD). It was peer-reviewed by Derek Byerlee and Don Larson (World Bank), and André Pouillès-Duplaix (AFD).

The results presented in this book draw extensively on two sets of seven country reports and data work developed by the country teams during the two phases of the RuralStruc program. The authors and contributors to the national reports are as follows:

Kenya: Lilian Kirimi, Mary Mathengue, John Olwande, and Betty Kibaara (Tegemeo Institute); Paul Gamba, Sam Onyuma, and Job Lagat (Egerton University).

Madagascar: Alain Pierre-Bernard, Rivo Ramboarison, Lalaina Randrianarison, Nicole Andrianirina, and Lydia Rondro-Harisoa (APB Consulting).

Mali: Amadou Samake, Bino Teme, Ousmane Sanogo, Manda Sadio Keita, and Aly Ahamadou (IER); Jean-François Bélières, Pierre-Marie Bosc, Christian Corniaux, Jacques Marzin, Denis Gautier, and Kako Nubukpo (CIRAD); Nango Dembele, John Staatz, and Valerie Kelly (Michigan State University); the late El Hadji Oumar Tall, and Bakary Sékou Coulibaly (CEPIA).

Mexico: Fernando Saavedra, Fernando Rello, Hector Robles, Christian Muñoz, and Claudio Gonzalez (FLACSO); Virginie Brun (IRD/CEMCA); Eric Leonard (IRD); Rafael Palma Grayeb (Universidad Veracruzana).

Morocco: Najib Akesbi and Driss Benatya (Institut Agronomique et Vétérinaire Hassan II), and Noureddine El Aoufi (Université Mohammed V) for Phase 1; Icon2e for Phase 2.

Nicaragua: Arturo H. Grigsby Vado, Francisco J. Perez, Ligia I. Gómez, Edna S. García, Miguel A. Alemán, and Yuri L. Marín (Universidad Centroamericana, Instituto Nitlapán).

Senegal: Cheikh Oumar Ba, the late Jacques Faye, Ibrahima Hathie, Pape Nouhine Dièye, Bocar Diagana, Adama Faye, Madické Niang, and Mamadou Dansoko (IPAR and ASPRODEB).

Jean Coussy (Ceri-Sciences Po) and Jean-Jacques Gabas (Université Paris X–Orsay and CIRAD) participated in the program's preparation and in its launching workshop in Senegal (April 2006), as well as several dissemination events. Jean-Jacques Gabas also led two Sciences Po Paris student workshops (2006 and 2007) and was involved in preparing several of the program's policy briefs. Eric Léonard (IRD) provided specific support on Mexico.

Additional contributions were received from Emmanuelle Benicourt (consultant) and Véronique Meuriot (CIRAD). Emilie Losch designed the program's logo and Erin O'Brien took charge of editing the national reports as well as draft versions of the final report.

World Bank staff who contributed to the overall RuralStruc program included Bruno Losch (TTL), Patrick Labaste and Michael Morris (successive TTLs of the RuralStruc multidonor trust fund), Eric Thomas White, Malick Antoine, Angela Lisulo, Benjamin Billard, James Keough, Beatriz Prieto-Oramas, and Ingrid Mollard. Hawanty Page and Germaine Mafougong-Ethy were in charge of the program's administrative support. Jeff Lecksell and Bruno Bonansea prepared the maps based on information provided by the RuralStruc national teams.

The program benefited from the guidance of its Advisory Committee, chaired by C. Peter Timmer (Cabot Professor of Development Studies, emeritus, Harvard University) and including Kirsten Albrechtsen de Appendini (Colegio de México), Pierre-Marie Bosc (CIRAD), Peter Gibbon (Danish Institute for International Studies), Catherine Laurent (Institut National de la Recherche Agronomique), Jean-Luc Maurer (Institut des Hautes Etudes Internationales et du Développement), Sandra Polaski (Carnegie Endowment for International Peace), Marc Raffinot (Université Paris–Dauphine), and Sibiri Jean Zoundi (Sahel and West Africa Club, OECD).

The program also benefited from careful follow-up by a Steering Committee consisting of RuralStruc's contributing donors (Agence Française de Développement, French Ministries of Foreign and European Affairs, and of Agriculture and Fisheries, Centre de Coopération Internationale en Recherche Agronomique pour le Développement, International Fund for Agricultural Development, and World Bank), chaired successively by Florence Lasbennes (Ministry of Foreign and European Affairs) and Marie-Cécile Thirion (Agence Française de Développement).

About the Authors

Bruno Losch is a Senior Economist at the World Bank and a Research Director at CIRAD (Centre de coopération internationale en recherche agronomique pour le développement). In his current position he has been leading the RuralStruc Program, a joint initiative of the World Bank, IFAD, and the French government. In Cirad, he was in charge of the Family Agriculture Program and then joined the University of California–Berkeley as a visiting scholar. He holds a Master's in political science and in geography and a PhD in economics and has published extensively in the field of rural studies, public policies, and the political economy of development.

Sandrine Fréguin-Gresh holds a Master's in Agricultural Sciences and in Geography and PhD in Agricultural Economics. She is research fellow at CIRAD, where she has developed research on contract farming and rural transformation in Africa, Central America, and the Caribbean. After a visiting position at the University of Pretoria, South Africa, she was seconded to the Institute for Research and Development Studies—Nitlapan—of the Central American University, Managua, Nicaragua, where she is in charge of research projects on the labor market, migrations, and agrarian transformation.

Eric Thomas White is a World Bank consultant and a Managing Associate at the international development consulting firm INTEGRA LLC, where he leads the firm's practice in Information and Communications Technology (ICT) for Agriculture. His previous consulting assignments have included the African Development Bank and the Millennium Challenge Account–Zambia. In a earlier career, he served as a Lieutenant in the U.S. Navy. He holds a Master's in Public Administration in International Development from the Harvard Kennedy School, and a BA in Economics from the University of Virginia.

Abbreviations

AFD	Agence française de développement
AgEAP	share of economically active population engaged in agriculture
AgGDP	share of agriculture in GDP
CAADP	Comprehensive Africa Agriculture Development Program
CAFTA-DR	Central American–Dominican Republic Free Trade Agreement
CIRAD	Centre de coopération internationale en recherche agronomique pour le développement
DDA	Doha Development Agenda
EAP	economically active population
EqA	equivalent adult
FAO	Food and Agriculture Organization of the United Nations
FDI	foreign direct investment
FTA	free trade agreement
FTZ	free trade zone
GAFSP	Global Agriculture and Food Security Program
GNP	gross national product
H1, etc.	Hypothesis 1, etc.
HHi	Herfindahl-Hirschman index
IAASTD	International Assessment of Agricultural Knowledge, Science and Technology for Development
ICT	information and communication technology
IFAD	International Fund for Agricultural Development
IFOAM	International Federation of Organic Agriculture Movements
ILC	International Land Coalition
ILO	International Labour Organization
IPCC	Intergovernmental Panel on Climate Change

kcal	kilocalorie
LCU	local currency unit
LDCs	least developed countries
LSMS	Living Standards Measurement Studies
LSMS-ISA	LSMS Integrated Surveys on Agriculture
MDGs	Millennium Development Goals
MoHS	mean of household shares
NAFTA	North American Free Trade Agreement
NbEAP	number of economically active population
NEPAD	New Partnership for Africa's Development
OECD	Organisation for Economic Co-operation and Development
PPP	purchasing power parity
REC	regional economic community
RIGA	Rural Income Generating Activities project
RNFE	rural nonfarm economy
RuralStruc	Program on the Structural Dimensions of Liberalization on Agriculture and Rural Development
SoRM	share of regional means
SSA	Sub-Saharan Africa
UNCTAD	United Nations Conference on Trade and Development
UNECA	United Nations Economic Commission for Africa
UN-Habitat	United Nations Human Settlements Programme
UNIDO	United Nations Industrial Development Organization
UNRISD	United Nations Research Institute for Social Development
WDI	World Bank's World Development Indicators
WDR	World Bank's yearly World Development Reports
WTO	World Trade Organization

Overview

The last 40 years of world history have witnessed dramatic changes. The population of the planet has grown by 3.2 billion people—a near doubling—and for the first time more people live in cities than in rural areas. The advent of a global open economy, boosted by technological progress and the growing importance of emerging economies in the international political landscape, has greatly modified the world's development prospects.

Over the next 40 years, the world's population will grow by an additional 2.3 billion people, and urbanization will come to affect 70 percent of humanity. The abrupt nature of this change in demography, occurring over less than a century, raises the issue of sustainability. The world's growth trajectory is simultaneously challenged by the depletion of natural resources, the consequences of climate change, and the high risks associated with asymmetric economic development among the world's regions.

A long-standing international debate about the multiple challenges of a 9-billion-person world (not least regarding how to feed all these people) is now growing more intense. However, focusing on overall figures tends to divert attention from other equally important facts related to the dynamics of population growth and distribution. A major shift is the continued marginalization, in terms of world population share, of the developed world (or the world of the "first developers"). In 2050, North America and Europe combined will account for only 15 percent of global population. Asia will remain the world's most populous region, but the relative weights of the populations of Sub-Saharan Africa (SSA) and Europe will be reversed compared with 1960 (10 percent for SSA and 20 percent for Europe in 1960, and the reverse in 2050). This major population realignment will exacerbate existing inequalities in access to resources.

Meanwhile, despite continued urbanization, 2.8 billion people will still live in rural areas in 2050. Rural populations will still be massive and will still earn their living primarily from agriculture. Regional differences in urban dynamics will strongly affect the distribution of rural populations: South Asia and Sub-Saharan

Africa will together account for nearly two-thirds of the world's rural population, and uniquely, in SSA the rural population will continue to grow.

These trends are of major importance because they challenge the prospects for development in much of the world. Agriculture is more than just the production of food. Because agriculture is the core activity and main source of livelihood for billions of rural people, its evolution will shape the process of economic, social, and environmental change. The situation is especially challenging in SSA, where the lack of economic diversification—reflected most notably in the region's anemic rate of industrialization—limits options for employment outside agriculture and the informal sector. Over the next 15 years, as a consequence of demographic dynamics, 330 million youth (who have already been born) will enter the labor market—a figure roughly equivalent to the current population of the United States. Of these, 195 million will live in rural areas, and rural activities will have to provide them with jobs. Otherwise they will migrate to cities or to neighboring countries, where they will contribute to the growing economic, social, and political difficulties that result from mega-urbanization and mass migration.

Economies characterized by a large rural population and slow industrialization will have to focus on creating rural employment, although economic diversification and management of urban growth remain critical objectives. The evolution of agricultural and rural development policy in the next two decades will be decisive for the continued fight against poverty, for economic development, and for political stability.

From the WTO Debate to the Food Price Crisis—A Missing Long-Term Vision

The RuralStruc program was initiated in 2005 in the context of an intense international debate about the liberalization of agricultural markets and the resulting consequences for farming in developing countries. RuralStruc's main goal was to provide a renewed perspective on agriculture and its role in development. Specifically, it aimed to reconnect the issues related to trade liberalization with the broader discussion of rural transformation and the evolution of rural economies in a rapidly globalizing world.

The program was carried out over a five-year period (2006–2010) during which time the scope of the international debate on agriculture changed dramatically. Three main issues affected this debate: (1) growing concerns about the consequences of global climate change, which culminated in the 2009 Copenhagen Summit; (2) the world food price crisis; and (3) the world financial crisis and its impacts on growth. These issues remain high on the agenda and continue to focus international attention on agriculture, as evidenced by the implementation of an Agricultural G20.

Amid the evolving international debate, the World Development Report 2008 on Agriculture for Development (WDR08) offered a strong and well-argued reminder of the central role of agriculture in the development process and its importance as a contributor to poverty alleviation. Although the report's full incorporation into the policy agenda was delayed by the food price crisis and the subsequent need to focus on more pressing short-term issues, its contribution to the debate is invaluable.

The originality of the WDR08 was in adopting a regional approach based on different stages in the process of structural transformation. It introduced the idea of the "three worlds of agriculture," which correspond to the different roles played by agriculture at different stages of a country's development. The first of these worlds consists of countries whose economies rely heavily on agriculture for growth and employment ("agriculture-based countries"); this world includes most of Sub-Saharan Africa. The second world of agriculture corresponds to "transforming countries," found mainly in South and East Asia, where rapidly rising rural-urban disparities and the persistence of extreme rural poverty are major sources of social and political tension. The third agricultural world refers to "urbanized countries," including most of Latin America, where agriculture can help reduce the remaining rural poverty through better integration into modern food markets and the development of environmental services.

Although the conceptualization of these three worlds facilitated the design of policy recommendations, some of the challenges countries face were overlooked. These included demographic issues (notably population growth and its consequences for employment) and asymmetries in competitiveness that result from globalization.

Consideration of these issues calls into question the viability of the historical pathway of structural transformation, which involves the progressive shift from agriculture to industry and then to services. The underlying dynamic of this economic transition (a key component of structural transformation) is increased productivity in agriculture, which fosters technical change and allows labor and capital to flow to other economic activities. Simultaneously, economies experience a broad geographic restructuring as labor moves from scattered activities (agriculture) to more concentrated ones (industry), and urbanization processes accelerate. This process of change translates into higher incomes, greater wealth, and improved living conditions, which, along with medical progress, initiate the demographic transition (the progressive, though staggered, reduction of mortality and birth rates). The result is a population that grows rapidly at first, then stabilizes.

This evolutionist vision, based on statistical evidence from past transitions, is challenged by today's world, which suggests that it is important to adopt a more contextual historical perspective to understand the ongoing process of structural change. The "moment in time" matters, because opportunities, constraints, and the balance of power evolve continuously throughout world history.

Three characteristics from previous transitions must be kept in mind. First, the Western European and North American transitions that occurred over the 19th and the better part of the 20th centuries cannot be disconnected from European and American political hegemony, which reduced or eliminated competition and created captive markets that were very lucrative. Access to these markets strongly facilitated economic specialization and industrialization. Second, the European transition was boosted by a unique outflow of international migrants that smoothed the adjustment of European economies and improved their ability to deal with labor surpluses. Between 1850 and 1930, nearly 60 million Europeans migrated to the New Worlds, 35 million to the United States alone. Third, the Latin American and Asian transitions started during a very specific period of self-centered national development that characterized the international regime between the 1929 crisis and the current era of globalization, which began at the end of the 1970s. This developmental regime was characterized by import substitution, protection, and strong state intervention, all of which contributed to economic modernization. In Latin America the economic transition started between the two World Wars; in Asia it began in the 1950s. Additionally, both regions benefited from massive assistance programs that resulted from the Cold War.

Today, the situation for developing countries in the early stages of structural transformation is drastically different. Sub-Saharan Africa—the last region of the world to embark on the structural transformation process—faces the challenges of an incipient economic transition and an unachieved demographic transition in the context of a global open economy and under the constraints of climate change.

Late developers—which include most of the countries in Sub-Saharan Africa—enjoy certain advantages that their predecessors lacked. They can reap the benefits of technological progress and past experience, and can take advantage of new opportunities to access global markets. At the same time, they face new constraints, such as huge asymmetries in productivity, increased international competition (notably from the big emerging countries), and environmental degradation. These contextual challenges, as well as the instability of the international environment, drastically constrain their room to maneuver in managing structural change, particularly when it comes to improving the livelihood prospects of fast-growing populations.

The Research Program

This challenging contextual background shaped the design of the RuralStruc program, which had three specific objectives: (1) contribute to the analytical knowledge base on structural change and its effects on agriculture and the rural economy in developing countries; (2) feed and improve international and national debates by promoting and reconnecting these issues; and (3) provide perspectives for policy making. The program's motto was "Better understanding for better policy making."

The program design was based on three interrelated hypotheses. The first hypothesis (H1) is that the global restructuring of agrifood markets and the increasing asymmetry of international competition are leading to growing differentiation among farm, marketing, processing, and distribution structures. The second hypothesis (H2) is that the income sources and activity patterns of rural households change to include more off-farm activities in response to these more competitive and challenging global markets. The third hypothesis (H3) is that marginalization processes in agriculture and the difficulties rural households encounter in adapting to this new context (especially in situations characterized by the absence of effective alternatives to farming) sometimes lead to impasses within the process of structural transformation. The third hypothesis is particularly relevant for the first of the three worlds of agriculture; namely, the agriculture-based countries.

The RuralStruc program used a comparative approach to address these hypotheses. To draw lessons from the various ways rural economies adapt to the global context of change, seven countries at different stages of structural transformation and economic integration were selected for study. Kenya, Mali, Madagascar, and Senegal are at an early stage of the economic transition, and are part of the first of the three worlds of agriculture. Morocco and Nicaragua are at an intermediate stage in their transformation process: Although agriculture remains critical in the economies of both countries, its role is declining. Mexico, an upper-middle-income economy, is much further ahead in its transformation process, has become deeply integrated with its northern neighbors through the North American Free Trade Agreement (NAFTA), and forms part of the World Development Report's "urbanized world" (WDR08).

Program activities were implemented through a collaborative process involving national teams in the seven countries: These teams were deeply involved at every stage of program development, including preparation, implementation, analysis, dissemination, and discussion of results. Phase 1 of the program was dedicated to the production of a series of broad overview documents summarizing what was known in every country about processes of rural change. This exercise exposed the weakness of the empirical knowledge base regarding the characteristics of rural economies, particularly concerning the livelihood structures and income-generating activities of households. The only information available came in the form of case studies, undertaken with various objectives and using various methodologies, which prevented them from being used systematically.

On the basis of this information, program developers decided to engage in primary data collection through field surveys. Around 8,000 rural households in 26 regions of the seven participating countries were interviewed in early 2008 (note that the survey was implemented before the full development of the food price crisis). The interviews focused on the activities and incomes of the participating households. The resulting data set provided a unique, single-shot representation of rural income structures that was comparable across the surveyed regions because it used a common methodology. Since the surveys were carried out at a single point in time, dynamic analysis was not possible. However, because the surveys used the same methodology at the same point in time, yet were carried out in different regions at different stages of economic development and featuring different levels of integration into the global economy, a dynamic interpretation of results at the cross-regional and cross-country levels was possible. This interpretation allowed the program to investigate the drivers of rural transformation and contribute to the debate on economic transition and structural change.

The Persisting Role of Agriculture and the Extent of Rural Poverty

The analysis revealed a diverse array of rural situations that nevertheless had a number of important characteristics in common. First was the continued dominance of agriculture as an economic activity in all the surveyed regions. Ninety-five percent of surveyed households were engaged in on-farm activities: producing crops, growing livestock, or processing products on the farm. However, some regions were significantly more diversified: Tequisquiapan (Queretaro state) in Mexico, where only 30 percent of households rely on on-farm activities, and Souss in Morocco, where no more than 75 percent of households are farm households.

In addition to high levels of involvement in agriculture, the surveyed regions were characterized by widespread poverty, particularly in Sub-Saharan Africa (SSA). Median incomes (which offer a better overview of the rural reality than regional averages) were estimated between $0.5 and $2 PPP (purchasing power parity) per person per day in the SSA regions (except Nakuru North in Kenya, where it is $3). The non-SSA regions had higher incomes (between $1.5 and $5.5 PPP). Dealing with averages, 70 percent of SSA surveyed households earn less than $2 PPP/person/day, and 40 percent suffer from $1/day poverty. In some regions, notably Mali, this figure can reach as high as 80 percent.

Examining the poorest 20 percent of households in a given surveyed region, rather than looking at the region as a whole, expresses the reality of poverty even more dramatically. This bottom quintile suffers from $1/day poverty in every region in the survey outside of Mexico, even in regions that were originally put in the "winning" group, owing to their good connections to markets and strong asset endowments. Further, average incomes in the top quintiles are usually pulled up by a very small number of households that are significantly better off than the others and that benefit from very specific social and economic conditions.

A consequence of high poverty levels is that households face very high levels of risk, which limit their investment capacity and their ability to innovate. This dire situation is complicated for households that also face food insecurity. When earnings are converted from $PPP into kilocalories (kcal) using local prices, a substantial share of households in all surveyed regions had difficulty meeting their minimum daily caloric requirements: In 11 of the 19 surveyed zones in SSA, the bottom quintile was, on average, unable to provide 2,450 kcal/person/day. Two regions in Nicaragua exhibited the same situation.

These results concerning the importance of on-farm income and the widespread prevalence of poverty, even in otherwise heterogeneous rural economies, colored the investigation of each of the program's three hypotheses. In the case of the SSA countries, the data suggested that, whatever farm differentiation processes have been initiated or strengthened by globalization and the subsequent increasing integration of world food markets, none have been deep or profound enough to have a macro-level effect on rural economies in the surveyed regions. The data also suggested that no matter what other activities households may have diversified into as a rural nonfarm economy developed, few have been able to leave agriculture altogether, and few of the households that stayed in rural areas escaped poverty. At the other end of the transition gradient, the case of Mexico showed that even when differentiation processes are extensive and many households leave agriculture, rural poverty can remain quite substantial. In these economies, many households in the lowest quintiles are still poor—below the $2/day line and sometimes below $1/day.

Similarly, the differences in income levels and patterns of income distribution observed among rural areas of the seven countries say something about structural transformation. In SSA, the overwhelming majority of rural households are poor, but inequality among them is limited (Gini indexes built on the sample range from 0.35 to 0.45). In Morocco and Nicaragua, which are moving more quickly in the transition, average rural incomes are notably higher, but inequality is quite severe (Gini indexes between 0.6 and 0.7). In Mexico, which had the highest median rural incomes in the sample, Gini indexes are quite low (0.4). There, the issue of inequality in rural areas has been displaced by that of rural-urban inequality. The concern in Mexico is the increasing marginalization of rural areas. Mexican regions had the largest gap in the sample between surveyed household incomes and national GDP per capita: The latter is four to seven times the former.

Farm Production, Markets, and Differentiation Processes

Over the past decade, the agricultural economics literature has brimmed with accounts of farmers in developing countries integrating into the market economy. Case studies abound that describe how producers have forged new connections with high-value markets, achieved vertical integration through contracts, and reaped the benefits of the so-called "supermarket revolution." Although these processes are under way in several regions of the developing world, their impact can be overstated, especially when it comes to the proportion of farmers involved in this new world of agriculture. New opportunities do exist, but they are often strongly localized in specific regions and, above all, affect a relatively limited number of producers. In any given country, while thousands or even tens of thousands of farm households may have benefited from the development of integrated value chains, hundreds of thousands or even millions of other households remain embedded in more traditional types of agriculture—a situation exemplified by the well-known Kenyan horticulture success story (the second-largest commodity export of the country, horticulture exports involve less than 50,000 of Kenya's more than 3.5 million farm households).

The Importance of Staples and Self-Consumption
Among surveyed households, a commonly observed characteristic of production is the importance of staples, usually a cereal: rice in Madagascar, Mali, and Senegal, complemented by millet and sorghum in the last two countries; wheat in Morocco; and maize in Kenya, Mexico, and Nicaragua. Ninety-eight percent of the surveyed households in SSA and 76 percent in non-SSA regions are engaged in staple production. In the RuralStruc sample, staples represent on average 62 percent of farm output. In SSA, they often constitute as much as 80 percent. In non-SSA countries, where more products are grown, the situation is more varied. Production of staples is around 45 percent in Nicaragua and Morocco, although the figure was lower in Morocco during the survey year, because drought affected the relative share of wheat. Specialization in maize in the surveyed regions in Mexico is related to specific incentives.

The pervasive importance of staples reflects the fact that risk levels, and sometimes food insecurity, have led a large proportion of SSA households to remain at least partly and significantly engaged in subsistence farming. These households do not simply produce staple crops; they consume a large portion of their own output. Self-consumption, depending on the region, accounts for about half of production. Extremes are found at one end of the spectrum in Mali (75 percent in Diéma or Tominian) and at the other end in Mekhé, in Senegal (less than 20 percent). Outside Sub-Saharan Africa, the self-consumed share of farm output is lower (20 percent to 30 percent), although poorer quintiles in Nicaragua rely heavily on subsistence farming (up to 60 percent). The extremely low level of self-consumption in the Mexican regions is the consequence of a restructuring of the nation's maize industry following the implementation of NAFTA.

Generally, the share of self-consumption decreases with rising wealth at both the household and regional levels. Surveyed households in Sub-Saharan Africa are less advanced in this process, because they are poorer. The prominence of self-consumption in the survey reflects two complementary effects that limit smallholder farmers' participation in markets. The supply effect refers to risk management strategies that households employ to retain control over their food supply—a direct response to incomplete and imperfect markets. The demand effect refers to weak demand for products because of poor access to and integration with markets, or the fact that production surpluses are too low to attract buyers.

Marketing by Traditional Means

These observations express a dual reality. Rural areas—notably in Sub-Saharan Africa—continue to engage in subsistence farming, even though improved connectivity to markets is an established fact. Households that do not sell any products are unusual, and a large majority of them also purchase food products produced by others.

In the surveyed regions in SSA, traditional marketing patterns persist. Most private collecting agents rely on informal strategies based on trust to obtain output from farmers, and contractualization remains low, even among farms that are firmly integrated into markets through ongoing relationships with wholesalers or agro-industries (this is the case in monopsonistic situations like cotton in Mali). However, some local agribusinesses do make use of contracts (tomatoes in the Haut Delta, Senegal; milk in Antsirabe and green beans in Itasy, Madagascar; sugar cane in Kenya), and modern marketing systems are more prevalent in non-SSA countries. Contractualization rarely occurs at the producer level and most often occurs downstream, between the wholesaler, collection unit, or producers' organization and the processing firm or procurement service (for example, the dairy industry in Nicaragua).

Where on-farm diversification has occurred, it has done so without any discernible pattern. The surveys revealed heterogeneous examples of on-farm diversification that have developed in response to region-specific opportunities. These include the legacy of a colonial cash crop (cotton in Mali, groundnut in Senegal, coffee in Kenya); a specific investment by a foreign firm (green beans produced by Lecofruit in Madagascar); or local entrepreneurship enabled by public investment in infrastructure (booming shallot production in the Office du Niger irrigation scheme in Mali).

With reference to the program's first hypothesis, the conclusion is that households in the RuralStruc surveys participate in rural economies that have not been radically reshaped by vertical integration and the supermarket revolution (the unique situation of the Sotavento region in Mexico is an exception). It is not surprising that new agricultural production systems featuring nontraditional connections to markets are rare. Farm differentiation, where it occurs, primarily reflects differences in levels of existing household assets rather than new kinds of connections to markets, and likely simply illustrates the characteristics of local agrarian systems.

The Importance of Household Assets

Additional evidence for this conclusion is provided by econometric work investigating the determinants of farm income in surveyed households. A strong finding of this regression work is that household earnings from farming depend largely on traditional determinants of income rather than on more modern factors. A particularly striking result is the widespread importance of land as a top determinant of farm income (significant in 22 of the 30 surveyed zones, making it the most commonly significant variable in the survey). This suggests that expanding acreage under cultivation is generally more worthwhile than using fertilizer or improved seed varieties.

A large herd and a small number of family members were found to be the next largest contributors to per capita household income, while market integration and the use of modern farm inputs (seeds and fertilizer) did not seem to matter as much. Although the survey did not collect detailed information on the practices of farmers and did not allow for a fine-tuned understanding of farming systems, a noteworthy finding was that market integration does not necessarily lead to improved incomes. A link between the two is context-specific. For example, the income effects of contractualization are highly differentiated, and depend on where the contracts are concentrated on the income spectrum (poor households can be in a situation of heavy dependence, tightly bonded to the processor) and on the regional context (especially the existence of competition).

Off-Farm Diversification and the Reshaping of the Rural Economy

Given the extent of poverty observed in the survey, the risk levels of households (including all types of risks related to climate, pests, prices, and market access) are a major issue and a major determinant of livelihood strategies. Households that face high levels of risk in their agricultural activities often seek income opportunities outside the farm; consequently, a large majority of surveyed households engage in off-farm activities (75 percent, on average). The figures are higher in SSA (80 percent to 95 percent) and lower in non-SSA regions, where more on-farm specialization is observed.

Despite these general tendencies, the degree of development of the rural nonfarm economy remains uneven, and the rural off-farm sector is often characterized by high levels of self-employment, provision of petty services, and few formal opportunities to earn a wage. The picture that emerges from the survey data is quite far removed from the buoyant rural economy frequently described in the literature.

Uneven Opportunities for Diversification

Diversification patterns are most often a combination of four main categories of income: agricultural and nonagricultural wage labor, self-employment, and transfers.

Agricultural Wage Labor. Agricultural wage employment is a common off-farm activity (reported by one-quarter of the sample) and can help the poor supplement their on-farm income between cropping seasons. However, agricultural wages are generally not very high. Quoted wages (which are usually listed in reference to the peak season, when labor demand is high) are $2–$4 PPP/day in the surveyed regions in SSA and $10–$15 PPP/day outside SSA. Agricultural jobs are almost always seasonal and provide a very limited return aggregated over the year. Although many rural households engage in this work, it is a limited complement to farming activities. The only way agricultural wage labor can help households escape from poverty is for a household member to secure a permanent job, which might pay $7 PPP/day in Senegal and as much as $9 PPP/day in Mexico. But these opportunities are too scarce to provide a sustainable solution for many.

Nonagricultural Wage Labor. Nonagricultural wage employment is a limited option, mostly found in regions with unique endowments of resources, infrastructure, and services. Only 15 percent of the surveyed households engaged in this activity, and the percentage varied considerably across the studied regions. Nonagricultural wage labor opportunities are found mainly in non-SSA countries; they appear only sporadically in SSA. An example is the maquiladoras (labor-intensive industrial units) in Tequisquiapan (Mexico) and Terrabona (Nicaragua), where an apparel industry has developed in rural areas. In SSA, especially in rural areas, this kind of manufacturing work is scarce; nonagricultural wage labor mostly consists of jobs in the service industries. These jobs are generally poorly paid and in the informal sector, although some formal sector jobs can be found (for example, in civil service or tourism). The most lucrative opportunities are usually available to households that are already well-off, with ample human and social capital.

Self-Employment. Self-employment is prevalent everywhere. It is the most common source of off-farm income in most of the surveyed regions and the main diversification option for the poorest households. In SSA, as well as in the Sotavento (Mexico), 40 percent to 80 percent of the surveyed households were engaged in self-employment. In Morocco, Nicaragua, and Tequisquiapan (Mexico), where there are more economic options (waged jobs), the incidence of self-employment is dramatically lower (5 percent to 15 percent). Self-employment activities are almost always carried out at the micro-level and are often based on the performance of odd jobs. Two main self-employment patterns can be distinguished: positive diversification (generally a full-time activity), in which self-employment contributes significantly to household income, and neutral diversification, in which the poorest and most marginalized households develop coping or survival strategies by engaging in minor self-employment activities with very low returns. Positive diversification is accessible mostly to better-off households—those with more or better assets and the ability to make an initial investment (for example, a grinder, a sewing machine, or welding equipment). Other types of self-employment, especially types related to coping strategies (for example, petty trade), could rightly be considered a form of underemployment and do not represent a good option for the alleviation of poverty.

Transfers. Transfers contribute significantly to the income of rural households. Although public transfers related to farm subsidies and safety nets were observed only in Mexico, they factored quite heavily in household incomes (for example, contributing between 12 percent and 20 percent in the Sotavento region). Private transfers related to migration (remittances) are more common but difficult to quantify. They were reported by 24 percent of the households in the sample, most of them in regions with strong historical patterns of migration. The importance of remittances depends on the type of migration (long term or short term) and the destination (national or international, to high-income countries or neighboring countries). However, remittances make up a significant share of income in only one region (40 percent in Diéma, Mali). In the other regions where they occur, they generally account for between 5 percent and 15 percent of total household income (Morocco, Nicaragua, and Senegal), except in Kenya and Madagascar, where they are insignificant. Households in poor quintiles often engage in short-term migration with the goal of reducing the number of mouths to feed during the dry season. In these cases, remittances are often very limited or even nonexistent, and the living conditions of the migrants can be dire.

Rural Adaptation That Mirrors Overall Structural Change

In addition to the direct income benefit of migration in the form of remittances, a network effect also can provide indirect returns. Improvements in transport and communication infrastructure allow for a new kind of household organization in which family members contribute to household income from different locations, where they are engaged in different economic activities. These "archipelago systems" facilitate greater diversification and risk management, improve the economic prospects of households, and offer new perspectives for rural change. This pattern was observed several times in the RuralStruc sample.

With reference to the program's second hypothesis (H2), the overall characteristics of off-farm diversification illustrate heterogeneous processes of adaptation and rural transformation. They somewhat mirror the economic transition as a whole: initial diversification that generates very low returns at the early stages of structural transformation and a more mature diversification that consolidates the process of change at later stages. These characteristics are a reminder that proximity to an area of high population density is not enough to stimulate economic growth. The characteristics of urbanization count, especially the infrastructure, public goods, and services that are critical for the intensification of rural-urban linkages.

The Diversification-Income Relationship and Rural Transformation

Many of the RuralStruc survey results are quite sobering. Most of the surveyed households in SSA, as well as significant shares of the sample in the three non-SSA countries, are very poor and continue to engage extensively in subsistence farming. For households in the lowest income quintiles, food security is a major challenge. Opportunities to engage in off-farm activities offer very weak returns or are accessible only to the already well-off, and vertical integration and contractualization processes are not well developed.

However, the surveys also turned up some more hopeful results. Levels of income vary among countries and regions, and—outside SSA—considerable evidence shows that average incomes are rising. The situation is also improving in some SSA regions; for example, Bas Delta in Senegal and Nakuru North in Kenya. In Morocco and Nicaragua, falling levels of risk and improving market opportunities have allowed some households to engage in more on-farm diversification. In these two countries and in Mexico, the increasing number of economic options has facilitated higher returns from off-farm activities. This trend is most obviously exemplified in Tequisquiapan (Mexico), where 70 percent of rural households are no longer directly engaged in agriculture. Although this trend can result in a critical form of marginalization for households that cannot access wage employment, the average household is better off. In this region, among households with farms (30 percent of the sample), those that have one member working in a wage-earning activity have the highest per capita income levels.

To explore the extent of these processes of change, the phenomena of diversification and specialization were studied more closely, as was their relation to income levels. Two indicators (the Herfindahl-Hirschman index and the share of income earned from off-farm sources) were used to illustrate the extent to which rural households and regions have moved away from on-farm activities as a source of livelihood. Several trends were identified. First, households in surveyed zones in the richer, non-SSA countries tend to have lower levels of off-farm diversification. This result was somewhat surprising, as structural change is generally considered to be associated with increases in income and moving away from a reliance on farming.

Second, at the subnational level, no clear pattern was seen. In some countries, richer surveyed regions were more diversified; in others, they were less diversified. Within surveyed regions, the effect was equally muddled. However, regardless of the direction of the diversification-income relationship, the difference in diversification levels among income quintiles was pronounced, indicating a strong interaction between the two factors.

The Inverted U: A Perspective on Processes of Rural Change

To explain these observations, it was hypothesized that the diversification-income relationship is characterized by an inverted U shape. At very low income levels (where households focus on survival strategies), diversification of income sources is uncommon and households are fully engaged in farming. As income levels start to rise and households become slightly richer, they remain at risk (especially from adverse shocks) but develop more room to maneuver and to build safety nets. As incomes continue to grow, households begin to diversify their activities to cope with risk and to find additional revenues. In this stage, diversification takes place only at the household level (within-household diversification), while the region remains highly specialized in agriculture. The process of diversification continues to the point at which households develop enough of a wealth and asset base that they can earn sufficient returns through specialization to meet their basic needs and manage their risks. At this point, households begin to specialize into different activities—some on-farm, others off-farm—and the result is a more diversified regional economy on the whole (between-household diversification).

An indicator was developed—the diversification gap—to serve as a proxy for a region's progress along this continuum. The very strong correlation observed between the diversification gap and household income suggests that regions in the RuralStruc survey tend to move along the inverted U path as they develop. The diversification-income relationship appears to include an exponential component: Once a region "turns the corner" and households begin to specialize economically, income growth at the aggregate regional level, which was previously quite slow, seems to take off rapidly and lead the region on a path out of poverty.

Poverty Traps and the Elusive Rural Nonfarm Economy

A significant finding of the RuralStruc analysis is that most of the surveyed regions in Sub-Saharan Africa are lagging in their progression along the inverted U. In fact, many African households seem to hit an invisible wall in the transition process where they cannot earn enough money through income diversification to become secure in their livelihoods (a result of low returns to available off-farm income-generating activities). Consequently, they never turn the corner and begin to specialize. They seem to be trapped in structural poverty, an observation that confirms the difficulty of rural transformation as well as the program's third hypothesis—that the globalization process includes the risk of transition impasses.

Finally, in the sample, the process of specialization at the final stage of the inverted U path occurs mainly in agriculture, while specialization in other economic activities is observed less frequently. This striking outcome can be explained by a methodological bias related to the fact that the survey was implemented only in rural areas and thus tends to inform mainly about specialization processes in the farming sector. Households that specialize in nonfarm activities often do so in urban areas, meaning that they frequently migrate. In addition, and perhaps more fundamentally, this result reflects the somewhat ephemeral nature of the rural nonfarm economy, which tends to simultaneously grow and dissolve itself as a result of the urbanization process. Not only do off-farm specializers migrate to urban areas, but urban areas expand as rural boroughs grow into small cities. This phenomenon of "cities moving to the country" is a consequence of increasing demographic densities and of the territorial expansion of cities related to the urban growth process itself.

Main Policy Outcomes

The RuralStruc survey results tell a story about rural transformation and provide a framework for understanding the evolving trends of diversification and specialization. Furthermore, they show the importance of national characteristics (for example, country assets, market functionality, business climate, institutional arrangements, overall governance, and political stability) that determine how much room to maneuver is available to households as they struggle to escape from poverty. The RuralStruc survey results provide important insights into the specific situation of the late developers, exemplified by the surveyed regions in SSA, where the fact that countries are still in a very early stage of the economic transition limits households' opportunities for income diversification and access to high-return activities.

The inverted U pattern is not deterministic; rather, it provides a conceptual framework to help explain where regions stand in the diversification-specialization process. This framework allows people to think systematically about changes that occurred in the past and to enumerate the possible causes of observed transition impasses. It does not predict future developmental paths, as these will depend on the idiosyncrasies of the local context and the nature of its interactions with the outside world.

For the many rural regions in Sub-Saharan Africa that are caught in a poverty trap, solutions will have to come from contextualized policy interventions at the country level, as well as initiatives capable of bringing about stronger regional integration. The best way to approach SSA's lagging transition is to introduce policies that can promote rural growth by simultaneously fostering and meeting rural demand. An important lesson from past transitions is that rising farm incomes trigger rural demand. To ensure that this demand is met with an adequate supply of goods and services, governments must support local investments through the provision of public goods.

This rural development strategy is sensible for all developing countries; it is critical for SSA countries. In non-SSA countries, the program also found a marginalized rural population combined with high urban-rural inequality—a situation that is not politically sustainable.

General Guidelines

The huge challenges of poverty alleviation, rural growth, and economic transition have no easy solutions. In the absence of a silver bullet, a long shopping list of potentially helpful policy measures has emerged from the past two decades of rural development practice. The main components of this list are the improvement of imperfect markets (by lowering transaction costs); the development of missing markets (for credit, technical support, and insurance); the provision of public goods (infrastructure, research, information, and capacity building); and the introduction of risk-mitigation mechanisms.

Procuring all the ingredients for an effective policy regime is challenging; finding the exact recipe for success is even more difficult. Policies must be tailored to local circumstances, so the most difficult task is to identify the combination of policy measures that will be effective in a particular context. This process includes making critically important choices in terms of prioritization and targeting. In most countries (not only the developing ones), an important issue for policy makers is the pressing need to address a multitude of problems at the same time, which is usually not possible owing to financial and human resource constraints.

On the basis of the program results, which show a very strong heterogeneity of situations among countries, among regions, and among households, two major recommendations for policy making can be advanced: (1) reengage in development strategies at both the national and subnational levels, and (2) implement regional diagnoses.

Reengaging in Development Strategies. Overall strategy design has been neglected over the past decades as a result of state withdrawal, excessive segmentation in sectoral policy making (leading to "stovepiping"), and the deterioration of public information and statistical systems—a major handicap for policy makers.

In this context, reinvesting in knowledge creation is an urgent priority. As illustrated by the country reviews carried out during Phase 1 of the RuralStruc program, general socioeconomic information is deficient, and the data needed to understand the dynamics of evolving rural economies are especially scarce. Public data collection and reporting systems (statistical systems) must be reinvigorated and redefined, and capacity in public agencies to collect and report data must be complemented by capacity to analyze the data and formulate relevant policy conclusions. If this does not happen, policy makers will be unable to design measures to deal with evolving rural economies, the increasing mobility of people, and the resulting new organizational patterns of households (such as the archipelago system). Reengaging in development strategies at both the national and subnational levels implies reinvesting in processes. Consultation is a requirement to secure ownership—the determining factor of shared vision and commitment. It takes time, adequate planning, and a significant effort in capacity building to manage information systems, analyze results, and monitor processes.

Implementing Regional Diagnoses. Regional diagnoses are indispensable to prioritize objectives, target interventions, and sequence actions. A useful approach is to identify the binding constraints to agricultural growth—the necessary first step for increasing rural demand and fostering rural diversification—and then design policies to address them. These policies must make choices, identity targets, plan, and then monitor the implementation of interventions. An important caveat is to avoid becoming trapped in monosectoral policy making (for example, focusing exclusively on agricultural problems) and to embrace broader approaches that reconnect agriculture to rural development and rural development to a comprehensive framework of integrated multisectoral and regional development (an approach sometimes referred to as "territorial development").

These two recommendations relate to the methodology of policy making and do not prescribe any particular set of interventions. Specific policy measures formulated on the basis of these recommendations should reflect country-specific circumstances and processes. Specific assets or strong natural advantages (for example, in mining or tourism) can offer additional room to maneuver in supporting new activities and rural transformation.

Building Blocks

Still, for a large majority of rural situations, where households are deeply engaged in farming, it is possible to suggest some major policy orientations or building blocks. Policy makers should keep these in mind when devising targeted development strategies aimed at overcoming poverty traps and facilitating the overall process of rural transformation. Three building blocks can help governments avoid shopping lists of urgent policy needs. They are relevant to the specific circumstances of the late developers (particularly countries in Sub-Saharan Africa) and are based on the main findings of the program. They focus on the following critical areas: (1) supporting family farms, (2) promoting staple crops, and (3) strengthening rural-urban linkages for territorial development.

Supporting Family Farms. The RuralStruc program results provide arguments for supporting family farms and contribute to the debate about optimal farm size, which has been reignited by the food price crisis of 2008 and the related increase in land grabbing, notably in Africa.

A false dualism lies at the heart of this debate. It sets smallholder and subsistence agriculture on one side against large-scale and commercial agriculture on the other, when the reality is a continuum in which family farming is nearly always the dominant mode of production. Family agriculture—as opposed to large-scale managerial or capitalist agriculture—feeds most of the world. Family farms can be subsistence oriented, commercially oriented, or a combination of the two. A large body of empirical evidence shows that family farms can be competitive in terms of production costs compared with large-scale managerial farms. In Sub-Saharan Africa, family farms are often competitive in the domestic market but disadvantaged in global markets owing to factors unrelated to their size (for example, the economic and institutional environment).

The current focus on food security has overshadowed the multifunctionality of agriculture (specifically its ecological, economic, social, and cultural roles); family farms, because they are embedded in the local context, are the major stakeholders in this sector. The concern for food security has also led many policy makers to overlook the role of agriculture as a source of employment and a driver of structural transformation over the medium term. Family farms, because they rely heavily on labor-intensive production methods, have the largest capacity to absorb the rapidly growing labor force (195 million rural youth in the next 15 years in SSA). In contrast, managerial agriculture, which is much more likely to be capital intensive, offers fewer prospects for generating major labor opportunities.

Investments in large-scale commercial agriculture (including foreign investments) can offer important opportunities for growth, diversification of markets, and development of sparsely populated areas, but they should be evaluated in terms of the employment they are likely to generate. Investments in large-scale commercial agriculture should be focused on segments of the value chain that lack capital (input supply, marketing, transformation), with the goal of unleashing the huge potential of family farms to increase production.

Supporting family farms can mean many different things, but this book avoids presenting a long list of recommendations. Rather, it suggests three kinds of action to address the most critical problems: (1) securing land rights, (2) providing public goods, and (3) supporting farmers' organizations.

Securing land rights. Farm households face high levels of risk. The first steps toward achieving a more secure environment are to facilitate access to farmland and to secure land rights, both necessary conditions for investment and innovation. There is a need to facilitate land access to youth and to ease the transmittal of farm assets to young family workers.

Providing public goods. Most family farms are severely constrained by their very low capacity for investment, a consequence of long-lasting poverty. Selective targeting of direct support can help overcome this constraint, but an even more effective measure is to increase the provision of public goods, notably information, training, and capacity building for farmers, as well as rural infrastructure (small-scale irrigation, roads, power generation and transmission structure). Infrastructure can also, when possible and appropriate, facilitate access to sparsely populated areas and encourage internal migration.

Supporting farmers' organizations. Because of their small size and limited production capacity, many family farms are unable to capture economies of scale in sourcing inputs, marketing outputs, and transforming products. This constraint can often be overcome through collective action: Providing support to farmers' organizations can improve integration into value chains, facilitate contracting with downstream agents, and strengthen the bargaining power of producers.

Promoting Staple Crops. In countries with agriculture-based economies, four major evidence-based arguments can be advanced for giving priority to staple crops. The first argument stems from the ubiquity of staple crop production. In most developing countries, the overwhelming majority of farm households are involved in staple crop production (90 percent, on average, in the RuralStruc survey), so targeted policies that promote the production and marketing of staple crops can have important effects on the overall rural economy in terms of labor, income, and growth. The ratio of producers involved in staple crop production to producers engaged in production of other crops is easily 10 to 1, and often much higher.

The second argument in favor of giving priority to staples is related to the critical role played by staple crops in risk management. Because food markets in rural areas often do not work well, many rural households are vulnerable to periods of food shortage and, consequently, often retain a significant share of their output for self-consumption. By reducing risk, increased production of staples can unlock the potential for technical innovation, speed on-farm diversification, and encourage participation in modern value chains.

The third argument in favor of priority for staples is related to the huge potential of the staple food sector. For the foreseeable future, demand for food will grow steadily, fueled by population growth and urbanization. Even if rising incomes lead to shifts in consumption patterns, staples—especially cereals—will account for the majority of food demand for years to come. Additionally, rising food prices are creating progressively better returns and preventing competition from low-priced imports.

The fourth and final argument for promoting staple crop production is that it can add value at the local level because of the huge potential for local processing of products. This scenario could strongly contribute to strengthening rural-urban linkages and rural diversification.

Policy measures to increase the productivity of staple crops and improve staple markets are diverse and varied. In the case of Sub-Saharan Africa, however, two entry points seem obvious: (1) reduce postharvest losses and (2) unlock regional trade.

Reducing postharvest losses. Postharvest losses are a recurring problem against which very little progress has been made. The economic cost of these losses is high (10 percent to 20 percent in cereals, and probably more in roots, tubers, and plantains), and the burden is borne mainly by farmers. Technical solutions are available, but efforts are needed to adapt institutional and financial arrangements to facilitate the cost-effective use of storage systems (for example, warehouse receipts).

Unlocking regional trade. Sub-Saharan Africa is a potentially huge market, but access is currently constrained by the political fragmentation of the continent and multiple recurring barriers to trade. Even though some progress has been made in fostering better regional integration, regional trade continues to lag as a consequence of nontariff barriers, lack of enforcement of regional trade agreements, and the high transaction costs associated with overland transportation. The most promising interventions for jump-starting regional trade are improving infrastructure networks and, above all, strengthening the political will of the members of regional economic communities.

However, supporting staple crops is not an overall strategy. Because of the relatively low value of these crops compared with other commodities—for example, horticulture crops or livestock and livestock products—productivity increases in staple crops cannot be the only solution for poverty alleviation. Other opportunities, when they exist, must be seized.

Strengthening Rural-Urban Linkages for Territorial Development. The development of strong linkages between small cities and their surrounding rural areas is particularly critical for development. Historically, rural-urban linkages were forged as a result of growth in rural demand for goods and services, which generated new productive activities that naturally concentrated in rural boroughs and small towns so as to benefit from economies of scale. In recent decades, this scenario has changed: Urbanization around the world has increasingly been characterized by rapid "metropolization" in and around large cities, which concentrates economic activity even more and offers superior job prospects. Metropolization is a consequence of better transportation and information networks, and it has given rise to large-scale migration directly from rural areas to metropolitan areas. In many cases, migrants completely bypass the smaller towns in which rural-urban and on-farm/off-farm linkages could be formed. And even when they stay in small and mid-size cities, they create an informal urbanization that takes place without adequate public goods and services. This constrains sustainable urban development and prevents the formation of strong urban-rural linkages.

Strengthening the intermediate level of territorial development by promoting the economic vitality of towns and small cities—the so-called "missing middle"—seems to be an important step for fostering rural transformation in the context of globalization (which tends to favor long-distance over short-distance networks). Interventions in this area can offer win-win solutions that not only create better local market opportunities, facilitate access to services, strengthen communities, and contribute to the weaving together of a region's economic and social fabric, but also reduce the burdens of mega-urbanization. This kind of regional rural-urban dynamic is more flexible and does not create such a stark contrast between urban and rural conditions; it allows for the possibility of working on both sides of the rural-urban divide and creates a strong basis for a more sustainable rural nonfarm economy. This perspective acknowledges the multifunctionality of agriculture and the fact that it can be a driving force for rural and regional development. Two kinds of action can strengthen rural-urban dynamics: (1) improve urban services and (2) empower local institutions.

Improving urban services in small cities. To link towns and small cities with their immediate surroundings and strengthen their economic functions, transportation infrastructure is key. However, as revealed by the RuralStruc surveys in the well-connected rural areas of western Kenya and Senegal's *bassin arachidier*, road infrastructure alone is not sufficient to foster growth and territorial development. The adequate provision of a range of other public goods and services is critical and should be a major objective for policy makers. Provision of health and education services—as well as assured supplies of water, electricity, and telecommunications—is paramount. Most of these goods and services cannot easily be provided by the private sector during the early stages of development, but fiscal incentives can be introduced that encourage private service providers and entrepreneurs to participate more actively in some of these areas. This kind of improvement in services and specific supports (especially in terms of capacity building and credit access) can strengthen nonfarm activities, especially the small-scale enterprises that complement a growing farm sector and are the main ingredient of a buoyant territorial development.

Empowering local institutions. Parallel to the improvement of public goods and services, it is important to strengthen local institutions and local governance systems, and to facilitate the decentralization process, which in many countries has been more de jure than de facto. Building strong capacity in the government agencies and civil society organizations that are active at that level is a major first step to foster an effective integrated local development strategy. Decentralized decision-making power embedded in well-functioning local institutions offers the most promising opportunity to identify local assets and resources that can be employed in the pursuit of balanced and sustainable territorial development.

Chapter 1

Setting the Scene and Selecting the Tools

The RuralStruc program, initiated in 2005 in the context of an intense international debate on the liberalization of agricultural markets and the resulting consequences on farming in developing countries, aimed to provide a new perspective on agriculture and its role in development. Specifically, the program was implemented to reconnect issues related to trade liberalization with the broader discussion of rural transformation and the evolution of rural economies within globalization (see box 1.1).

This initiative was motivated by the lack of systematic information on the processes under way in the rural economies of developing countries and by the question of what these processes mean for structural change and economic development. Themes such as farmers' integration into global value chains, migration and remittances, the development of a rural nonfarm economy, and possible futures for agriculture are commonly investigated and discussed by scholars engaged in development and agrarian studies. The international community of donors and governments, as well as local stakeholders, also refer to these themes. The many comprehensive works published in these areas provide a wide range of information on the dynamics of rural change. However, this information often relies on scattered local case studies, making it difficult to draw general conclusions, and analyses are rarely connected to structural change. This situation creates a "knowledge challenge," because a comprehensive understanding of rural dynamics is the foundation for development strategies and agricultural policies.

These initial objectives shaped the RuralStruc program and its general framework, which was a broad comparative approach involving seven countries at different stages of their structural transformation and economic integration into the global economy (from west to east: Mexico, Nicaragua, Senegal, Morocco, Mali, Kenya, and Madagascar). The objectives also underpinned the program's collaborative design—a key feature of its implementation. RuralStruc formed strong partnerships with local research teams in each country,

BOX 1.1

RuralStruc: What's in a Name?

The official title of the program is Structural Dimensions of Liberalization on Agriculture and Rural Development. The selection of RuralStruc as the acronym reflects a desire to bring structural issues back into a debate that was mainly focused on trade.

RuralStruc refers to both rural structures and the implications of overall structural change on agriculture and rural economies. The program's logo draws on the iceberg image: Trade liberalization is the visible tip, while structural transformation is the large portion under the waterline.

---

with the objective of strengthening local evidence-based approaches and fostering the local debate.[1]

A Disconcerting and Quickly Evolving Global Context

Over the past five years, during the in-depth fieldwork implemented by the program, the international landscape as well as the scope and issues of the international debate have dramatically changed. It is important to keep track of this permanent shift in policy agendas, because these changes are the immediate reality to which policy makers refer.

The Starting Point

When the RuralStruc program was being planned (2005–06), two major frameworks structured the international debate about development: the United Nations Millennium Development Goals (MDGs) and the World Trade Organization (WTO) development cycle or Doha Development Agenda (DDA), set at the Doha ministerial conference in 2001. Agriculture was clearly a part of these two frameworks, but although it sometimes occupied a key position (as in the case of the DDA), it was never the core issue.

The MDGs provided a global framework based on poverty alleviation. The first goal—"To halve poverty and hunger before 2015"—is clearly agriculture-related. First, 70 percent of the world's poor (who make up 45 percent of the world's population) live in rural areas and rely mainly on agriculture as a livelihood. Second, alleviation of hunger depends on improved food availability and access. Agriculture's decisive role in "pro-poor growth" was also reaffirmed by broad cross-country analyses performed by the World Bank (2005). However, poverty remained the central issue, while agricultural development was only one of the means cited to fight poverty, along with many other thematic and nonsectoral options.

The WTO negotiations logically focused on trade liberalization, in which agriculture was one sector among others to be liberalized. However, agriculture became the main stumbling block in the negotiation process. It was used by developing countries as a core argument to engage with developed countries on the broader issue of the liberalization of industrial products and services, which led to the failure of the 2003 Cancún ministerial and initiated a debate on the costs and benefits of trade liberalization for agriculture. This focus on agriculture and trade, as well as its domination of the international debate, was one of the main justifications for the RuralStruc initiative.

Since 2005, the global perspective on development has shifted dramatically. The MDGs have waned in importance; they remain a somewhat distant reminder of the international community's commitment to poverty alleviation and global development. They briefly gained renewed attention during the UN Summit of September 2010, which assessed the progress so far and concluded that not every goal will be achieved (United Nations 2010).

At the same time, the WTO debate has faded for several overlapping and interlinked reasons. The first reason is, of course, the emergence of new issues at the forefront of the international agenda, including a new debate over agriculture (see next section). Another reason is the profusion of research that has provided mixed estimates of the expected gains from liberalizing trade. This body of work highlights the unique situations of many developing countries, particularly in Africa, where trade liberalization could result in net losses rather than gains, adding some doubt—if not confusion—to the discussion.[2] These findings helped shift negotiations to a narrower focus on OECD (Organisation for Economic Co-operation and Development) countries' agricultural subsidies and developing countries' access to OECD markets. The findings strengthened the opposition to the Doha Round and resulted in successive impasses, particularly regarding agriculture: The unsuccessful Hong Kong SAR, China, ministerial (2005) led to the suspension of negotiations (July 2006), followed by failed attempts to reach an agreement on agriculture and nonagriculture market access (Geneva meetings in July 2008) and, since then, recurring postponements of the conclusion of the Doha Round. "Negotiation fatigue" is another explanation for the fading of the WTO debate; it also explains why increasing attention was dedicated to bilateral or regional free trade agreements (FTAs), and why major stakeholders decided to carry on bilaterally what was impossible to achieve at the global level.

The New Issues
Over the past five years, three major issues have affected the global debate about agriculture: growing concerns about the consequences of global climate change, and the eruption of the food price and financial crises.

Climate change has been firmly on the global agenda at least since the Rio Earth Summit (1992) and the Kyoto Conference (1997). However, concern has increased over the past few years as a result of two broad research works: the *Stern Review on the Economics of Climate Change* (Stern 2007) and *Climate Change 2007*, the Intergovernmental Panel on Climate Change (IPCC) report (Pachauri and Reisinger 2007). These analyses heightened the international community's awareness and refocused the ongoing negotiations, which led to the Copenhagen Summit of December 2009. They emphasized the various adverse effects climate change is expected to have on natural resources and agriculture, such as extreme weather events (droughts, floods, heat waves) as well as changes in temperature, rainfall, and sea levels. All these consequences are likely to compound the challenges faced by farmers and agricultural workers in securing sustainable livelihoods. Of all the world's regions, Sub-Saharan Africa is expected to suffer most from climate change: The IPCC projects annual agricultural losses of between 2 percent and 7 percent of GDP in the region by 2100. World Development Report 2010, *Development and Climate Change* (WDR10) (World Bank 2009a), provided a comprehensive update on the challenges faced by developing countries, which will bear most of the costs (75 percent to 80 percent) of the damages related to climate change. These challenges include the reliance of these countries on ecosystem services and natural capital for production (mainly agriculture), the concentration of their populations in physically exposed locations, and their limited financial and institutional capacities for adaptation. Special mitigation measures will be necessary to prevent an additional 120 million people from suffering from hunger, and agriculture will occupy a central role in resource management and carbon sequestration.

The second issue is related to the rapid emergence of the food price crisis (2007–08), which contributed to renewed international interest in food and agriculture issues, especially given the projections of a 9-billion-person world in 2050. Prices had been increasing progressively since 2006 and rose sharply at the beginning of 2008, leading to mobilization of international assistance. Although prices declined, forecasts have predicted greater volatility and relatively high prices in the medium term; at the end of 2010, prices rebounded. Various factors lead to high food prices, and the relative importance of these factors has triggered debate. On the supply side, weather-related production shortfalls combined with increasing fuel costs and a trend toward lower stock levels are the main explanations. On the demand side, the major factors are the long-term changing structure of food demand related to quickly evolving diets in emerging countries, the development of biofuels as a response to growing oil costs, and speculation (even if limited) in financial markets. Regardless of the relative importance of these factors, everyone agrees that there is no global food shortage in the medium term—the issue is the *cost* of food rather than a global *lack* of food. Thus, the main concern is the functioning of food markets and access to food for low-income consumers. The challenge is to avoid an excessive focus on short-term issues and to concentrate simultaneously on helping farmers reap the benefits of the current high prices, mitigating price impacts on the poorest consumers, increasing local food production to counteract rising local prices, and improving producers' incomes through increased bargaining power and higher yields.

The third issue is the unexpected and sudden onset of the global financial crisis in September 2008 and its dramatic effect on the world economy. The recovery has been a slow and fragile process. The rapid transmission of the downturn in the U.S. housing sector to the global financial system deeply affected both rich and poor countries, causing contraction and recession in several developed economies and a sharp slowdown of growth rates in many developing countries. This slowdown has been particularly challenging for countries with limited financial resources and those that face drastically reduced revenues (through reduced foreign direct investment, fiscal revenue, foreign aid, and remittances).

The food price and financial crises generated different (and disconnected) sets of discussions on remedies. However, to a certain extent, both crises have triggered temporary protectionist reactions, such as tariff increases, new non-tariff barriers, and the provisional return of quotas and export bans. The possible risk of a "protectionist tide" is a sharp move away from the arguments about trade liberalization that had previously characterized the international debate. The food price crisis and the new resource forecasts it engendered have also led to new strategies targeted at food security. These strategies focus on new production options based on quick investments or reinvestments in inputs (sometimes with subsidies), infrastructure, irrigation, and large-scale agricultural schemes. Land-grabbing by foreign investors, particularly in Sub-Saharan Africa, has been an increasing matter of concern (International Land Coalition [ILC] 2009; World Bank 2010b). It has led to conflicting situations among local stakeholders in several countries and launching anew the old debate about the merits of small-scale versus large-scale farming (wrongly considered as, respectively, smallholder and commercial agriculture).

Which Role for Agriculture?

Fortunately, during the past five years, two major contributions to the debate on agriculture have boosted its profile in the international community. The first is the International Assessment of Agricultural Knowledge, Science and Technology for Development (IAASTD), a broad international effort to review the existing stock of knowledge about agriculture and assess its adequacy in light of current global challenges to sustainable development. In a cooperative effort involving 110 countries, the results were reviewed and ratified at the Johannesburg International Plenary Meeting (2008), then published (IAASTD 2009).

The second contribution is the publication of the World Development Report 2008, *Agriculture for Development* (WDR08) (World Bank 2007). Prepared in

2006–07 and launched at the end of 2007, the WDR08 supplied the necessary momentum for a new focus and a new perspective on agriculture. It strongly reaffirmed the role of agriculture as a main sector of economic activity in most developing countries (as a source of labor, growth, and comparative advantage); as an important social sector, owing to the large share of the population involved; and as an important user of natural resources. After nearly 30 years of marginalization of agriculture in development economics—a consequence of the Washington consensus reforms (de Janvry 2009)—the WDR08 provided an insightful review of what is known about the mechanisms of agricultural development and how agriculture can serve as a catalyst for development. It is based on a regionalized vision of world agriculture and reviews the specific roles and challenges of agriculture in the development process, depending on its importance in the regional economy (box 1.2).

Though the scope of the report is somewhat limited with regard to links between agriculture and other sectors,[3] the regionalized and targeted approach has strongly contributed to the WDR's success; and the broad dissemination of the document has facilitated agriculture's comeback in the international debate on development. However, its momentum, as well as that of the IAASTD report, was somewhat slowed by the hectic international agenda and the short-term issues that arose from the food price crisis. Additionally, only a few months after the publication of the WDR08, different and, to some extent, contradictory messages were disseminated by the same and other international bodies. For instance, the United Nations Industrial Development Organization's (UNIDO) Industrial Development Report 2009 (UNIDO 2008) highlighted the role of industry as the main driver of change, particularly for the "bottom billion" and middle-income countries.[4] Adopting a different perspective, the next World Development Report, *Reshaping Economic Geography* (WDR09) (World Bank 2008a), stressed the need for higher demographic densities, shorter economic distances, and fewer political divisions (see box 3.1). The WDR09 demonstrated that these objectives can be achieved through increasing agglomeration and integration processes, highlighting the role of urbanization.[5]

In the end, despite this very unstable and somewhat confusing environment, agriculture is firmly back on the agenda, and donors and governments are reengaging. The UN Secretary-General's High Level Task Force on the Global Food Security Crisis, launched in April 2008, helps coordinate international efforts. At the L'Aquila Summit (July 2009), the Group of Eight industrialized countries (G8) pledged to mobilize $20 billion over five years to boost food security; this pledge was confirmed at the G20 Summit in Pittsburgh in September 2009. In April 2010, the Global Agriculture and Food Security Program (GAFSP) was officially launched with a first contribution of close to $1 billion. Finally, at the Seoul G20 Summit in November 2010, it was decided to launch an "agricultural G20" to foster international cooperation, especially in combating food price volatility.

BOX 1.2

The WDR08 and Its Three Worlds

The WDR08 proposes a tiered approach to agriculture for development and identifies three distinct worlds of agriculture that depend on agriculture's contribution to growth and the rural share of total poverty in a country. The three worlds are agriculture-based, transforming, and urbanized. In each world, the agriculture-for-development agenda differs in pursuit of sustainable growth and poverty reduction.

In *agriculture-based countries*, which include most of Sub-Saharan Africa, agriculture and its associated industries are essential to growth and to reducing mass poverty and food insecurity. They provide jobs, activities, and incomes. In *transforming countries*, which include most of South and East Asia and the Middle East and North Africa, rapidly rising rural-urban income disparities and persistent extreme rural poverty are major sources of social and political tension; rural diversification and agricultural income growth are the answers to these challenges. In *urbanized countries*—including most of Latin America, much of Europe, and Central Asia—agriculture can help reduce the remaining rural poverty if smallholders become direct suppliers in modern food markets, good jobs are created in agriculture and agro-industry, and markets for environmental services are introduced.

The WDR08 suggests three paths out of rural poverty: (1) agricultural entrepreneurship, (2) the rural labor market, and (3) the rural nonfarm economy and migration to

Box Figure 1.2.1 Agriculture's Contribution to Growth, 1990–2005

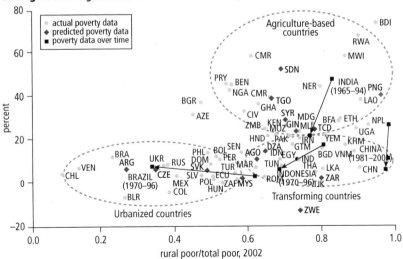

(box continues on next page)

cities or other countries. Often two or more paths operate simultaneously, and the complementary effects of farm and nonfarm activities can be strong. But although rural households engage in farming, labor, and migration, one of these activities usually dominates as a source of income.

Box Table 1.2.1 Characteristics of the WDR08's Three Worlds of Agriculture

	Ag. based	Transforming	Urbanized
Rural population (millions), 2005	417	2,220	255
Rural population (%), 2005	68	63	26
GDP per capita (2000 US$), 2005	379	1,068	3,489
Agriculture in GDP (%), 2005	29	13	6
Annual Ag. GDP growth (%), 1993–2005	4.0	2.9	2.2
Annual Non-Ag. GDP growth (%), 1993–2005	3.5	7.0	2.7
Rural poverty rate (%), 2002	51	28	13

Source: World Bank 2007, p. 31–33.
Note: The poverty line is $1.08 a day in 1993 PPP.

Although food security is narrower in scope than agricultural and rural development as a whole, this context does provide an opportunity to broaden the debate and to propose a perspective that does not restrict agriculture to food supply but embraces its other functions as well (environmental, economic, social, cultural). As stated by the IAASTD, this multifunctionality[6] is a unique feature of agriculture, given that the sector is the core activity for rural livelihoods and rural poverty alleviation; is the basis for rural diversification and the development of rural-urban links; and is central to the provision of environmental services. Its role as a driver of structural change must be reaffirmed, and questions must be asked about the viability of possible pathways out of rural poverty in the era of globalization.[7] This critical issue has to be pushed to the front of the policy debate and should justify reengaging in the development of policy frameworks that adopt the necessary long-term focus.

Main Objectives and Hypotheses of the Program: Reconnecting the Dots

Originally, the RuralStruc program had three specific objectives: (1) to contribute to the analytical knowledge base about structural changes related to liberalization and economic integration, and the consequences of these changes on developing countries' agriculture and their rural economies (box 1.3); (2) to feed and improve the international and national debates by promoting and reconnecting these issues; and (3) to provide perspectives for policy making.

BOX 1.3

Liberalization or Globalization?

In the early definition of the RuralStruc program, liberalization was understood in a broad sense as a global process of change, begun in the early 1980s, that included trade and domestic reform, state withdrawal from economic activities, privatization, and, in many developing countries, the reform of the state through decentralization.

The aim of the RuralStruc program was to focus on all the structural dimensions of this new context, which explains the choice of a title for the program. However, although the program adopted this broad definition of liberalization, the official positioning of the program's name quickly appeared inadequate. First, because the understanding of its objectives was often restricted to the policy package dimension of the reform process associated with liberalization, the program was often perceived as a critique of the reforms, which was not its purpose. Second, this misinterpretation implicitly limited the understanding of the scope of the processes at play.

After discussions with both the donor community and the national partners, it appears that it would have been clearer to use "globalization" rather than "liberalization" in the program's name. Although the use of "globalization" might suggest an excessive scope, the context to which the program refers clearly corresponds with the new international regime that emerged in the early 1980s and its consequences for agriculture, rural economies, and the process of economic transition as a whole. This new regime is characterized by new roles for the state and private actors, as well as by a broad and deep movement toward integration of the world economy.

The RuralStruc program has progressively adopted this broader positioning for the presentation of its results. "Globalization and Structural Change in Rural Economies" has been used as a title for the Phase 2 national reports and policy briefs, and the title of this book clearly refers to globalization.

The third goal relied directly on the program's design and the operationalization of its research results, while the first and second goals were more subjective. They implied a clear positioning, and the program chose to place the discussion of agriculture and rural change into the context of the structural transformation framework—to reconnect the development debate to global issues and avoid discussions trapped in sectoral approaches.

The structural transformation of economies and societies is a core issue in development studies. Historical records and statistical evidence[8] show a progressive shift from agriculture (the original primary activity of every sedentary population), to industry (the secondary activities), and then to services (the tertiary activities). The well-known underlying dynamic of this structural transformation—the economic transition from one configuration to the next—is productivity gains in agriculture, based on innovation that fosters technical change and allows labor and capital transfers toward other economic activities.

This process is accompanied by progressive spatial restructuring from scattered activities (typically agriculture) to more concentrated ones (typically industry), with migration of labor and people from rural areas to cities. Alongside this process of growing urbanization, overall economic transformation creates higher incomes and an increase in wealth, which translate into improved living conditions. This, in turn, along with medical progress, initiates a demographic transition: the progressive reduction of mortality and birth rates, the difference between which explains population growth dynamics.

Although this process of global structural transformation occurs at different paces and can follow various paths, its basic pattern has been observed throughout the world. It started with the closely related agricultural and industrial revolutions of Western Europe at the end of the 18th century, and continued in European offshoots (mainly the United States), other European regions, the majority of Latin America, and various parts of Asia.

Reference to this process has forged the classical development paradigm that underlies development economics.[9] Currently, one of the main challenges is the acceleration of the pace of change related to globalization and, thus, the growing asymmetries among regions of the world characterized by their different stages in this process of structural transformation.

This conceptual positioning strongly shaped the rationale of the RuralStruc program and its hypotheses. While the trade liberalization debate focused on expected gains from the liberalization process and their consequences for growth and poverty,[10] the program's objective was to reengage in the debate on economic transition within globalization and to elaborate on possible structural difficulties rather than just on transitional problems.[11] RuralStruc aimed to reconnect the discussion of agriculture with some challenging issues, such as the increasing productivity gaps among countries, lagging economic diversification, and the demographic challenges faced by several regions. These issues are recurring blind spots in the international debate, but they are critical for the structural transformation of developing countries.

Three hypotheses were advanced to structure the research process with regard to the debates on agriculture, food markets, and rural diversification (box 1.4). The first hypothesis (H1) refers to the global restructuring of agrifood markets and the increasing asymmetry in international competition. It states that these processes lead to the development of increasing differentiation among farm structures and among marketing, processing, and retailing structures. This hypothesis raises several questions: What is the balance between the potential integration of farmers in modern emerging value chains and their possible exclusion? What are the scope, speeds, and characteristics of these processes? Do they induce a segmentation dynamic with concentration, marginalization, and, sometimes, exclusion within and from the farm sector, leading to the emergence or consolidation of multiple-track agriculture?

BOX 1.4

The RuralStruc Program's Three Hypotheses

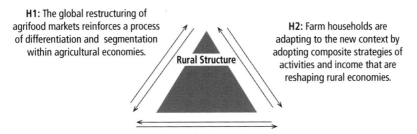

H1: The global restructuring of agrifood markets reinforces a process of differentiation and segmentation within agricultural economies.

Rural Structure

H2: Farm households are adapting to the new context by adopting composite strategies of activities and income that are reshaping rural economies.

H3: Marginalization trends introduced by these processes lead to risks of transition dead ends linked to the relative scarcity of alternative activities and sources of employment.

The second hypothesis (H2) relates to the existing processes of adaptation among rural households as a response to the many changing factors in agriculture and their impact on farm viability. Rural households engage in new configurations of activities and income systems characterized by the changing role of agriculture and the growing importance of off-farm activities and transfers (private transfers related to migration and, possibly, public transfers linked to specific support systems). The following questions are relevant to this hypothesis: What are the characteristics of these new configurations? How do they differ among countries? Are these dynamics new or do they follow the historical paths of structural transformation? How do they reshape the characteristics of rural areas and of rural-urban links? Are they effective approaches to sustainability in rural livelihoods?

The differentiation dynamics in agriculture and the possible difficulties of rural households' adaptation (in the absence of effective alternative activities and incomes) could create transition impasses in the process of structural transformation. This is the third hypothesis (H3), which refers primarily to the characteristics of what the WDR08 called "agriculture-based countries." In these countries, the weight of agriculture in employment and activity structures, the strong urbanization process without significant industrialization or job creation, limited economic diversification in a context of growing international competition, and heavy demographic pressure create a unique challenge for development. Will some countries face impasses in escaping poverty owing to a lack of alternatives (Kydd 2002) and limited migration opportunities? What are the potential social, economic, and political consequences of such dead ends in the economic transition?

General Design of the Program: Country Case Studies, Regional Surveys, and Collaborative Processes

To assess the relevance of the hypotheses and answer the questions posed, the RuralStruc program attempted to identify the primary similarities and differences in countries' processes of adaptation to the new context, taking into account the characteristics of their rural transformation and their own trajectories of structural change. The program design was supported by a collaborative framework that engaged local teams in an internal process of analysis with the dual objective of "better understanding for better policy making" (the motto of the program).

A Comparative Approach

Comparison is a powerful tool for analytical work because it highlights convergences and divergences, and identifies key explanatory factors. However, a comparative approach is risky and can lead to deep methodological errors. Rural-Struc did not make comparisons between countries (for example, Mexico and Madagascar), as this would have made little sense and would have induced classical selection bias.[12] Likewise, facing the classical challenge of ex post analysis, the goal was not to evaluate impacts, because that would have led to information difficulties (particularly the lack of years of reference for evaluation) and to a risky discussion on the direction of causality. In fact, the word "impact" was purposely avoided in the official title of the program; "dimensions" was preferred.

The objective of the comparative approach was to illustrate processes of change in agriculture and the rural economy related to liberalization, economic integration, and globalization to identify and understand patterns and differences that can be useful for policy making. In its implementation, the program endeavored to adopt a global, multidisciplinary, and historical perspective on the dynamics of change by focusing on national trajectories and their critical junctures,[13] which can modify the nature of relationships among agriculture, the rural sector, and the overall economy.

Country Selection. The process of selecting country case studies for comparative purposes involves trade-offs among objective criteria related to research goals and operational issues (which refer to local partnerships); conditions for implementation (especially allocated time and financial and human resources); and contributing partners' buy-in and their own interests.

In preliminary discussions, the program's contributing donors decided that a focus on Sub-Saharan Africa was justified by the critical structural situation of the continent and the many efforts already undertaken to revitalize its agricultural sector. Concurrent with the progressive reengagement of the donor community in agriculture, African governments are notably dedicated to the implementation of the New Partnership for Africa's Development (NEPAD) Comprehensive Africa Agriculture Development Program (CAADP).[14] This program has become the African—indeed, the international—reference for action in agriculture and is currently being operationalized.

To engage in the comparative approach, it was decided to select a small sample of countries. These countries were not intended to represent the large diversity of possible development trajectories, but they did correspond to a spectrum of situations in the process of structural transformation. Some countries were far ahead in this process; in others, economic transition and the pace of integration into the world economy had been slow or unequal.

Among the program's seven country case studies, Mexico was chosen as an example of advanced economic transition, with a high urbanization level and a limited role for agriculture in the economy. The Mexican rural economy showed evidence of being broadly affected by huge migration flows to the United States and by deep integration and liberalization processes, accelerated 15 years ago with the implementation of the North American Free Trade Agreement (NAFTA).

On the other hand, Sub-Saharan Africa (SSA)—represented by Kenya, Madagascar, Mali, and Senegal—illustrated the initial stage of economic transition, with partial integration and liberalization processes initiated through state and market reforms, and an important enduring role for agriculture and other primary activities.

Morocco and Nicaragua illustrated an intermediate stage of structural transformation, corresponding to countries characterized by rapid integration processes owing to their proximity to powerful economic zones in which free trade agreements had recently been implemented.[15] In these countries, agriculture (characterized by dualistic structures) remains a major political issue and international migrations play a big role in the political economy.

In addition to the criteria of gradual and differentiated integration, three specific macro-economic criteria were used to select countries for the program: GDP per capita, the share of agriculture in GDP (AgGDP), and the share of the economically active population engaged in agriculture (AgEAP) (see table 1.1).[16] These criteria are basic indicators of a country's stage of economic transition. With the exception of Mexico, the selected countries are low-income or lower-middle-income countries. They display a wide range of situations in terms of poverty, human development, governance, and business climate, with stark contrast between SSA and non-SSA countries and clear gradual indicators results among countries.

Using the WDR08 typology, the selected countries represent the three worlds of agriculture: (1) agriculture-based (Kenya, Madagascar, Mali); (2) transforming

Table 1.1 Selected Indicators for the RuralStruc Countries

	Country	Mali	Senegal	Madagascar	Kenya	Morocco	Nicaragua	Mexico
Number								
1	ISO code	MLI	SEN	MDG	KEN	MAR	NIC	MEX
2	Income group 2009	Low	Low	Low	Low	Lower middle	Lower middle	Upper middle
3	GDP per capita 2007 (US$)	552	952	395	718	2,373	1,023	9,715
4	GDP per capita 2007 ($ PPP)	1,084	1,666	935	1,437	3,980	2,578	12,780
5	$2 / day (PPP) 2005 (% of pop.)	77.1	60.4	89.6	39.9	14.0	31.9	4.8
6	National Gini index 2005	39.0	39.2	47.2	47.7	40.9	52.3	48.1
7	% AgGDP 2007	37	14	26	25	14	20	4
8	Transition stage (WDR08)	Ag. based	Transforming	Ag. based	Ag. based	Transforming	Transforming	Urbanized
9	Population 2005 (Thds)	11,833	11,281	17,614	35,817	30,495	5,455	105,330
10	Urbanization stage (WDR09)	Intermed.	Intermed.	Intermed.	Incipient	Intermed.	Intermed.	Advanced
11	% rural 2005	69.5	58.4	71.5	79.3	45.0	44.1	23.7
12	% AgEAP 2005	78	72	72	73	29	18	19
13	Human development (index 2010)	0.37	0.45	0.49	0.50	0.62	0.63	0.79
	Human development (rank 2010)	128	121	110	106	98	96	46
14	Rule of law (Gov. Indicator 2008)	−0.35	−0.31	−0.46	−0.98	−0.11	−0.86	−0.64
	Political stability (Gov. Indicator 2008)	−0.21	−0.16	−0.42	−1.25	−0.47	−0.39	−0.62
15	Doing Business (rank 2010)	155	151	138	94	114	119	41

Sources:

1. International Standard Organization country codes.
2. World Bank—Classification of economies 2010. http://data.worldbank.org/about/country-classifications/country-and-lending-groups. *Economies are divided among income groups according to 2009 gross national income (GNI) per capita, calculated using the Atlas method. The groups are: low income, $995 or less; lower middle income, $996–3,945; upper middle income, $3,946–12,195; and high income, $12,196 or more.*
3. World Bank—Data Development Platform 2010.
4. World Bank—Data Development Platform 2009 using the poverty purchase parity conversion factor calculated for January 2007–April 2008.
5. World Bank—Data Development Platform 2010. Poverty headcount ratio at $2 a day (PPP) (% of population).
6. World Bank—Data Development Platform 2010.
7. World Bank—Data Development Platform 2010.
8. World Bank, World Development Report 2008—see Box 1.2 for definition.
9. United Nations—World Population Prospects: The 2008 Revision http://esa.un.org/unpp.

10. Word Bank, World Development Report 2009. The urbanization classification refers to urban shares: incipient is below 25%, intermediate is between 25 and 75%, and advanced is above 75%.
11. United Nations—World Urbanization Prospects: The 2007 Revision. http://esa.un.org/unup/default.aspx
12. FAO—FAOSTAT 2010. http://faostat.fao.org/site/452/default.aspx
13. UNDP—Human Development Indicators. http://hdr.undp.org/en/statistics/. *The HDI is combining indicators of life expectancy, educational attainment and income and is rated from 0 to 1. It ranks 135 countries.*
14. World Bank & Brookings Institution—Worldwide Governance Indicators 2010. http://info.worldbank.org/governance/wgi/index.asp. *The Worldwide Governance Indicators (previously KKZ index) scores six indicators from −2.5 to +2.5. The six indicators are: voice and accountability, political stability, government effectiveness, regulatory quality, rule of law, control of corruption. Only two are provided here.*
15. World Bank & IFC—Doing Business 2010. http://www.doingbusiness.org/rankings. *The Ease of Doing Business indicator ranks out of 183 countries.*

Notes: for numbers 5 and 6, Mali and Mexico values are for 2006.

(Senegal, Morocco, Nicaragua); and (3) urbanized (Mexico).[17] In the selected countries, agriculture contributes less and less to economic growth but maintains a significant role in national employment—between 70 percent and 80 percent of the labor force for the SSA countries, and less than 30 percent in Mexico, Morocco, and Nicaragua.[18] The seven countries also correspond to the three urbanization stages of the WDR09: incipient, intermediate, and advanced.[19]

Population size also played a role in the selection process. To avoid extreme situations, both the most populous countries (for example, China, India, Indonesia, and Brazil) and the very smallest were not chosen.[20] This decision is disputable because there is no direct correlation between economic transition and demographic size. However, the WDR09 reminds us that "size matters," and it can be a strong asset facilitating structural transformation. Large domestic markets offer economies of scale and accessible demand, which provide substantial maneuvering room for domestic firms in the context of increasing competition linked to globalization. This is especially the case in industrialization, research, and capacity building.[21] Therefore, the selected countries have a small to medium demographic size—except for Mexico, they all have between 5 million and 35 million inhabitants. These criteria precluded the selection of any Asian countries.[22]

The selected SSA countries reflect the diversity of situations among low-income countries (Madagascar, Mali, and Senegal are included in the least developed countries [LDC] group). They display a diversity of geography (Southern, East, and West Africa, including a landlocked country, Mali); colonial history (former French or British colonies); activity structure (including the role of migrations); and the state of the national debate around agriculture and privatization.[23]

The choice of Mexico, with its demographic and economic characteristics, violated many selection criteria: Mexico is an upper-middle-income country, an OECD member, and an emerging economy. The point in selecting Mexico was to provide a useful background picture that showed the restructuring of a rural economy in a context of strong liberalization and economic integration.[24]

There is no perfect sample; however, the RuralStruc country cases offer a wide range of situations that fit with the program's objectives and help draw a differentiated picture of the processes of change under way. These countries shed light on the structural characteristics of economies with different degrees of economic diversification and urbanization, various migration patterns, different types of public policies, and diverse agricultural sectors. Agricultures are characterized by the goods they produce, the size of their main value chains, and their market orientation (domestic or international, staple or high-value). All these factors are related to natural and historical conditions that have shaped local agrarian systems and markets. Thus, the agricultural sectors of the selected country cases are generally focused on annual crops (mainly cereals), including irrigated crops, but also include traditional commodities such as sugar cane, cotton, groundnut, and coffee. The sample could have benefited from including a strong plantation-based agricultural economy (such as some countries of the Gulf of Guinea in West Africa), where perennial crops (coffee, cocoa, palm oil) have long shaped the agrarian systems.[25]

Operationalizing the Comparative Work. The RuralStruc program was conceived to include two phases. The main objective of Phase 1 was to generate broad country overviews based on desktop studies on the role of agriculture in the economy. These studies specifically examined market structures and their evolution, the development and differentiation of farm structures, and the risks of transition impasses and possibilities for adaptation. Phase 1 also provided an opportunity to identify missing information related to the processes of structural change in agriculture and to share views with national partners on the general approach of the program.

Phase 2 was originally designed to produce specific information at the regional and value-chain levels, based on qualitative interviews with farmers, middlemen, and other economic agents, and targeting issues identified in the first phase. However, the Phase 1 results highlighted the weakness of the knowledge base and identified significant information gaps regarding the process of rural transformation, particularly with regard to rural household activities, income, and integration into markets. Consequently, Phase 2 was modified to include more direct primary data collection at the household level.[26]

The objective of the household surveys in each country was to generate original information—both qualitative and quantitative—on the processes under way in agriculture and the rural economy. It was hoped that this information would facilitate understanding of the roles of agriculture in local economies and rural livelihoods, for example, types of rural income generation, combination of activities and income sources, and multifaceted livelihoods.[27]

Regional Fieldwork

The overall design of the fieldwork and the selection of regions were as follows.

Design and Limitations. The decision to implement rural household surveys focusing on activities and incomes shaped the operationalization of the program and its outputs. The preference for *rural* and not just *farm* households was justified by the need to more precisely identify agriculture's role with respect to other rural activities and sources of income. This choice made it necessary to deal with analytical categories whose definitions can be complicated, like the official definition of "rural," which varies among countries (see box 1.5).

Targeting household incomes led the program to focus on the core issue of income estimates, which, in rural areas, means dealing with farm incomes and

BOX 1.5

Rural versus Urban: What Definition for Each Country?

Although the definition of "rural" varies from country to country, there does seem to be a commonality: The definition is rarely positive. In most cases, rural refers to the residual population after subtracting the urban population from the total population (FAO definition). There is no uniform definition for "urban"—it is most often based on the size of settlements but can also be based on population density or administrative boundaries, and sometimes on the provision of services. The RuralStruc countries define rural in the following ways:

Kenya: The Kenya National Bureau of Statistics defines rural as a locality with a human population of less than 2,000.

Madagascar: Rural areas are districts in which the proportion of agricultural economically active population (as defined for the Agricultural Census) exceeds 50 percent (RS 2 Madagascar, 26).

Mali: Rural households include all households in rural areas, which are defined as the opposite of towns. Through at least one of the members, rural households are involved in agricultural activities, broadly defined (RS 2 Mali, 20).

Mexico: A rural locality is defined by the national statistical system as a place with fewer than 2,500 dwellers. However, this threshold is debated, and the country team used the common reference of 5,000 inhabitants instead (RS 2 Mexico, 6).

Morocco: Rural areas are defined by default as any areas that are not included in the scope of an urban area. Urban areas change their boundaries over time owing to the expansion of cities and the reclassification of rural localities to urban. There is no statistical definition of the rural population (RS 2 Morocco, 6).

Nicaragua: The official definition of rural areas is districts with fewer than 1,000 dwellers (RS 2 Nicaragua, 11).

Senegal: Rural is defined in opposition to urban, which has an administrative definition: All "communes" are classified as urban, even if they have all the attributes of rural areas, including a farm-based economy (RS 2 Senegal, 39).

the difficulties of approximating them. The program dealt with these difficulties by employing a heavy survey framework with extensive questionnaires.[28]

The survey work encountered a few localized difficulties (such as delays and missing information resulting from Kenya's postelection violence in early 2008), but the main constraint was the limitation inherent in a one-shot survey, a consequence of the duration of and funding for the program. The one-time nature of the fieldwork was a major difficulty due to the program's hypotheses, which were developed in dynamic terms. It is also a source of bias owing to the interannual variation in farm incomes (for example, the impact of drought on yields).

One way to mitigate this severe restriction would have been to benchmark the surveys on the basis of existing panels, but this option was not feasible. In the first place, it would have been difficult within the allocated time frame to deal with several different baselines, survey frameworks, and methodologies. Second, panels with a specific focus on rural incomes are scarce. In developing countries, household panel data (when they exist) have usually been developed to estimate poverty, notably in the context of structural adjustment programs started in the 1980s–90s. These data most often deal with household expenditures and frequently target urban households, which typically constitute the main share of the country samples.[29]

Although many local case studies exist, few data are available on rural incomes. This situation is often a consequence of the depletion of national statistical systems, but it also frequently results from statistical frameworks that do not target the rural economy, just agriculture. This makes it hard to conceptualize the ongoing processes of rural change. A rare exception is the Rural Income Generating Activities (RIGA) project, developed by FAO in collaboration with the World Bank, which offers a coherent framework for a cross-national comparison of rural income sources (box 1.6).[30]

The RIGA results were used extensively by the WDR08, most notably to discuss the roles of rural activity and income source diversification as a way out of poverty.[31] However, they were not directly usable for the RuralStruc analysis owing to different years of reference and missing country cases.

Because the program lacked easy options for benchmarking the household surveys, the drawbacks related to the one-shot data collection were mitigated by complementing the surveys with specific fieldwork and desk reviews on selected value chains and the characteristics of the surveyed regions. These activities allowed for contextualization—a fine-tuned analysis of the household survey results that incorporates the historical background of the processes of change under way, especially the restructuring of agricultural markets. The value chains were selected by the national research teams according to their importance in the economy at both the national and regional levels. Each value-chain analysis presented characteristics of supply and demand, their evolution in the context of liberalization, and the existing integration and differentiation processes resulting from the global restructuring of agrifood markets.

The selected value chains, which included both staples and commodities, are listed in table 1.2.

Selection of the Surveyed Regions. The purpose of the household surveys was not to obtain a statistically representative sample but rather to provide a comprehensive picture of rural realities. Consequently, in each country, the pro-

BOX 1.6

The Rural Income Generating Activities Project (RIGA)

The RIGA project was intended to fill some of the major gaps in the understanding of the rural nonfarm economy (RNFE) by using a database constructed from a pool of Living Standards Measurement Study (LSMS) and other multipurpose household surveys made available by the World Bank and the FAO. It analyzed sources of rural household income from 32 household surveys in 18 countries: Albania 2002 and 2005; Bangladesh 2000; Bolivia 2005; Bulgaria 1995 and 2001; Ecuador 1995 and 1998; Ghana 1992 and 1998; Guatemala 2000 and 2006; Indonesia 1992 and 2000; Kenya 2004–05; Madagascar 1993–94 and 2001; Malawi 2004; Nepal 1995–96 and 2003–04; Nicaragua 1998, 2001, and 2005; Nigeria 2004; Pakistan 1991 and 2001; Panama 1997 and 2003; Tajikistan 2003; and Vietnam 1992–93, 1997–98, and 2002.

The RIGA database is composed of a series of constructed variables about rural incomes created from the original data sources. The sample of countries and the indicators built offer geographic coverage, as well as adequate quality and sufficient comparability to allow for cross-country analysis, despite pervasive differences in the quality and level of information available in each survey.

Numerous analyses based on the RIGA project have been published. The database allows researchers to (1) evaluate the participation in and income received from RIGAs; (2) analyze the role of household assets in participation in each activity; (3) analyze the role of household assets in the income received from each activity; and (4) disaggregate rural nonfarm activities by industry.

Source: Carletto et al. 2007, and http://www.fao.org/economic/riga/en/.

Table 1.2 Main Value Chains Analyzed in the RuralStruc Country Studies

Country	Value chains
Mali	Meat and dairy, dry cereals, rice, onion, cotton
Senegal	Groundnut, cassava, rice, dairy, maize, tomato
Madagascar	Rice, maize, potato, dairy, green bean
Kenya	Maize, milk, sugarcane
Morocco	Cereals, red meat, olive oil, tomato, citrus
Nicaragua	Basic grains, vegetables, dairy, coffee, sesame
Mexico	Maize, dairy, fruit, and vegetables

Source: RuralStruc Phase 2 reports.

gram selected regions that illustrated underlying trends that had been previously identified.

Regions were chosen by the national teams on the basis of Phase 1 results and their own expertise. The goal in selecting regions was to illustrate the regional

Table 1.3 Selected Surveyed Regions in the RuralStruc Countries

Country	Ex ante classification		
	Winning	Intermediary	Losing
Mali	Koutiala	Diéma	Tominian
	Macina		
Senegal	Senegal Delta	*Bassin arachidier:*	Casamance
		North (Mekhé)	
		South (Nioro)	
Madagascar	Antsirabe	Alaotra	Morondava
		Itasy	
Kenya	Nakuru North	Bungoma	Nyando
Morocco	Souss	Saïss	Chaouia
Nicaragua	El Viejo	Muy Muy	Terrabona
	El Cuá		La Libertad
Mexico	Tequisquiapan (Querétaro)	Sotavento (Veracruz)	Ixmiquilpan (Hidalgo)

Source: RuralStruc Phase 2 reports.

dynamics relevant to understanding the processes of change currently under way in the country. Various criteria were used depending on the country, but all related to market access (infrastructures and proximity to cities), the presence of integrated value chains, the level of public investments and public goods, and the situation regarding natural resources.

Three kinds of regions were specified:

- Winning regions, where the ongoing dynamics of integration to markets (whether related to specific value chains, the proximity of urban centers, or good infrastructure) provide opportunities and are strong drivers of change
- Losing regions, characterized by trends toward marginalization owing to local constraints (low factor endowment, lack of public goods), poor connection to markets, or high poverty rates, and where household sustainability appears to be increasingly difficult
- Intermediary regions, where the trends are imprecise and depend on the evolution of the local economic and institutional contexts, which will either provide new opportunities and reduce the existing constraints or not.

Using this general typology, at least three regions (one per type) but sometimes more were selected for data collection in the seven study countries (see table 1.3). Surveyed localities were chosen by the national teams in every region on the basis of their local knowledge, with the objective of illustrating the regional dynamics. In each locality, the selection of households to survey was randomized.

For certain surveyed regions, fine-tuning based on the first survey results led to the identification of significant differences between areas in the same region. Consequently, a few of the original surveyed regions were split in two to provide a more accurate representation of regional characteristics (to avoid misleading effects from averaging opposite extremes). This choice was usually made on the basis of statistically significant differences in household incomes between surveyed localities in the same region and sometimes on particular local conditions, such as remoteness or natural characteristics. This was the case in Senegal, Madagascar, and Mexico, where several regions were split in two.[32] These choices enabled the program to take into account different households' asset endowments and agrarian structures, reflected in income patterns.[33]

Thus, owing to the characteristics of the sampling method, the RuralStruc surveys are statistically representative at the local level (village or community) only. However, because the program relied on national teams of experts to select the surveyed regions, with reference to their factor endowments and connection to markets, the results provide an accurate estimate of the country's existing regional trends in terms of agricultural development, rural incomes, and rural diversification. They illustrate the diversity of the rural situations at the national level, which is confirmed by the Phase 2 national reports (see chapter 3).

Approximately 8,000 rural household surveys encompassing 57,000 people were implemented in 26 regions[34] of the seven selected countries between November 2007 and May 2008—before the full development of the food price crisis. The data collected primarily reflect the 2007 crop season. Forty percent of the surveyed households are in the three non-SSA countries.

Surveys in each region were based on the same positioning and questioning, and used the same survey instrument framework. Despite data limitations, this design offers a set of comparable statistics referring to the same period of time (a key difference from RIGA) that documents both overarching patterns of development and the great diversity within rural societies.[35]

The Partnership at Work

One of the original characteristics and strengths of the RuralStruc program was the methodological choice to develop activities through local partnerships and rely on national teams. This choice facilitated the implementation of the program, notably the process of data collection, but it also strongly improved the quality of both the data and the analysis by providing an additional safeguard in terms of accuracy and consistency of the collected information and of the general understanding of the processes under way. In the end, it facilitated both local ownership and the public policy debate.

Between the launching workshop in April 2006 and the publication of the first draft of this synthesis in June 2009, the national and coordination teams engaged in continuous exchanges, which intensified during the launching and ending stages of each phase, during joint field missions, and at several collective events.

The same terms of reference, adjusted collaboratively, were used for each phase, and a consultative process was adopted for the design of the survey instrument. The same methodological framework was used in each of the seven countries, including common definitions and selection of core transversal variables to be used for the analysis, with the necessary local adaptations. The major difficulties related to variable definitions and data analyses were discussed at a workshop, as was the outline of the Phase 2 report. Also, a common effort was employed to build an aggregated merged database focusing on a core set of variables that each national team extracted or calculated from the national data sets. Finally, the country results were thoroughly discussed on the basis of the cross-country data analysis and national reports to consolidate the final outcomes of the program.

The teams disseminated results in each of the surveyed countries after Phase 1, and the results of Phase 2 have been disseminated in some of the participating countries. The format and pace of these dissemination events (which should continue after the formal end of the program) depend on the local political agenda and the willingness of the local partners and contributing donors to participate in the events.

Formal dissemination events for Phase 2 have been held in two countries so far (Mali in April 2010 and Senegal in June 2010), and both were structured the same way. The country team prepared a set of "policy briefs" on program results and recommendations that were discussed during a workshop involving representatives from farmer organizations, civil society, national government, local government, the private sector, and donors.

International dissemination will continue and will involve the country teams. In addition to several presentations of the program and its first results in various forums since 2006, a preconference workshop was held during the 27th International Conference of Agricultural Economists in Beijing (August 2009).[36]

Synopsis of the Book

This book, presenting the final results of the RuralStruc program, offers a comparative analysis of rural change articulated with the existing debate on agriculture, rural development, and structural transformation. It relies on the extensive fieldwork and analyses developed by the country teams, based on rural household surveys and desk reviews, and presented in 14 country reports.[37] The country-based material is complemented by a literature review that provides the necessary background for interpreting the program's results and highlighting its contribution to thematic research and the policy debate.

The book consists of six chapters; figure 1.1 shows how they fit together. The reader can follow the progression or go directly to the chapters of inter-

Figure 1.1 A Tool to Navigate the Report

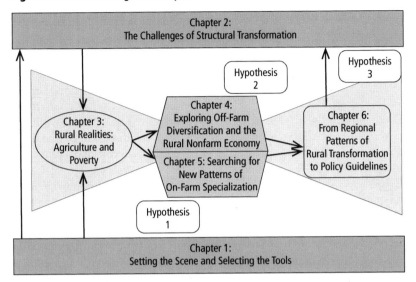

est. Technical annexes were not included due to editorial constraints. They are accessible in the appendix posted on the RuralStruc web page and provide additional information on the methodology, the local partnerships, the description of surveyed regions, and data results that did not fit into the core document.

This first chapter has explained the motivation behind the program, with reference to past and ongoing international debates, as well as the methodology used. It described how the program employed a two-stage process that involved both qualitative and quantitative research, and it presented the program's three hypotheses related to (1) the extent of integration processes in agriculture and their consequences on farm households and the agricultural sector; (2) the development of the rural nonfarm economy (RNFE) and how it reshapes rural realities; and (3) the risks of transitional dead ends, in which some households and regions are left behind in the process of structural transformation.

Chapter 2, Challenges of Structural Transformation, is a summary of the overall processes of structural change, particularly the characteristics of economic and demographic transitions. It provides a frame of reference for the discussion in the rest of the report and addresses the question of the viability of the historical sequence of structural transformation in a globalizing world. It cites the situation of the least developed countries—mainly in Sub-Saharan Africa—which remain at the early stages of their transition processes. The chapter also presents the characteristics of the RuralStruc countries with regard to their demographic and economic structures, and highlights their main challenges and the various roles played by agriculture.

Chapter 3, Rural Realities, examines the surveyed regions by focusing on the role of agriculture in household activities and incomes, and the extent of poverty. After underlining the central role of agriculture across very different regional settings, the chapter uses micro-level survey data to present the income characteristics of the households. Two themes dominate this review: the strength and persistence of absolute poverty, and the extent to which households are still engaged in agriculture, especially in Sub-Saharan Africa. The chapter shows that this poverty holds when calculated a number of different ways: per head, per adult equivalent, and even in kilocalories. The last section of the chapter discusses the livelihood strategies observed in the survey in the context of the WDR08 typology, which refers to three pathways out of rural poverty: farm specialization, rural labor, and migration. Two large groups of households are defined: those that are strongly specialized in on-farm activities and those that are more diversified. Households with significant off-farm specialization are limited in number.

Chapter 4, Exploring Off-Farm Diversification and the Rural Nonfarm Economy, examines the extent of diversification in the surveyed regions, investigates the different types of off-farm activities and incomes (agricultural wage labor, nonagricultural wage labor, self-employment, public and private transfers, and rents), and identifies characteristics of the households that are involved in these activities. It reviews the current debate and clarifies the definitions of "rural nonfarm economy" (RNFE) and "off-farm," which includes agricultural wage labor and is the lens used by the program. The chapter focuses on the second hypothesis and discusses how patterns of off-farm diversification contribute to the process of change and the reshaping of the rural economies. It differentiates coping strategies at the initial stage of diversification from more mature and positive diversification at a later stage.

Chapter 5, Searching for New Patterns of On-Farm Specialization, focuses on agriculture. After reviewing the patterns of the "big restructuring" related to market liberalization and the new agrifood markets, it investigates the characteristics of on-farm activities in the surveyed regions. The chapter explores the first hypothesis with regard to the consequences of changes under way in the sector. Rather than the "new agriculture" suggested in the literature, the program results highlight the persistence of old agricultural patterns, including the importance of self-consumption and staple production (connected to risk-management strategies and weak market environment), and the limited role of contractualization. However, the connection of farm households to markets is significant everywhere.

Chapter 6, From Regional Patterns of Rural Transformation to Policy Guidelines, discusses the determinants of the regional levels of income and elaborates on the core diversification-specialization relationship that is central to the process of structural transformation. On the basis of statistical analyses, it identifies an inverted U pattern that helps explain the process of rural transformation. It highlights the specific situation of Sub-Saharan Africa, where obstacles along the transformation path appear to trap most of the regions surveyed in poverty. This illustrates the risk of transitional impasse cited in the third hypothesis. The second part of the chapter draws on the accrued evidence to propose possible policy guidelines. It suggests methodological orientations and three building blocks specifically targeted to SSA's early-transitioning regions that could help them overcome risks of persistent traps.

Notes

1. National reports were produced for each phase of the program. They are referenced in the document using RS 1 [country] for Phase 1 reports and RS 2 [country] for Phase 2 reports. The list of reports is provided at the beginning of the bibliography.
2. Among recent and often contradictory research work, see, for instance, Bouët et al. (2005); Boussard, Gérard, and Piketty (2005, 2006); Polaski (2006); or, more recently, Peréz, Farah, and Grammont (2008) on Latin America; Zepeda et al. (2009) on Kenya; and the work coordinated by Anderson on "Krueger/Schiff/Valdés Revisited" (Anderson 2010).
3. Specifically, the limitation is in regard to the scope of intersectoral linkages in the context of globalization. This discussion is developed in chapter 2. For criticism of the WDR08 framework, see, among others, Akram-Lodhi (2008) and Oya (2009).
4. The "bottom billion" refers to Paul Collier's 2007 book that focuses on 50 so-called "failing states" that are stuck in poverty; 70 percent of these states are in SSA. Collier, who is one of the two authors of UNIDO's report, fed the controversy about the role of agriculture, noting that it will not be able to alleviate poverty and that the only option is a broad migration to cities (Collier 2008, 2009). For more on this debate, see chapter 6.
5. Two departments of the World Bank—the Poverty Reduction and Equity Group and the Finance, Economics and Urban Department—have launched a joint work program on poverty reduction during the rural-urban transformation in developing countries, with the objective of combining the two WDR perspectives. See Simler and Dudwick (2010). This work was completed in 2011 (Dudwick et al. 2011).
6. There has been a long and tense international debate about recognizing multifunctionality as a feature unique to agriculture, and it has been heavily intertwined with ongoing policy discussions. Many European states adopted policies promoting multifunctionality in the 1990s despite strong opposition in the WTO from countries (mainly the Cairns Group countries and the United States) that denounced their actions as market distortions. On these debates and on the multifunctionality of agriculture in general, see Barthélémy et al. (2003), Losch (2004), Caron and Le Cotty (2006), and Groupe Polanyi (2008). In addition, FAO implemented a Roles of Agriculture project between 2000 and 2006 that developed a broad set of case studies and analyses on the roles of agriculture at the different phases of development (FAO 2007).
7. A long tradition of stimulating research in agrarian studies questions the consequences of ongoing processes of change and the related risks of economic and social impasses. See the *Journal of Agrarian Change* and, for a recent review of the current debates and their evolution, Akram-Lodhi and Kay (2009a and b).

8. See, for example, Johnston and Kilby (1975), Chenery and Syrquin (1975), and Timmer (1988, 2009).

9. Development economics emerged at the end of World War II with the idea of catching up the growth process of industrialized countries, with reference to the take-off of 19th century Western European countries. It established a debated evolutionist vision of development in which countries must go through "necessary stages." Economic and demographic transitions are further discussed in chapter 2.

10. Economic research rarely addresses other consequences of liberalization. For the potential employment dimensions of liberalization, see, for instance, Hoekman and Winters (2005). For environmental dimensions, see Cook et al. (2010).

11. In the economic literature, difficulties related to liberalization are generally perceived as temporary. This is the case for unemployment, which is supposed to reflect the time needed for adaptation to the new context and for reaching a new equilibrium (Winters, McCulloch, and McKay 2004).

12. Owing to the selection process and the self-selection of the country cases, any conclusion from direct comparison to explain variables would suffer from systematic error (Collier and Mahoney 1996).

13. The concept of critical juncture is found in path dependence approaches and refers to the identification of key choice points at which a particular option is selected by governments, coalitions, or social forces and leads to the creation of recurring institutional patterns. See Mahoney (2001) and Pierson (2000).

14. CAADP is one of the flagship programs of the New Partnership for Africa's Development (NEPAD). Launched in 2003, it aims to increase agricultural investment to 10 percent of national budgets (Maputo Declaration) and facilitate the preparation of investment plans. CAADP focuses on four pillars to improve productivity and growth: land and water management, market access, food supply and hunger, and agricultural research. See http://www.nepad-caadp.net.

15. The European Union and the United States in the case of Morocco, and the United States in the case of Nicaragua (with the Central American–Dominican Republic Free Trade Agreement [CAFTA-DR]).

16. In table 1.1 and in the document as a whole, country data have been sorted from left to right, first by region (SSA, North Africa, and Latin America) and then by income level based on the survey results (see chapter 3).

17. The appearance of Senegal, a country with 72 percent of its economically active population (EAP) in agriculture, in the "transforming world" illustrates the ambiguity of using rural or rural poverty instead of AgEAP as a criterion for the analysis. The definition of rural varies among countries (see box 1.5) and has a restrictive definition in Senegal. Nicaragua is not mentioned in the WDR three worlds analysis, which excludes countries with fewer than 5 million inhabitants (even though Nicaragua passed this limit in 2000). However, using the same criterion, Nicaragua would be part of the transforming countries group.

18. AgEAP shares are computed from FAO based on International Labour Organization (ILO) data. In the case of Nicaragua, the share of the active population engaged in agriculture seems to be strongly underestimated. According to the Central

Bank of Nicaragua, 29 percent of the labor force was employed in the sector (RS 1 Nicaragua, 28).

19. Country groupings are always debatable. However, qualifying Kenya as a country facing incipient urbanization is somewhat surprising, given the huge urban growth observed in the country. See box 3.2 and Harre, Moriconi-Ebrard, and Gazel (2010).

20. "Small" and "large" are relative values. Among the 192 member states of the United Nations, only 11 countries have more than 100 million inhabitants; 25 countries have more than 50 million people; and 50 countries have more than 20 million—but 80 countries have fewer than 5 million inhabitants. The median country population is 7 million.

21. If the case against the most populous countries in the selection is easily understandable, the case against the smallest is trickier. They can also face difficulties in their economic transition in today's world, but the population numbers at stake are globally less illustrative of the transition challenges and the risks of dead ends.

22. If China and India are global exceptions, most of the Asian countries (for example, Thailand, Vietnam, Indonesia, and the Philippines) have large populations. If we exclude the republics of the former Soviet Union and the conflict and postconflict countries (Cambodia and Sri Lanka), the alternatives are limited. Within this demographic range, Nepal or Malaysia could have been interesting cases, the latter being already deeply engaged in structural transformation. The selection of Nicaragua is disputable—it is a postconflict country, affected by a civil war between 1978 and 1989, and its population is limited. Guatemala and Honduras were discussed as alternative options to illustrate the CAFTA-DR countries, but Nicaragua was selected for operational reasons.

23. Owing to its insularity, Madagascar is a unique country case study in Southern Africa. Mozambique and Zambia were other possible case studies but, again, the availability of local partners prevailed.

24. Mexico also holds a special status among developing countries as a result of its longstanding agricultural policy, initially based on the revolutionary agrarian reform that ran from the 1920s to the 1970s. In spite of liberalization of the land market in 1992, this trajectory has shaped the structure of the Mexican agriculture (RS 1 Mexico).

25. The selection includes regions engaged in tropical perennial crops. Among the country cases, examples are found in Kenya and Nicaragua (coffee). Perennials are also strongly represented in Morocco (mainly citrus and olive trees).

26. Decision of the first Advisory Committee meeting in March 2007. The program benefited from a governance structure that included a 10-member Advisory Committee from academia and a Steering Committee of contributing donors.

27. Phase 1 was implemented between April 2006 and March 2007. Phase 2 was scheduled for implementation between June 2007 and June 2008, but the new choices related to the household surveys required a new schedule. Phase 2 was launched in September 2007 and lasted until June 2009, with extensions for Kenya, Morocco, and Mexico until January–March 2010.

28. See annex 1 in the appendix posted at http://www.worldbank.org/afr/ruralstruc, which presents the detailed methodology used for the fieldwork (units of analysis, sampling procedures, dates of collection); the difficulties; and the technical solutions that were adopted to deal with them.

29. This is broadly the case for the Living Standards Measurement Studies (LSMS) initiated by the World Bank in the 1980s, which include 32 countries. In Africa, most of the poverty household surveys were implemented on a national basis, using a very similar approach.

30. In the coming years, the LSMS-ISA program (LSMS Integrated Surveys on Agriculture), launched in 2009 by the World Bank and the Bill and Melinda Gates Foundation in seven SSA countries, will provide panel data focusing on agriculture and linkages between farm and nonfarm activities.

31. RIGA results are also a main reference of the International Fund for Agricultural Development (IFAD) *Rural Poverty Report 2010*, which also makes use of the Rural-Struc survey results (IFAD 2010).

32. In Senegal, the Senegal River Delta region was divided in two—Lower Delta (Bas Delta) and Upper Delta (Haut Delta)—as well as the north of the *bassin arachidier:* Mekhé 1 and 2. In Madagascar, the Antsirabe and Alaotra regions were also split in two: Antsirabe 1 and 2, and Alaotra 1 and 2. In Mexico, it was decided to drop the results of Ixmiquilpan, in the Otomi region of the Hidalgo state, which had been selected as a losing region, because the inconsistencies in the survey results were insurmountable. Then, the Sotavento (Veracruz state) was divided into the lowlands (Tierras Bajas) and the mountains (Sierra de Santa Marta). The Sotavento subregion of Sierra de Santa Marta, characterized by remoteness, low provision of public goods, and a primarily indigenous population, offers the characteristics of a losing region and mitigates the dropping of Ixmiquilpan.

33. Maps of the surveyed regions are displayed at the end of the book. Their main characteristics are provided in annex 3 in the appendix posted at http://www.worldbank .org/afr/ruralstruc.

34. Owing to the regional fine-tuning, the results are displayed for 30 regions and subregions (among the 26 surveyed regions, 5 regions are divided in two, minus the dropped Mexican region of Ixmiquilpan). See the table in annex 1 in the appendix posted at http://www.worldbank.org/afr/ruralstruc.

35. The contributing donors agreed to provide public access to the RuralStruc databases (country databases and core merged database). This dissemination, including adequate documentation using international standards (metadata and variable description), will be progressively implemented with support from the Accelerated Data Program coordinated by the World Bank and the PARIS21 Secretariat. Data are already available through the World Bank's Micro Data Library at http://microdata. worldbank.org/index.php/catalog/670.

36. International dissemination events are listed in annex 2 in the appendix posted at http://www.worldbank.org/afr/ruralstruc.

37. The 14 RuralStruc country reports are posted on the World Bank's RuralStruc Web page: http://www.worldbank.org/afr/ruralstruc.

Chapter 2

The Challenges of Structural Transformation

The previous chapter underscored several new issues that have emerged as growing international concerns in the policy debate in recent years, issues that have changed the policy landscape. Among them, the financial crisis unexpectedly contributed to the resurrection of a theme that had long been ignored in the policy agenda: structural transformation. Although this topic had remained fully relevant in academic circles, it was largely absent from the discussions of policy makers. Reconnecting structural issues with the policy debate was a core motivation for the RuralStruc program.

The political comeback of structural transformation is still very limited. Short-term issues and rescue plans demand most of the attention of governments and donors, and consequently limit their ability to strongly reengage in long-term structural policies. However, two recent contributions are worth citing: the United Nations Research Institute for Social Development report *Combating Poverty and Inequality: Structural Change, Social Policy and Politics* (UNRISD 2010), and the African Union and Economic Commission for Africa Economic Report on Africa 2011 titled *Governing Development in Africa: The Role of the State in Economic Transformation* (UNECA 2011). Interest on the donor side can also be identified: Justin Lin, the World Bank's chief economist, has repeatedly called for a "new structural economics" as a framework for rethinking development (Lin 2010).

Two factors can be put forward to explain this progressive new focus on structural issues. First, the financial crisis has raised questions about the sustainability of the existing growth model and its global imbalances. Thus, new structural solutions are being sought to allow a more sustainable and inclusive development regime, a process exemplified by the many attempts to improve world governance through international regulations and the growing role of the G20. Second, the dramatic actions of rich country governments in dealing with the consequences of the financial crisis through bailouts is a clear reminder of the limits of market-only approaches and suggests that states still have a role to play, particularly in dealing with regulatory and structural issues.

With this evolving context in mind, the main objectives of this chapter are to provide background on the processes of structural change currently under way and to discuss specific challenges faced by the RuralStruc countries and regions with respect to their economic and demographic transitions. The chapter addresses the situation of Sub-Saharan Africa in particular, as it was the last region in the world to begin its structural transformation.

Regional Differences and Positioning of the RuralStruc Countries

There are major differences between the economic and demographic structures · of the RuralStruc countries, which are illustrative of their stage in the process of structural transformation and, more broadly, of the dynamics of the world's regions.

Uneven Economic Transitions

The seven RuralStruc countries were selected because they demonstrate different stages of the structural transformation process. Although a deep analysis based on macroeconomic data could have been presented for each country,[1] this book restricts the discussion to simple and comprehensive figures, and to the most important stylized facts. This allows for a clear presentation of the seven countries' positioning within the process of structural change.

Figure 2.1 is a reminder of the wide differences in income levels among world regions and, above all, of the dramatic differences in their growth over time. It compares SSA as a whole with the three non-SSA RuralStruc countries and other comparators, and underscores the long stagnation of Sub-Saharan Africa compared with other regions (with the notable exception of Nicaragua, whose growth trajectory reflects the consequences of its civil war).

Figures 2.2 and 2.3 show the economic transition of each of the RuralStruc countries (and some comparators) from 1965 to 2005 using three basic indicators: GDP per capita, the share of agriculture in GDP, and its share in employment. This is an efficient way to measure the structural evolution of an economy away from one entirely centered on agriculture. The figures demonstrate very significant differences in the extent and pace of structural change.

Figure 2.2 shows the share of agriculture in employment and in GDP over time. The squiggly lines could be termed the countries' "signatures," not only for their visual resemblance but also because they summarize each country's unique development trajectory. The figure illustrates the importance of agriculture over time, highlights the positioning of world regions through country examples, and shows how the share of agriculture in GDP decreases from SSA

Figure 2.1 Evolution of GDP per Capita among Selected Countries and Regions, 1960–2009

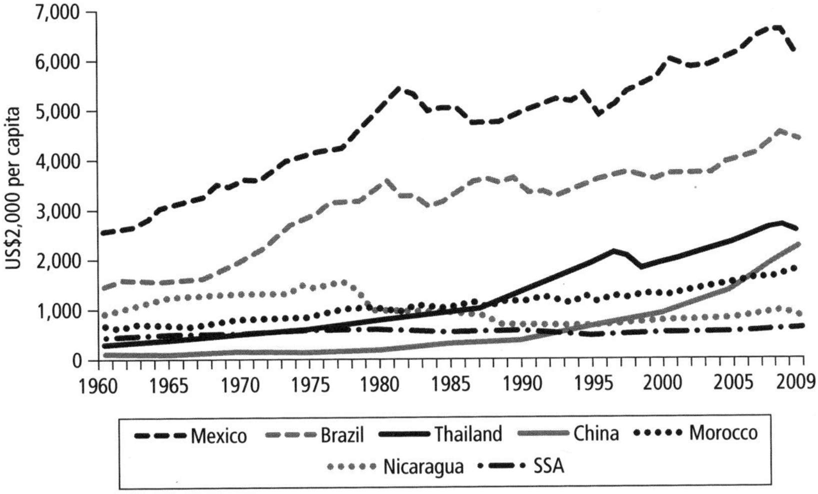

Source: World Development Indicators (WDI).
Note: To avoid clutter, the graph displays an aggregate line for Sub-Saharan Africa rather than a line for the four RuralStruc SSA countries. At this scale, the differences among the SSA countries in terms of evolution are slight.

to Asia and Latin America. It also shows the decreasing share of agricultural employment in the labor force. This change occurs slowly at first, exemplified by the stagnant employment structure observed in Sub-Saharan Africa, and also by China, where the decrease is similarly very slow.

The difference between agriculture's share in GDP (AgGDP) and its share in employment (AgEAP) illustrates a well-known characteristic of structural transformation: an inequality of incomes between agriculture and the other sectors of the economy that reflects differences in factor productivity (Timmer and Akkus 2008). Figure 2.3 shows this structural gap, which clearly highlights rural-urban income differences. The structural gap widens during the early stages of economic development, a consequence of rapidly expanding economic activity in cities and the resultant accumulation of wealth. It narrows as the economy diversifies overall and as urbanization continues, leading to the progressive convergence of rural and urban sectors into a fully integrated economy, with a gap near or equal to zero.

Among the RuralStruc countries, the comparison of gap values confirms that Mexico is deeply engaged in its structural transformation. It is a diversified economy in which agriculture no longer plays a major role (5 percent of GDP). However, even after this transition, the risks of growing marginalization in Mexico's rural economy continue to exist: 25 million people still live in rural

Figure 2.2 Share of Agriculture in GDP and in EAP over Time, 1965–2005
percent

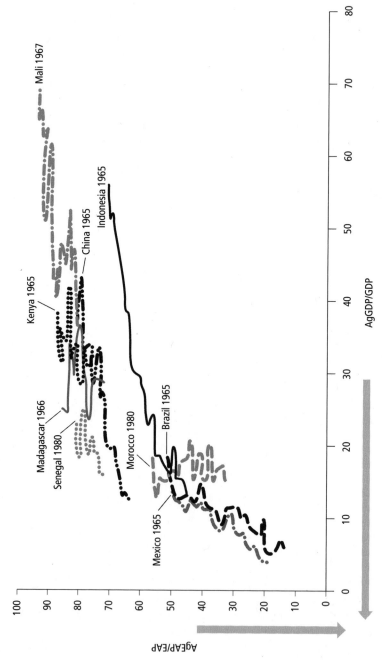

Sources: WDI; FAO.
Note: Final year is 2005. Starting year is given with the country name.

Figure 2.3 Structural Gap and GDP per Capita, 1965–2005 (5-Year Averages)

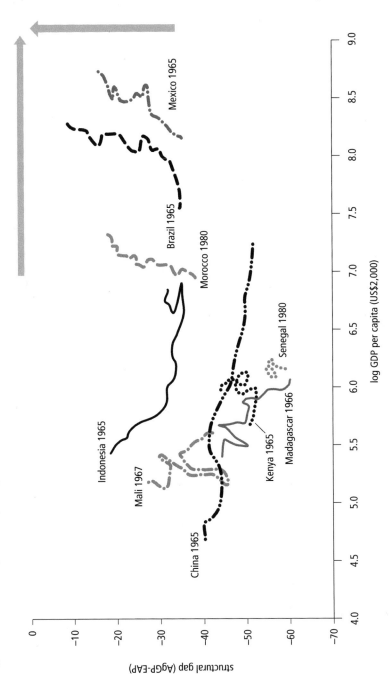

Sources: WDI; FAO; authors' calculations.
Note: Final year is 2005. Starting year is given with the country name.

areas, and between 15 percent and 20 percent of the labor force is in agriculture. Mexico's difficulties in this convergence process are shown through a comparison with Brazil, whose gap value is decreasing much more rapidly.[2]

The cases of Morocco and Nicaragua[3] are more tenuous, because agriculture still plays a significant role in overall value added (15 percent and 20 percent, respectively). The convergence between the rural and urban sectors is well under way, and this process has been especially quick in Morocco. However, the successful deepening of these two countries' economic transitions will rely on their capacity to skillfully manage their internal economic integration in a way that avoids marginalizing remote areas (the mountain zones in Morocco and Autonomous Caribbean Regions in Nicaragua). Agricultural policies could play a significant role in limiting the exclusion processes. The Moroccan government has addressed this issue; in 2008, it launched a new rural development strategy—Le Plan Maroc Vert—based on two pillars: the development of the agro-industrial sector (mainly based on a nucleus of smallholders supplying export-oriented processors called "aggregators") and the promotion of family agriculture. The relative levels of attention afforded to the two pillars and how different approaches would affect the marginalization of rural households continue to be strongly debated (RS 1 and RS 2 Morocco).

In Sub-Saharan Africa, the process of structural change has barely begun. Fifty years after their political independence, SSA countries continue to be characterized by the weight of the agricultural sector in GDP. On average, it stands at about 20 percent, but in most countries—including Kenya, Mali, and Madagascar—it is over 30 percent.[4] SSA countries are also notable for the weight of agriculture in their employment structures. Except in South Africa, agriculture employs, on average, 65 percent of the subcontinent's economically active population; in many countries, including the four RuralStruc countries, the figure is between 70 percent and 85 percent. Thus, agriculture is still the principal source of economic activity and household income.

The most striking phenomenon is the great inertia of SSA's economic structures. Trajectories in the transition are stagnant (see figures 2.2 and 2.3), although the populations show significant mobility, demonstrated most effectively by the speed of urbanization. With an urbanization ratio (percentage of the population living in urban areas) approaching 40 percent, the urban population has increased by a factor of 12 since 1960 (see table 2.5). However, this dynamic has not been accompanied by any sort of significant industrialization. The urbanization-without-industrialization phenomenon so widely observed in Sub-Saharan Africa contrasts with patterns seen in other developing regions, notably Asia, where changes in the economic structure happened very quickly (see figure 2.4). This has resulted in an overwhelmingly high share of services in SSA economies, mainly related to informal urban activities and to the marketing of agricultural products.[5]

Figure 2.4 Evolution of GDP Structure: SSA versus Asia, 1965–2005

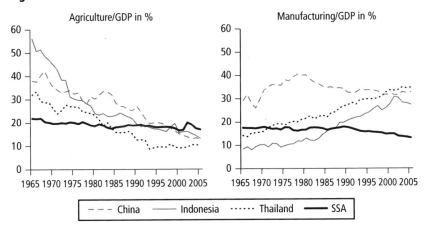

Sources: WDI; World Bank 2009.
Note: Latin American countries are not included as comparators because most of their economic diversification occurred before 1965.

The lack of a dynamic manufacturing sector in SSA has meant that increases in the economically active population have mainly occurred in agriculture or the informal urban sector, which play the role of shock absorbers for Africa's population. The informal urban sector represents about 30 percent to 45 percent of nonagricultural GDP and 70 percent to 90 percent of overall nonagricultural employment (Jütting and De Laiglesia 2009).

With a fragmented regional market consisting of 42 states (continental SSA only), limited success in effective regional integration, and deep levels of poverty that limit local capital accumulation, the growth of SSA's economies is highly dependent on external forces. It is prone to trade shocks related to price volatility and to foreign direct investment and public aid budgets that are often pro-cyclical. These characteristics, along with low labor productivity (a result of the sectoral distribution of labor discussed above), frequent political instability, and rapid population growth (see next section), explain SSA's very weak economic growth and high volatility compared with the rest of the world (table 2.1). This chaotic growth pattern has greatly contributed to the short-term vision of many political leaders and private investors.

In the past two years, the literature on African economic development has been brimming with very optimistic titles: *Lions on the Move* and an *Emerging Africa* Where *Poverty is Falling . . . Much Faster Than* [we] *Think!*[6] However, these victory statements must be carefully weighed against the historical perspective.

Although the recent growth period and Africa's apparent resilience to the global financial crisis are good news, it is not clear that they are the result of

Table 2.1 Compared Dynamics of GDP per Capita Growth among Regions, 1960–2007

Region	% per year	Variation coef.
North Africa and Middle East	2.06	1.68
Sub-Saharan Africa	0.72	3.10
Latin America and the Caribbean	1.73	1.38
East Asia & Pacific	5.44	0.76
South Asia	2.72	0.99

Source: Arbache and Page 2007.

structural solutions that will sustain growth in the long term.[7] With some exceptions (situations of catching up and improvements in governance), growth has initially been brought about by a boom in raw materials. Growth was slower in SSA than in other developing countries (notably East Asia) and it was mainly concentrated in services and construction—the investment rate remained the lowest of any developing region (Ali and Dadush 2010). So far, recent progress has not changed the structural anemia of the subcontinent; in fact, gaps between it and the rest of the world have continued to widen.[8]

New Patterns in Demographic Transitions

Economic and demographic transitions are closely intertwined. World population growth is rapid and characterized by differential growth rates across societies. Consequently, countries are at different stages in demographic transition—a process characterized by a successive reduction in both mortality and birth rates.[9] As a result of these differences, an increasing share of the world's population comes from developing countries. This trend will challenge economic growth, exacerbate the existing asymmetries among regions, and ultimately affect every region's economic structure.

According to UN estimates, the world's population should reach 9.2 billion by 2050—more than 2 billion more people than today (see table 2.2).[10] Although these statistics are widely discussed,[11] the distribution of this population increase across regions receives less attention. While Europe shows characteristics of the final stage of demographic transition (with an aging and declining population), Sub-Saharan Africa and South-Central Asia are still booming. However, the latter two regions are growing at different rates: SSA's population should double by 2050, reaching 1.7 billion people, while South-Central Asia should "only" grow by 40 percent.[12] Thus, by 2050, Sub-Saharan Africa should be the second most populous region of the world, after South Asia. At the same time, East Asia's population growth (mainly China) should come to a halt as a consequence of a huge increase in incomes and possibly a result of the radical

Table 2.2 World Population by Region, Absolute and Share, 1960–2050
millions

Year	1960		1990		2010		2050		2010–50	
Eastern Asia	779	26%	1,337	25%	1,564	23%	1,600	17%	36	2%
South-Central Asia	627	21%	1,250	24%	1,780	26%	2,494	27%	713	40%
Sub-Saharan Africa	229	8%	518	10%	863	12%	1,753	19%	890	103%
Latin America and the Caribbean	220	7%	442	8%	589	9%	729	8%	141	24%
Northern America	204	7%	283	5%	352	5%	448	5%	97	28%
Europe	604	20%	721	14%	733	11%	691	8%	−42	−6%
Other regions	359	12%	739	14%	1,028	15%	1,434	16%	406	40%
World	**3,023**	100%	**5,290**	100%	**6,909**	100%	**9,150**	100%	**2,241**	**32%**

Source: United Nations, *World Population Prospects,* 2008 revision.
Note: For the definition of regions, see http://esa.un.org./wpp/Excel-Data/definition-of-regions.htm.

birth policies in place in China since the 1970s, the consequences of which are debated. As a result, East Asia will progressively face the problem presently seen in Europe—the burden of an aging population—which will weigh heavily on the region's growth rate. Japan is already confronting this situation.

The main result of differential population growth rates (which could change in the event of exceptional circumstances) will be a new mapping of the world and a likely shift in the balance of power. Guengant (2007) says that by 2050, SSA should have regained its former share of the world population—around 20 percent—and overtaken China. (Interestingly, the two had very similar populations in the 16th century—around 100–120 million.) Europe and North America combined should represent fewer than 15 percent of the world's total population (table 2.2).

The different demographic prospects of the RuralStruc countries illustrate variations around these overall regional trends. Three SSA countries—Kenya, Madagascar, and Mali—exceed the regional average increase. Nicaragua's growth is very similar to that of Central America (38 percent), while Mexico—part of the same UN subregion—shows a clear slowdown consistent with the end of its demographic transition (table 2.3).

The main economic concern regarding the demographic transition relates to the evolution of the population's activity structure, which in turn reflects its age structure (Bloom, Canning, and Sevilla 2001). This evolution is revealed in dependency ratios (or activity ratios) that summarize the proportions of active and inactive people in the economy.[13] In the first phase of demographic transition, the population is young, with a high share of inactive youths; during the second stage, these cohorts become active and—if the conditions for growth exist (good economic, institutional, and political environment)—offer a potential bonus to the economy referred to as the "demographic dividend."

Table 2.3 Population of the RuralStruc Countries, 1960–2050
millions

Country	1960	1990	2010	2050	2010–50	
Kenya	8.1	23.4	40.8	85.4	44.5	109%
Madagascar	5.1	11.2	20.1	42.7	22.5	112%
Mali	5	8.6	13.3	28.3	14.9	112%
Senegal	3	7.5	12.8	26.1	13.2	103%
Morocco	11.6	24.8	32.3	42.6	10.2	32%
Nicaragua	1.8	4.1	5.8	8.1	2.3	40%
Mexico	37.9	83.4	110.6	128.9	18.3	17%

Source: United Nations, *World Population Prospects,* 2008 revision.

The third stage corresponds to the aging of these cohorts, which increases the dependency ratio (or decreases the activity ratio).

Figure 2.5 illustrates these staggered and differentiated demographic transitions. As a result of its high population growth rate since the 1960s (higher than 2.5 percent per year over 40 years, with a peak of 3 percent in the 1980s), Sub-Saharan Africa during the 1980s and 1990s faced the weakest activity ratio ever recorded, with only about one active person for every inactive person.[14] Understanding this heavy burden helps provide perspective on SSA's two decades

Figure 2.5 Activity Ratio by Selected Regions, 1950–2050

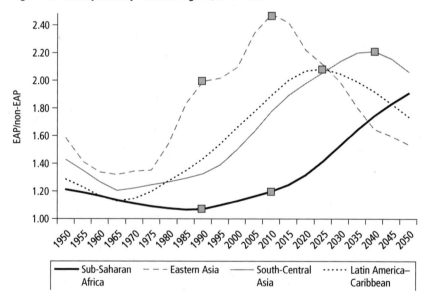

Source: United Nations, *World Population Prospects,* 2008 revision.

of economic crisis and structural adjustment, as well as its current situation. During the same period, East Asia benefited from an outstanding demographic dividend. Its activity ratio grew beyond two active people for every inactive one and fueled the economic growth of the region.[15] South Asia, whose transition lags behind East Asia's by about 30 years, should see this demographic windfall around 2035–40, while SSA will have to wait until after 2050 to reap the benefits of a more favorable demographic structure.

When examined in terms of yearly cohorts of people—particularly yearly cohorts of young labor market entrants—these different demographic trends reveal a coming surge in the labor supply over the next decades in SSA and South Asia.

Figure 2.6 shows the size of the yearly cohort of labor market entrants and illustrates the same trends in the world's most populous regions (Asia and SSA).[16] It provides an estimate of the labor absorption needs of the various regional economies. Currently, Sub-Saharan Africa's yearly cohort of new EAP is around 17 million; it should reach 25 million in 15 years. The peak will occur after 2050. For a medium-size SSA country (15 million people), the yearly cohort was 250,000 in the 2000s; it is expected to reach 400,000 in the 2020s. This means that SSA will see a surge of around 330 million new market entrants in the next 15 years—

Figure 2.6 Yearly Cohorts Entering the Labor Market by Selected Regions, 1955–2050

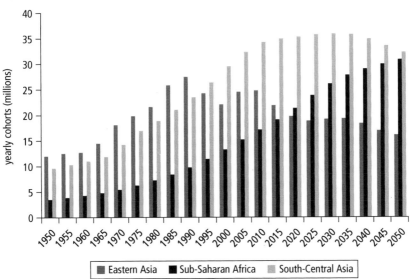

Source: United Nations, *World Population Prospects*, 2008 revision.
Note: Yearly cohorts correspond to 1/10 of the 15–24 age group.

Table 2.4 Labor Market Entrants in the RuralStruc Countries
thousands

Country	New labor market entrants in 2010	Peak of annual additional labor supply	Peak time
Kenya	847	1,545	> 2050
Madagascar	405	736	> 2050
Mali	278	524	> 2050
Senegal	269	452	> 2050
Morocco	638	644	2005
Nicaragua	125	129	2015
Mexico	1,984	2,008	2015

Source: United Nations, *World Population Prospects,* 2008 revision.

roughly equivalent to the current U.S. population.[17] This number is not a projection: These 330 million new labor market entrants have already been born.

Table 2.4 shows what these trends mean for the RuralStruc countries. In SSA, the peak period for labor supply will be after 2050; this is the major difference between SSA and non-SSA countries, where the peak period has already passed or will soon pass. During the next decades, achieving adequate economic growth to create demand for the coming labor surge will be a major concern for Sub-Saharan African societies and governments (World Bank 2009c; UNRISD 2010).

Structural Transformation in a Global Open Economy

The evolutionist view that underlies the canonical model of economic transition is insufficiently questioned today, given the new configuration of the global economy. The globalization process that began at the end of the 1970s is unique and too often mischaracterized as a second globalization, with reference to a first globalization that occurred between the 1860s and World War I. This period was characterized by an increasing movement of goods, labor, and capital among Europe, its immediate periphery (Russia and the Ottoman Empire), and the new worlds—mainly the United States (Berger 2002), but it did not affect the whole world. Rather, it was a process of convergence in the North Atlantic economy, driven by migration flows (O'Rourke and Williamson 1999) and governed by a geopolitical order that included European colonial empires and an American sphere of influence in Latin America.

The processes at play today reflect the growing integration of the world. This globalization is facilitated by continuous technological progress in the transportation of goods, capital, and information; strengthened by the liberalization policies begun in the early 1980s; and characterized by a greater concentration of assets being held by global firms and institutional investors, as well as the development of intrafirm trade and the outsourcing of production. Globalization is also characterized by a convergence in thinking related to common concerns about global change, especially with regard to the impact of human activities on natural resources and climate.

These characteristics foster a deep interconnection of markets and of human societies and, in the process, greatly affect the structures of both. They tend to simultaneously weaken local links in favor of more distant relations (notably in terms of production) and widen existing asymmetries among the different regions of the world.

Is the Historical Sequence of Structural Change Viable Today?

One of the main questions is whether or not, or to what degree, the historical sequence of structural change is viable for today's late developers. This debate includes many traps. Although it has many variants, the historical path of structural transformation is a stylized fact of history, confirmed by statistical evidence.[18] This is a positive, not a normative, statement. However, notions such as "development" and "emergence" are ambiguous and carry certain overtones related to the European (or western) view of world history.[19] In this view, the structural trajectory of today's developed countries is used as the evolutionary measuring stick against which changes in economies and human societies are judged (Gabas and Losch 2008). Despite the limitations and biases inherent in this framework, this book refers to "first" or "late" developers to describe a country's position with regard to the observed historical transition processes.

Timmer and Akkus (2008) argue that if countries are lagging in the process of structural change, it is mainly related to economic growth difficulties and does not imply failure of the historical transformation process. Although this is true in absolute terms, it understates the role of specific historical conditions in past transitions and the potential difficulty of replicating the structural transformation in the same way today.

Importance of the Moment in Time. Prospects for change in any country or region depend not just on internal conditions in terms of population, education, natural resources, and so on, but also on the relationship with the outside world (Gore 2003). For example, limited competition for a country's industrial exports could mean easier industrialization. Because opportunities, constraints, and the balance of power are always evolving, historical context matters. Thus, it is important to highlight the need for a historical perspective in discussing the ongoing processes of structural change.

Today, the evolutionary frame of reference tends to omit three major characteristics of previous transition processes. The first is the global balance of power at the time of the Western European and North American transitions over the 19th and the better part of the 20th centuries. These early transitions from agrarian societies toward more diversified economies cannot be disconnected from European political and military hegemony, which began to develop in the 16th century and was expressed most overtly through colonization and unfair treaties.[20]

This hegemony, which is fully embedded in the history of world capitalism (Braudel 1979; Wallerstein 1989), reduced or eliminated competition[21] and allowed for very attractive situations of both supply and demand with captive markets. Together with the agricultural revolution of the 18th century (Mazoyer and Roudart 1997), it made specialization and industrialization possible (notably through consistent food supplies based on cheap imports) and facilitated high business profitability, which resulted in increased capital accumulation and investment. When the United States went through its own transition in the mid- to late 19th century, it reproduced and deepened many of the features of the European transition.

The second omission is the huge outflow of migrants from Europe during the transition, an opportunity that was fully intertwined with European hegemony (Hatton and Williamson 2005). Between 1850 and 1930, nearly 60 million Europeans migrated to new worlds: the Americas, Australia, New Zealand, and Africa (mainly Algeria and Southern Africa).[22] These "white migrations" (Rygiel 2007) facilitated the adjustment of European economies and their management of the labor surpluses resulting from their demographic transitions, more specifically from rural depopulation and from the insufficient pace of job creation in urban sectors, despite a strong process of industrialization (Losch 2008).

The third omission is specific to the Latin American and Asian transitions, which are frequently cited to confirm the infallibility of the pattern of structural change. Latin American and Asian countries began their transition processes during a very specific period of national self-centered development (Giraud 1996) that characterized the international regime between the 1929 financial crisis and the 1970s (the beginning of the globalization period). Throughout the world, nation-states implemented their own "development projects" (McMichael 1996), characterized by import substitution, protection, and strong state intervention (Chang 2002). Public policies were of paramount importance for both industrialization (Evans 1995; Amsden 2001) and agriculture modernization (Djurfeldt et al. 2005), and they initiated the so-called "developmental state." The independent Latin American countries engaged in this process between the two world wars and continued these policies during the three decades after WWII.[23] They were followed by many of the newly independent Asian countries in the 1950s, and in both cases Cold War funding played its role. Although state-led development strategies produced mixed results and were eventually dropped for reasons of inefficiency, in most countries they contributed to the creation of a strong economic and institutional fabric (skills, processes, experiences). Once the scaffolding of strong state support was rolled back, this foundation helped facilitate the countries' adaptation to globalization.

Sub-Saharan Africa has followed a different path. Its lack of structural transformation over the past 50 years can be largely explained by the historical sequence that led to the continent's late insertion into the global economy and the conditions under which this was finally accomplished. A primary factor was colonial rule, with its captive markets and explicit obstacles to industrialization and education, which led to a deep specialization in primary sectors. Another was the political conditions under which African states were created, especially their inherited colonial borders and adoption of external administrative systems, which resulted in young states that lacked "institutional thickness" (Amin and Thrift 1993). This situation made attempts at national political integration very difficult and costly.

Finally, and perhaps most important, during the early 1980s African states faced a trifecta of globalization, the restrictive policies of structural adjustment, and the heavy burden of their demography (notably, their lowest ever activity ratios). At that time, most African states were only 20 years old. Their youth strongly restricted their institutional capacity to effectively deal with these issues—an important fact that is too often forgotten. They did not have the necessary room to maneuver to engage in strong modernization policies and to create and implement coherent development strategies, as was done in Asia and Latin America.

The Difficulties of Replication. Past transitions occurred within the specificities of their own time, and late developers have to deal with the characteristics of a global open economy. This offers significant new opportunities but eliminates others, exacerbating asymmetries.

Growing Gaps and Shorter Distances. Although each country may be at its own stage of economic and demographic transition, they look out on the same world. As a result of their specific development trajectories and diverse modalities and sequences of integration into the global economy, they have different comparative advantages. However, comparative advantages are not necessarily deterministic. Late developers can benefit from the technological progress and past experiences of the first developers to help build their own skill and asset bases. At the same time, they can seize new opportunities to access growing global markets.

However, these advantages to late-developing countries are constrained by the fact that they must also deal with huge and still growing asymmetries in productivity and competitiveness, not just in the international market but in their domestic markets as well. They must compete on a "stormy open field" (Birdsall 2006), where their productivity is challenged by firms from abroad (particularly from the major emerging countries), while dealing at the same time with the instability of the world economic environment and the growing consequences of global change. These are dramatic challenges for the structural transformation of the late developers.

The overall productivity gap faced by SSA is about 1 to 5 compared with other developing countries and 1 to 100 compared with OECD countries.[24] Such a gap is a major and enduring obstacle to global competitiveness: Even if comparative advantages exist for specific factors (for example, the cost of labor), these are not enough. Competitiveness is not based on production costs alone but includes an economy's responsiveness to the quality requirements of markets and the volume of product a country is capable of supplying. Thus, although quality requirements are a primary barrier to entry into the production of sophisticated products, the volume of supply determines market share, which is the core indicator of competitiveness.

This observation is valid for all sectors of activity, for manufacturing as well as agriculture, and for all countries. Thus, the current context of increasing food demand and high prices is equally favorable to producers around the world, but producers in late-developing countries will have a harder time taking advantage of the new opportunities. They will have to quickly upgrade the quality of their products and increase the supply. If they cannot do this, the new demand will be met by others, and their market shares will suffer.

These asymmetries of productivity and competitiveness in the context of an open economy affect the local dimension of structural transformation as well. Trade across any distance was greatly facilitated by the liberalization process and is quicker than ever as a result of modern telecommunications and transportation. A major consequence of this trend is that the strong local linkages among agriculture, industry, and urbanization—which powerfully contributed to the foundations of old economic transitions—are increasingly weakened by the propensity to rely on imports (UNRISD 2010). While imports are often more cost-efficient and timely—a significant advantage—they do not strengthen the local dimension of development.

The reliance on imports has resulted in changes in patterns of urbanization in many developing countries, where cities (particularly large ones) often depend significantly on imports rather than on their own resources or the resources of their surrounding regions. This situation has contributed to the dramatic expansion of the informal sector, which acts as a buffer in dealing with the differential between labor supply and labor demand. This process of "informalization" is exacerbated in Sub-Saharan Africa, where a long history of very slow economic growth did not affect the fast pace of urbanization (Fay and Opal 2000). Even without the promise of jobs, cities retained their allure: services, potential opportunities, way of life, and so on.

Despite a significant level of heterogeneity in the informal sector,[25] it can be characterized as one of low productivity, marked by underemployment, a lack of job security, and low returns.[26] These factors contribute to the development of urban slums, which are proliferating around cities in the developing world (UN-Habitat 2003; Davis 2006).

Restricted Room for Maneuver. In addition to competitiveness gaps and the changing geography of trade, late developers' transition prospects are hindered by two constraints that were not present during previous transitions: limits on the range of available policy interventions and limits on the opportunities for international migration.

A number of the policy interventions that characterized the transitions of many Latin American and Asian countries are not available to late developers, owing to the current policy agenda. The existing global economic consensus is built on market liberalization and the suppression of policies deemed to be distortive. This perspective prohibits many interventions that in the past were used to promote modernization and increase productivity in both agriculture and manufacturing, notably in Asia (Chang 2002). For example, the policies under which the Republic of Korea and Taiwan modernized in the second half of the 20th century might not be possible under today's WTO regime (Birdsall, Rodrik, and Subramanian 2005).

In the case of agriculture in Sub-Saharan Africa, Bezemer and Headey (2008) show how these external restrictions were endogenously exacerbated by a persistent urban bias in African domestic policy agendas.[27] This was manifested in the extensive taxation of agricultural exports and limited protection from food imports, which favored cheaper food access for urban dwellers. These policies contributed to the heavy burdens faced by African farmers.[28]

However, some of the policy restrictions related to the international consensus are softening, for example, with so-called "smart subsidies." But even with more room to maneuver, many governments do not have the financial capacity to engage in this sort of support while continuing to procure public goods. Budget constraints are severe in a global context marked by an unstable economic environment and volatile levels of international assistance. Additional means will have to be found through fiscal reform.

The second constraint relates to international migrations, which are no longer a viable option for large numbers of people leaving agriculture and unable to find other employment opportunities in their own countries. International migrations have been a growing issue in development studies, although primarily with reference to the impact of remittances,[29] which, in aggregate, account for more international capital flows than does official overseas development assistance. However, the relative ease with which migrants can remit their earnings masks the fact that migration itself is relatively restricted. Even though the total number of international migrants (people living outside their home country) is estimated at 200–210 million, one cannot imagine the repetition in the current geopolitical order of the mass migration from Europe beginning in the mid-19th century. If international borders were opened, "people would certainly come" (Pritchett 2006). But migration is a touchy political issue and borders remain closed to people, although largely open to goods, capital, and many services.[30]

The most active and remunerative migration routes are concentrated in regions peripheral to the European Union and the United States,[31] and future options for migration will likely depend on the demographic evolution of the high-income countries (plus China) and their demand for foreign labor. This demand will likely continue to be met by countries on their periphery, so most late developers will not be able to replicate the migration patterns of the rich world's border countries. Countries such as Mexico and Morocco have approximately 10 percent of their nationals living abroad, and the opportunity for migration at this scale plays a big role in their political economies: It provides large-scale cash transfers and serves as a relief valve for internal tensions associated with structural transformation. To illustrate the impracticality of this model for Sub-Saharan Africa, if 10 percent of the region's population were to migrate, it would mean an outflow of 85 million people, mainly to Europe. This is a politically unfathomable scenario.

Transition Options for Late Developers

All these conditions limit the ability of the late-developing regions to replicate the historical transition process, and there is a growing debate in the development community and in academia about the best options for transition under these circumstances. Discussions refer particularly to SSA and frequently compare the subcontinent with Asia. One of the most critical questions is how to manage the labor supply that exits agriculture (Headey, Bezemer, and Hazell 2010).

The division of population between rural and urban areas will determine the extent of the geographical and sectoral challenges related to a fast-growing labor supply. Although its figures are debatable, the UN's World Urbanization Prospects database offers useful estimates.

Table 2.5 shows the urbanization ratio for the principal regions of the world over time and into the future. It illustrates the very rapid process of urban growth under way in SSA, even when compared to South Asia's urban growth. However, the subcontinent should remain primarily rural until sometime around 2030.

Another feature of SSA's demography is that it is the only region in which rural populations will still be growing in absolute terms in 2050 (see table 2.6). While other regions should register a significant decrease in their rural populations between 2010 and 2050 (−50 percent in East Asia, −10 percent in South Asia, −45 percent in Europe), SSA's rural areas are expected to add 150 million people (nearly 30 percent).

As mentioned earlier, 330 million of today's children will enter SSA's labor market over the next 15 years. On the basis of the forecast urbanization ratios

Table 2.5 Urbanization Ratio by World Regions, 1960–2050
percent

Region	1960	1990	2010	2025	2035	2050	Urban population multiplier
Eastern Asia	20.2	33.0	48.5	59.2	65.5	74.1	4.8
South-Central Asia	18.1	27.2	32.2	39.6	46.5	57.2	5.1
Sub-Saharan Africa	14.8	28.2	37.3	45.2	51.2	60.5	9.5
Latin America and the Caribbean	48.9	70.6	79.4	83.5	85.7	88.7	4.4
Northern America	69.9	75.4	82.1	85.7	87.6	90.2	2.0
Europe	56.9	70.5	72.6	76.2	79.5	83.8	1.5
World	32.9	43.0	50.6	57.2	62.2	69.6	3.5

Source: United Nations, *World Urbanization Prospects,* 2007 revision.

Table 2.6 Rural Population by World Regions, 1960–2050
millions

Region	1960		1990		2010		2050		2010–50	
Eastern Asia	622	*31%*	896	*30%*	805	*24%*	414	*15%*	−391	*−49%*
South-Central Asia	513	*25%*	910	*30%*	1,207	*35%*	1,067	*38%*	−140	*−12%*
Sub-Saharan Africa	195	*10%*	372	*12%*	541	*16%*	693	*25%*	151	*28%*
Latin America and the Caribbean	112	*6%*	130	*4%*	121	*4%*	82	*3%*	−39	*−32%*
Northern America	61	*3%*	70	*2%*	63	*2%*	44	*2%*	−19	*−30%*
Europe	261	*13%*	213	*7%*	201	*6%*	112	*4%*	−89	*−44%*
Other regions	*264*	*13%*	*425*	*14%*	*474*	*14%*	*369*	*13%*	*−105*	*−22%*
World	2,029	*100%*	3,016	*100%*	3,413	*100%*	2,782	*100%*	−631	*−18%*

Sources: United Nations, *World Urbanization Prospects,* 2007 revision, and *World Population Prospects,* 2008 revision; authors' calculations.

(figure 2.7), 195 million of them will be in rural areas (59 percent) and 137 million in cities (41 percent). These workers will present the region with both an opportunity for growth and a serious challenge for employment.[32]

What are the options for employment creation? More broadly, what policy priorities will facilitate sustainable growth and foster economic transition on the one hand and both benefit from and support the demographic transition on the other?

In this debate, views are often strongly divided between industrialists and agriculturists (urbanists and ruralists). For the former, manufacturing is the only real driver of African development and thus of the subcontinent's structural transformation. The industrialists believe that agricultural productivity is too low, the challenges are too great, and the expected progress is too slow; thus, it is more realistic to develop manufacturing and services. The agricultur-

Figure 2.7 Yearly Cohorts Entering Rural and Urban Labor Markets and Rural Population Share in Sub-Saharan Africa, 1955–2050

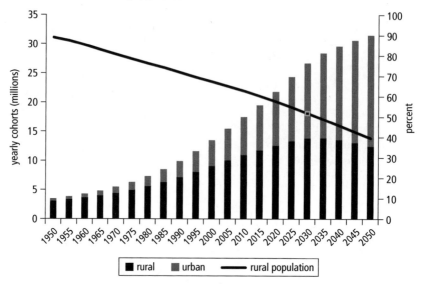

Sources: United Nations, *World Urbanization Prospects*, 2007 revision, and *World Population Prospects*, 2008 revision; authors' calculations.

alists point out that poverty is above all a rural issue and that the rural poor are deeply engaged in agriculture. Thus, agriculture can be a major tool for poverty alleviation, especially in light of the rapidly rising demand for food. Additionally, agricultural development creates opportunities for diversification through the processing of products and an increase in rural demand driven by increased agricultural incomes.

To help clarify this long-standing debate, it is useful to look more closely at the economies of cities and of rural areas, and review their respective capacities to absorb a growing labor force.

On the urban side, the decades of structural stagnation in SSA economies are a strong reminder of the failure of traditional models of transition in the region.[33] As previously noted, rural depopulation and the exit of labor from agriculture mainly fed the informal urban sector. Manufacturing never really took off, and much of the industrialization that did occur later fell victim to its own failures or to the policies of the structural adjustment period.

Although manufacturing is a very narrow sector in SSA, many believe that current conditions present a new opportunity for industrialization. Among the main arguments put forward in support of this view are an improved business climate in many countries, the progressive growth of Asian industrial costs related to increasing wages (notably in China), and new opportunities for task-based production or light manufacturing (UNIDO 2008). The last argument refers to specialization in certain segments of a value chain, rather than engaging in the manufacture of end products. This opportunity is a consequence of the development of outsourcing and intrafirm trade that characterizes globalization. It is appealing to late developers because it requires less capital and fewer skills, and is possible in a weaker economic and institutional environment.

Some economists cite new possibilities for the development of a service industry. The multiple possibilities offered by outsourcing and options related to the development of information and communication technology (ICT) and cloud computing are frequently discussed, especially in the context of leapfrogging the industrialization stage. Opportunities exist, but whether or not they are large enough to enable countries to bypass industrialization is debatable, particularly in an environment in which services are becoming increasingly tradable. Competition will be fully at play, and the challenges associated with winning an effective market share will be high (UNRISD 2010). Countries should not underestimate the requirements associated with such a strategy.

As noted earlier, industrialization did not occur over the past four decades in SSA, despite a huge process of urbanization that offers all the economic advantages of density vaunted by the WDR09 on economic geography. But upgrading from the current environment to a buoyant manufacturing sector will require more than just the exploitation of a country's comparative advantage (for example, labor costs); it will take heavy investment. The government should play a large role, procuring infrastructure and offering incentives to encourage private investment, although the specific types of incentives it should offer are highly debated (Lin and Chang 2009). However, given the challenges SSA will face over the short and medium term (the 15-year period to which this chapter frequently refers), it is difficult to imagine the creation of hundreds of thousands jobs a year in manufacturing. Thus, first priority should be upgrading the existing productive base, which means providing adequate incentives and supporting the most promising parts of the informal sector—those with potential for modernization.

On the rural side, echoing the title of Christiaensen and Demery's 2007 book, there is a need to get "down to earth" or, more precisely, down to basic arithmetic (Headey, Bezemer, and Hazell 2010). The "big figures" presented in this book are unambiguous: Approximately 65 percent of SSA's population still lives in rural areas, 65 percent of the labor force is engaged in agriculture, and 60 percent of the new workers entering the labor market between now and 2025 will be rural. Thus, rural issues must be addressed to deal with poverty and also manage the economic and demographic transitions. Rural activities will account for the "major part of the equation of youth employment" (World Bank 2009c), and failure in rural development will accelerate depopulation of the countryside and create an additional burden for cities.

"Rural activities" refers to both agriculture and the rural nonfarm economy (RNFE), which are strongly interrelated. As described by an abundant literature, increasing farm income drives rural demand, which in turn fosters the development of new activities, rural transformation, and economic change.

Because of the growing demand for food that has resulted from booming populations and increasing urbanization, agricultural growth will be steady for decades to come. For the late developers, the critical question is which growth model will be encouraged. This choice will condition the labor absorption capacity of agriculture, as well as the overall sustainability of its development. Favoring family farms and labor-intensive practices will not have the same consequences on labor absorption as favoring large-scale managerial enterprises and capital-intensive production techniques. Similarly, promoting the multifunctionality of agriculture with a specific focus on resource management will have a different effect on absorption and sustainability than promoting a strong intensification based on industrial inputs.

Limited natural resource endowments could pose a major obstacle to sustainable labor absorption in agriculture and to agricultural development in general (Alexandratos 2005). This is particularly the case for the stock of arable land, which is frequently unknown because of the lack of reliable information systems. And land availability is a relative concept. Its potential for output and employment depends on the way people use it—their level of technology, the infrastructure resources available, and the extent to which public goods are provided (water access and irrigation, roads, eradication of endemic diseases, and so on). Each situation has its own constraints and opportunities, which directly affect the options for development.

This discussion has stressed the need to understand the characteristics of rural situations as a prerequisite for assessing the constraints and room to maneuver, and for identifying the options for fostering rural transformation. But although a better appreciation of factor resources and their availability is indispensable, it is not enough. The realities and the economic environment under which rural households sustain their livelihoods and develop their activities must be understood. This includes the nature and extent of each activity and source of income, and how these might be modified by ongoing dynamics related to globalization. The following chapters explore this reality through the results of the fieldwork implemented by the RuralStruc program.

Notes

1. This work was undertaken during the first phase of the program. It relied on international sources to facilitate the overall positioning of the program and the background of the country studies developed by the national teams.
2. The situation of China is worth noting: Although the country has experienced rapid growth, a strong increase of GDP per capita, and a dramatic decrease in the eco-

nomic weight of agriculture, the structural gap is still widening. This very specific situation is the result of booming cities, mainly along the coast, and lagging rural areas, where a significant share of the population still lives (760 million people, or 56 percent, in 2008). This population remains principally engaged in agricultural activities (according to FAO—which possibly overstates the weight of agriculture— the AgEAP is around 500 million people), and the gap between urban and rural incomes is a source of increasing social and political tension.

3. Nicaragua is not included in figure 2.3 because its time series is too short.

4. The weight of agriculture is very significant in foreign trade. It is the primary foreign exchange earner for nonmining and non-oil-producing countries.

5. The other main sectors are extractive industries and construction, which were dropped from the primary and secondary sectors, respectively, to highlight the specific trends of agriculture and manufacturing.

6. These titles are, respectively, those of McKinsey (2010), Radelet (2010), and Sala-i-Martin and Pinkovskiy (2010). McKinsey's African lions seem to have been shrewdly named to complete the "zoo of emergence" (Gabas and Losch 2008) that includes the Asian dragons and tigers, and the Latin American jaguars. Note that the "lions" counted by McKinsey include the entire African continent, the GDP of which is shared among North Africa (41 percent), South Africa (21 percent), and the rest of SSA (38 percent) based on Africa's GDP breakdown for 2008 in constant 2000 US$ (World Development Indicators).

7. GDP per capita grew about 3.5 percent a year between 2004 and 2008, and bounced back to 2.3 percent in 2010 after the 2009 drop.

8. Using the World Bank's World Development Indicators, Arrighi and Zhang (forthcoming) compare SSA's GNP per capita (including South Africa) to the GNP of what they call the First World (North America, Southern and Western Europe including Scandinavia, Israel, Australia, New Zealand, and Japan). They show that the share of SSA (as a percentage of the First World's GNP per capita) dropped from 5.6 percent in 1960 to 2.3 percent in 2005 (table 1, 43).

9. In the first stage of the transition, the drop in the mortality rate before any comparable decline in the birth rate leads to high population growth, which then progressively diminishes as birth rates slow down. Today, progress in health care and welfare exacerbates the scale of the process and shortens its cycle.

10. The United Nations World Population Prospects are a major reference. The projections are based on a set of assumptions—notably the fertility rate—that is revised every two years. The "medium variant" results of the 2008 revision have been selected.

11. According to many specialists, the UN projections are underestimated (Guengant and May 2009). They are based on a convergence paradigm with a fertility rate target for 2050 that is contradicted by many national censuses. As an example, the 2009 Malian population census (INSTAT 2009) reports a 3.6 percent yearly increase in the Malian population between 1998 and 2009, a far higher rate than the 2.4 percent cited in the World Population Prospects.

12. Beyond this overall picture of a booming Sub-Saharan African population are significant differences among countries. The growth rate of many countries, mostly in Southern Africa, has been affected by the HIV pandemic, and total fertility (num-

ber of children per woman) is unevenly declining. Most of the Sahelian and Central African countries, as well as the African Horn, still report very high fertility (six to seven children per woman), while some countries (for example, Senegal, Nigeria, and Kenya) have begun a gradual and halting slowdown (four to five children per woman). These two groups encompass 85 percent of SSA's population. The countries that are clearly engaged in their transitions (three to four children per woman) are Ghana, Côte d'Ivoire, and Southern Africa (with the exception of Mozambique). South Africa is far ahead in the process (2.5 children per woman). See United Nations, World Fertility data 2008, Guengant (2007) and Gendreau (2010).

13. The ratio commonly used is the dependency ratio, which relates the economically active population (EAP, ages 15 to 64) to the economically inactive population (non-EAP, under 15 and over 64). The ratio is calculated by dividing the total number of non-EAP by EAP. However, the program decided to use the activity ratio (EAP/non-EAP), which is more illustrative. Note that these EAP ratios overestimate the active population: The "working age" group includes many inactive and unemployed persons. Thus, real dependency or activity ratios, including the employment rate, should be used. In many developing countries, and notably in SSA, this approach is complicated by the size of the informal sector and poor information on the labor market. For more on this topic, see, among others, Oudin (2003).

14. The ratio was less than 1 in some countries. The real activity ratio, including the effective employment rate, would be worse.

15. The activity structure's gap between SSA and East Asia is higher today: 1.2 versus 2.5 (see the dots in figure 2.5).

16. Cohorts are commonly calculated by taking 1/10 of the 15–24 age group, creating an estimate of the new entrants in the labor market; that is, youth looking for a job or an activity that provides an income. This is different from the increase in the labor force, which can be estimated by using the net increase (n+1–n) of the EAP (15–64 age group). The second calculation gives a lower yearly cohort than the first: 12 million in 2010 for SSA compared with 17 million. In addition to the imprecision of the EAP, it can also be misleading because the labor markets in most developing countries include many people who continue to work after 65, notably in the agricultural and urban informal sectors, and also retirees from the formal sector who try to augment their pension incomes. Thus, the yearly cohort of labor market entrants gives a clearer estimate in terms of new labor supply.

17. The figures for South and Central Asia are as follows: a yearly cohort of 35 million people in 2010, 37 million in 2025, and an accrued amount of 575 million new labor market entrants over the 15-year period.

18. Timmer and Akkus (2008) have tested the evolution of the structural pattern in 86 countries. The results confirm the robustness of this historical process. The authors included the seven RuralStruc program countries in their sample; they do not diverge much from the general pattern.

19. Rist (1996) refers to development as a "European belief" grounded in a unilateral vision of history, or what Goody (2006) calls the "theft of history." The term "new worlds" reflects the same European perspective, which gave little credence at that time to indigenous peoples.

20. The conditions that led to European hegemony cannot be developed here, but the "discovery" and domination of the Americas appear to have been critical (Grataloup 2007). Pomeranz (2000) notes that hegemony was also related to the fortunate location of coal in Western Europe, which profoundly changed the continent's relationship to natural resources compared with that of China.

21. Bairoch (1997) notes that in 1750 India and China accounted for slightly over half of world manufacturing production.

22. The estimates vary, depending on whether migrants who returned to their home countries are counted. European migrations to the Americas were primarily to the United States, which took in up to 1.3 million immigrants a year at the turn of the 20th century (Daniels 2003), for a total of about 35 million migrants. Canada and the southern part of South America (Argentina, Southern Brazil, Chile) were other important destinations.

23. See the huge work produced by the United Nations Economic Commission for Latin America (CEPAL).

24. Overall productivity is calculated by applying value added to the total working population. The average constant values per worker—based on 2000 to 2005 series—are around $500 for SSA, $2,500 for the other developing countries, and $50,000 for OECD countries (UNCTAD 2006).

25. Ranis and Stewart (1999) distinguish between two informal subsectors: a traditional subsector of the so-called "sponge type," stemming from the surplus of agricultural labor, with incomes sometimes lower than rural incomes; and an informal subsector, now undergoing modernization, that revolves around the formal urban sector.

26. These underemployment traps were detected by Todaro (1971) 40 years ago.

27. There has been an extensive literature on this urban bias and its effect on development since Lipton's initial work (1977) and Bates's contribution (1981), which overlooks some factors related to the idiosyncrasies of every country. The primary explanations for the bias are the legacy of colonialism and an adverse political context, in which the rural African populations had difficulties expressing their voice, while urban constituencies were more directly able to put pressure on governments. Among the cited obstacles to voice were authoritarian political regimes, low threat of rural-based communist insurgency (compared to Asia), low population density, and communication barriers.

28. Anderson and Masters (2009) show a 40-year trend of "disprotection" while other developing countries were protecting their agriculture, notably OECD countries.

29. See, among others, Maimbo and Ratha (2005) and Lucas (2005, 2008).

30. Discussions on the liberalization of migration often refer only to the liberalization of trade in labor. The main reference here is mode 4 of WTO's General Agreement on Trade in Services (GATS) on "movement of natural persons" (individuals traveling from their own country to supply services in another, that is, migrant workers). On this trade perspective, see Winters et al. (2003).

31. Migrations between developing countries must not be underestimated. Half of developing country migrants reside in other developing countries. However, as demonstrated by Ratha and Shaw (2007) who explore these "South-South migrations," 80 percent of these migrations take place between countries with contigu-

ous borders and with relatively small differences in income. Consequently, they accounted for only 10 percent to 30 percent of developing countries' remittance earnings in 2005. These major differences in returns between destination countries are fully confirmed by the RuralStruc surveys (see chapter 4).

32. In comparison, the labor force surge in South-Central Asia (the other booming region) will result in 575 million new workers over the same period, 64 percent (370 million) in rural areas and 36 percent (205 million) in cities.

33. The dualistic model proposed by Lewis (1954), suggesting labor transfers from a traditional agriculture-based sector (with low productivity and a surplus of labor) toward a modern urban industrializing sector, was a major contribution to development economics. See a recent application of Lewis's perspective on the role of agriculture in transition in Berthelier and Lipchitz (2005).

Chapter 3

Rural Realities: Agriculture and Poverty

When the RuralStruc country teams began implementing the surveys it was expected that each region would present different trends in terms of integration into markets, regional dynamism, and economic returns (translated into income levels). After all, the surveyed regions include representatives from countries in each of the WDR08's three worlds of agriculture. More specifically, the expectation was to find very different situations among regions with different a priori classifications—winning, losing, and intermediate—that corresponded to different opportunities for pathways out of rural poverty and different situations in the process of structural transformation.

The results, however, were surprisingly nuanced. Differences among regions are important, and the largest gap is between the surveyed regions in Sub-Saharan Africa and those elsewhere, reflecting very different levels of wealth and development outside of the sub-continent. But despite this diversity, two similarities stood out: the consistent importance of agriculture in the activities of rural dwellers and the staggering magnitude of poverty, almost across the board, in both absolute and relative terms.

This chapter provides an overall picture of rural realities in the surveyed regions. It focuses on agriculture's role in activities and incomes, proposes a comparison of estimated rural incomes to international and domestic poverty lines, and notes their distribution. It goes on to fine-tune the income estimates and address the situation of the lowest income households by assessing their food vulnerability. Finally, it relies on the WDR08 typology to identify the main categories of households on the basis of their income structure, which can indicate trends in rural diversification and possible pathways out of rural poverty.

The Central Role of Agriculture across Different Regional Settings

The regions surveyed by RuralStruc are primarily agricultural regions, without any major extractive industries.[1] They are primarily engaged in an annual crop-type agriculture centered on the production of staples, mainly cereals. The specific crop is often maize in Mexico, Nicaragua (together with beans), and Kenya; rice in Madagascar; rice, millet, and sorghum in Senegal and Mali; and durum and wheat in Morocco. Traditional commodities produced for export or local agro-industries are present in every region, as well as fruits and vegetables and livestock with, in some cases, dairy production (see chapter 5).

Consequently, it was not a surprise to find a deep involvement of the surveyed households in agriculture in the broad sense; that is, crops, livestock, hunting, fishing, and gathering of natural resources, as well as processing of related products. What was surprising was the observed share of "farm households"—rural households engaged in on-farm activities.[2] The RuralStruc teams expected to find more rural dwellers fully participating in other activities, but in most regions, 95 percent to (more often) 100 percent of surveyed households were farm households (figure 3.1). Excluding the landless families of Alaotra in Madagascar (one of the main rice baskets of the country, where some households rely on agricultural waged labor), the two major exceptions are the Souss region in Morocco and the Tequisquiapan region in Mexico, both characterized by strong ties to cities and a more diversified local economy, which is consistent with the development of the country.

In Souss, 25 percent of the households are fully engaged in off-farm activities. This diversification results from the proximity of several surveyed zones to Agadir (a city of nearly 800,000 people and Morocco's fifth largest) and its tourism industry, and above all from the development of agricultural waged labor in the coastal plain's commercial fruit and vegetable sector. Although the Sotavento region in Mexico also shows a slightly higher share of nonfarm households than in the other surveyed regions (15 percent), Tequisquiapan is the most dramatic outlier. There, only 28 percent of households are farm households. The surveyed region of Tequisquiapan corresponds to six localities selected in a valley north of the city of San Juan del Rio (around 210,000 inhabitants), 150 km southeast of the city of Querétaro (whose metro area is home to around a million inhabitants). With a strong urban network, the region has been a fast-growing zone over the past two decades.[3] It has seen the development of both agribusinesses (vegetables and poultry exported to the United States) and manufacturing (*maquiladoras,* as well as high-tech industries such as aeronautics), which has led to the emergence of a strong labor market and the exit of many rural dwellers from agriculture (Rello and Morales 2002).

The examples of Souss and Tequisquiapan highlight the importance of regional contexts and show how they affect rural households' activities. Population densities and urbanization rates (which reflect different stages in the processes of demographic and economic transition), characteristics of the urban network (its concentration and its hierarchy), and the development of transport infrastructure (which determines the fluidity of flows of people and goods) all shape regional landscapes. These features contribute to the observed heterogeneity among rural

Figure 3.1 Share of Surveyed Rural Households with Farms

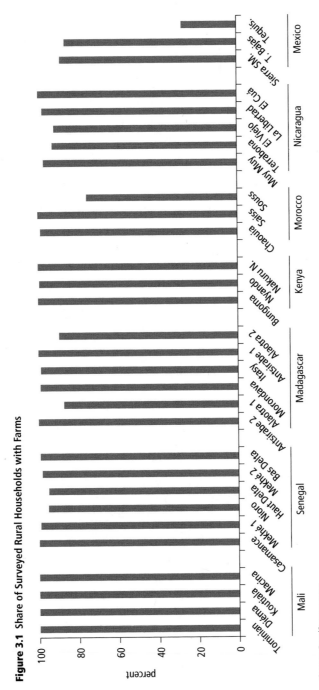

Source: RuralStruc surveys.

BOX 3.1

Density, Distance, and Division: The Three Major Geographic Features of Economic Development according to the WDR09

The World Development Report 2009, titled *Reshaping Economic Geography* (World Bank 2008a), distinguishes three geographic dimensions of economic development that shape market forces: (1) density (economic output per km²); (2) distance (between lagging and leading regions where activity is concentrated); and (3) division (thickness of barriers related to borders, currencies, regulations, ethnicity, and so on).

The three Ds—density, distance, and division—correspond to three scales: local, national, and international. They create disparities in welfare both regionally and among countries that can destabilize parts of a country, entire nations, and even some world regions (p. 22). Governments have many instruments to reduce these disparities. The WDR09 distinguishes three types of instruments: (1) institutions (land, labor, and trade regulations), which are "spatially blind"; (2) infrastructure (which facilitates movement of goods, people, services and ideas), which is "spatially connective"; and (3) interventions (for example, fiscal incentives and preferential trade access), which are "spatially targeted."

The WDR09 proposes a rule of thumb for economic integration: "An I for a D." For a one-dimensional problem (density, distance, or division), spatially blind institutions; for a two-D challenge, institutions and infrastructure; and for a three-D predicament, all three instruments.

Although the report offers tools for analyzing existing asymmetries, its standardized and evolutionist approach (see chapter 2) has led to criticism of its unilinear vision of rural-urban transition and its blind spots, such as the role of financial markets in redrawing the map of the world (see, for instance, Hart 2010).

---

economies in particular and within and between countries in general—the core theme of the WDR09 on economic geography (see box 3.1).

Access to markets and public goods (often provided in urban areas) and ease of networking owing to the quality of communication infrastructure strongly affect the scope of diversification of rural households. Maps in figure 3.3 show the travel time in hours to the nearest city of 50,000 inhabitants. They reflect both the urban structure of the country and the efficiency of its transportation network, and illustrate a remarkable heterogeneity among the RuralStruc SSA countries.[4]

Nevertheless, and despite clear differences among regional contexts, the average regional share of household income earned from on-farm activities is high in the RuralStruc sample and confirms the strong role of agriculture in the surveyed regions.[5] In 22 of 30 regions, on-farm income makes up more than 50 percent of overall income; in 11 regions, the share is 70 percent or more (figure 3.2). The significant role of agriculture is illustrated by another interesting pattern that will be discussed later: The share of household income from on-farm

Figure 3.2 Average Share of On-Farm and Off-Farm Income per Region

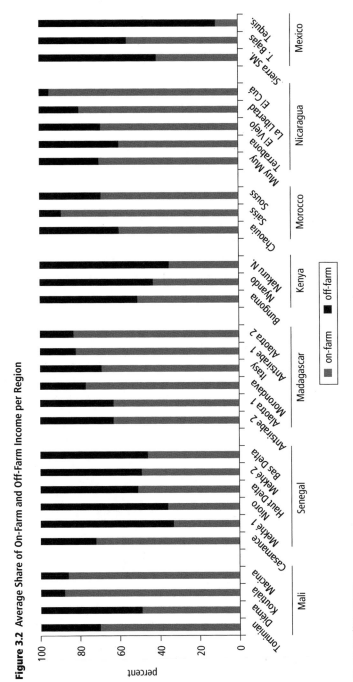

Source: RuralStruc surveys.

BOX 3.2

Urbanization, Transportation Networks, and Rural Livelihoods

The Sub-Saharan African countries are broadly part of the WDR08's agriculture-based world (although Senegal, one of the very few exceptions, is classified as a transforming country). However, the RuralStruc SSA countries reflect very different economic dynamics. Levels of population and population densities, rates of urbanization and types of urban networks, and the quality and density of communication infrastructure all affect the strength of market connections and, consequently, shape rural household activities.

Maps in figure 3.3 show the size of remote areas and the regional imbalances in terms of market access. They also show how different countries are at different stages of urbanization and have divergent population patterns. Mali and Madagascar illustrate highly polarized situations in which the transportation network shapes the overall pattern, while Kenya and Senegal illustrate dramatic processes of densification.

In Kenya, where urbanization is booming (the share of urban population jumped from 32 percent to 45 percent over the past 10 years), rural people living in the central highlands, the central part of the Rift Valley, and the western regions can access cities of at least 50,000 inhabitants in less than two hours. Nakuru North, one of the surveyed regions, is very close to the city of Nakuru, which is the fourth largest city in the country (estimated 2010 population, 544,000) after Nairobi, Mombasa, and Kisumu. However, over the past 20 years, the western part of the country has witnessed a spectacular process of progressive densification of its rural areas and the emergence of two conurbations. One, the western conurbation north of Lake Victoria's Kendu Bay, is home to around 3.9 million people and includes a network of 13 cities, the largest being Kisumu and Bungoma. The other is the Nyanza-Kisii conurbation south of Kendu Bay, home to 2.1 million people and four main cities (Harre, Moriconi-Ebrard, and Gazel 2010). The Bungoma survey zone is part of the rural area of the western conurbation, while the Nyando zone is between the two conurbations (east of Kendu Bay) and enjoys similarly high population densities.

In Senegal, the historical trend of populating the western part of the country has accelerated since the mid-20th century with the development of the *bassin arachidier* and its main cities (Thiès, Kaolack, Diourbel), which flourished with the groundnut industry. However, the past three decades have seen a progressive shift toward the coastal area. A majority of the Senegalese population is located within 100 km of the Atlantic coast and in less than two hours can reach Dakar, Mbour, Thiès, or St Louis. The contrast in densities with neighboring Mali is remarkable.

However, these maps say nothing about the asymmetric distribution of a country's urban population among its cities. When using the primacy index (population of the largest city/population of the second city), Senegal and Mali reveal the extreme weight of their capital cities. Although West African urbanization is becoming more dense in general, the persisting situation in these two countries weakens their urban structures. See the *Africapolis* study (Denis and Moriconi-Ebrard 2009) and the earlier West Africa Long-Term Perspective Study (Club du Sahel-OECD 1998).

Box Table 3.2.1 Level of Urban Concentration in the RuralStruc Countries

Country	Largest city	Second city	Primacy indices	Reference year
Kenya[a]	Nairobi	Mombassa	4.2	2010[e]
Madagascar[b]	Antananarivo	Toamasina	7.8	2005
Mali[a]	Bamako	Sikasso	11.3	2010[e]
Senegal[a]	Dakar	Thiès	10.5	2010[e]
Morocco[a]	Casablanca	Rabat	1.9	2010[e]
Nicaragua[b]	Managua	León	6.5	2005
Mexico[b]	Mexico	Guadalajara	4.9	2003

Sources: [a] e-Geopolis/Menapolis & Africapolis, [b] UnStats.
Note: [e] = estimates.

sources grows with regional wealth in five of the seven surveyed countries: the two exceptions are Kenya and Mexico.[6]

Surveyed regions in Mali, Madagascar, Morocco, and Nicaragua are most heavily involved in farm activities; unsurprisingly, Mexico shows a very different profile (though the Tierras Bajas zone does illustrate some agricultural specialization). Senegal and Kenya reveal different patterns: With the exception of Casamance, where many regional characteristics are similar to those in Mali, all Senegalese and Kenyan surveyed regions display a high level of off-farm income—around 60 percent. Strong connections to cities owing to higher densities and better infrastructure networks (box 3.2) are part of the explanation. However, the amount of off-farm activity does not necessarily imply a disconnection from agriculture; many of these activities are related to agriculture, notably trade of agricultural products and waged labor in agro-industries.

Widespread Rural Poverty

If agriculture's role remains so important in the surveyed regions, what are their characteristics in terms of income level and income distribution? In response to this question, the following section uses household results aggregated at the regional level to provide a general positioning of the sample with reference to existing baselines and discusses income differences within and among countries.[7] Because of the methodology adopted, the comparison is indicative only.

Average Incomes and Poverty Levels

The survey results show a wide range of situations in terms of income levels and income distribution which help to further characterize the regions, their similarities and differences.

Figure 3.3 Travel Time to the Nearest City of 50,000 in the Four SSA Countries

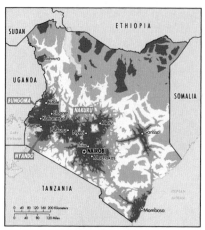

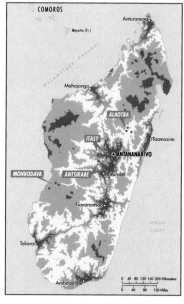

IBRD 38602
JUNE 2011

TRAVEL TIME TO THE NEAREST CITY > 50.000 (in hours)

<2   2–4   4–8   8–16   >16

HOUSEHOLD SURVEY ZONES

○   CITIES > 50.000 PEOPLE

✪   NATIONAL CAPITAL

Source: These maps are part of background knowledge products prepared for the Africa Infrastructure Country Diagnostics study published in Foster & Briceño (2010). See www.infrastructureafrica.org for more detail. They were generated by Siobhan Murray.

This map was produced by the Map Design Unit of The World Bank. The boundaries, colors, denominations and any other information shown on this map do not imply, on the part of The World Bank Group, any judgment on the legal status of any territory, or any endorsement or acceptance of such boundaries.

Overall Presentation. A striking observation is the very low level of income in the surveyed regions, even making a distinction between SSA regions, where poverty is overwhelming, and non-SSA regions (see table 3.1 and figure 3.4).[8] Not surprisingly, owing to the strong and well-known rural-urban divide in terms of welfare, the average income in these rural areas is below the national GDP per capita: Only the surveyed zones of Alaotra 2 (Madagascar) and El Cuá (Nicaragua) exceed this threshold.

The largest gap between observed household incomes and published national GDP per capita is recorded in Mexico, where average incomes in surveyed regions are four to seven times below the national average ($12,780 PPP). The situation in Mexico is worth exploring, because the country is by far the most engaged in its structural transformation and can therefore inform discussion about the major characteristics of the process of change. The observed gap confirms the high level of income inequality in the country and the uneven spatial distribution of poverty, which is highly concentrated in rural areas, as confirmed by the national Gini indexes (RS 1 Mexico).[9] The gap reflects the difficulty of bringing about convergence between rural and urban incomes, one of the most sensitive structural problems during the transformation process, and one that is a particular challenge in fast-transitioning countries such as China (see the structural gap discussion in chapter 2). This gap further reveals a rural pattern that is exacerbated by the survey methodology, but which also has a more generic dimension. Because it focused on localities defined as rural according to the selected definition (below 5,000 inhabitants), the survey excluded many better-off households (including some farm households) who migrated to large rural boroughs or small towns, where they access better services (RS 2 Mexico, 28). As discussed in chapters 4 and 6, this complicates the task of capturing an evolving rural reality in which the "rural" is progressively dissolved within the "urban" through rural depopulation and urbanization.

When considering poverty rates as defined by "absolute" and "relative poverty" lines of $1 and $2 PPP per day, the difference between SSA and non-SSA countries is staggering.[10] In SSA, nearly all the surveyed regions are near the $1 line, with the poorest region of Mali well below the line. Only the richest regions of Senegal, Madagascar, and Kenya are above $2 a day. While Nyando and Bungoma in Kenya are as poor as the other SSA regions, Nakuru North is a notable exception—it has an estimated average income comparable to those in the other non-SSA countries (figure 3.4).

The gap in average income per capita between the poorest and richest zones, highlighted when the focus is on income differences among regions, is an indicator of regional differentiation. The smallest gap is found in Morocco, with a ratio of only 1.8, and the highest is in Madagascar and Kenya (3.5).[11] Income distributions show strong inequalities—a common feature of most agrarian systems—evidenced by the very high incomes of the richest 5 percent of households; this

Table 3.1 Overall Annual Income in the Surveyed Regions

Country	Region	Ex ante classification	#HH	Global annual income per capita in $PPP						
				Mean	Median	Min	Max	Perc 05	Perc 95	GINI
Mali	Tominian	losing	155	196	155	29	2,229	50	405	0.37
	Diéma	intermediary	148	303	205	33	5,568	60	727	0.47
	Koutiala	winning	153	301	265	13	995	82	613	0.30
	Macina	winning	154	422	350	31	1,595	64	942	0.37
Senegal	Casamance	losing	239	360	263	1	3,059	33	1,022	0.47
	Mekhé 1	intermediary	111	436	323	23	2,442	55	1,166	0.44
	Nioro	intermediary	252	376	305	16	2,828	78	988	0.41
	Haut Delta	winning	61	443	268	26	2,238	78	1,106	0.47
	Mekhé 2	intermediary	113	641	511	38	2,996	125	1,578	0.39
	Bas Delta	winning	121	1,014	757	64	6,696	182	2,675	0.56
Madagascar	Antsirabe 2	winning	303	340	247	56	2,640	102	822	0.40
	Alaotra 1	intermediary	385	429	315	41	2,679	133	1,078	0.38
	Morondava	losing	506	493	384	39	2,440	132	1,255	0.38
	Itasy	intermediary	503	520	404	95	3,678	176	1,221	0.36
	Antsirabe 1	winning	206	626	440	65	6,272	130	1,456	0.43
	Alaotra 2	intermediary	115	1,181	788	125	7,521	180	3,309	0.53

Kenya	Bungoma	intermediary	299	527	341	5	4,484	30	1,629	0.48
	Nyando	losing	285	568	259	6	11,224	29	1,924	0.56
	Nakuru N.	winning	289	1,973	1,077	14	22,222	197	6,375	0.51
Morocco	Chaouia	losing	228	1,960	882	11	25,833	77	9,832	0.63
	Saiss	intermediary	261	2,941	1,242	9	73,849	81	10,144	0.67
	Souss	winning	240	3,583	1,493	20	54,054	106	12,497	0.66
Nicaragua	Muy Muy	intermediary	299	1,140	543	24	38,466	64	3,783	0.63
	Terrabona	losing	281	1,136	560	4	20,616	71	3,663	0.60
	La Libertad	losing	288	2,038	895	12	106,712	75	3,179	0.60
	El Viejo	winning	290	1,908	1,006	7	50,864	132	5,919	0.68
	El Cuá	winning	300	2,835	1,166	27	32,946	179	11,246	0.65
Mexico	Sierra SM.	intermediary	175	1,571	1,162	264	15,922	391	4,049	0.41
	Tierras B.	intermediary	145	2,728	2,024	216	16,907	548	8,225	0.41
	Tequis.	winning	364	2,486	1,888	50	21,808	470	6,575	0.39
Total			7,269							

Source: RuralStruc surveys.

Figure 3.4 Average Annual Income per Capita in the Surveyed Regions

$PPP

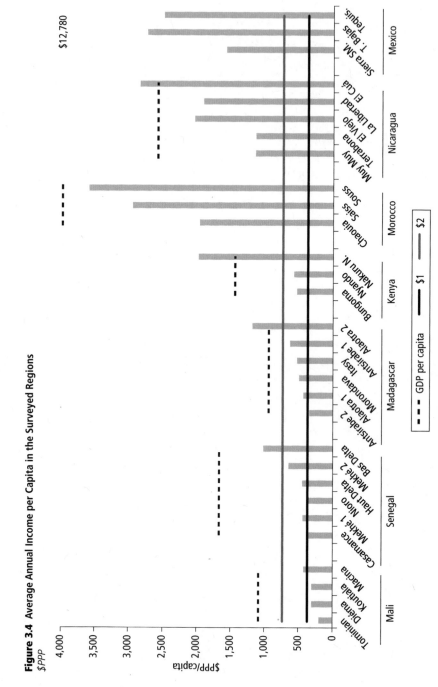

Sources: RuralStruc surveys for household incomes; WDI database for GDP data.
Note: Mexico's GDP per capita is $12,780.

is a reminder of the shortcomings of average values.[12] When median income per capita is used, the patterns within and among the surveyed regions are modified. Although the ordinal ranking of regions from poorest to richest is unchanged, the profiles are more compact, particularly in Morocco and Nicaragua (figure 3.5).

In spite of the limitations of the survey sample, the differences in income levels and income distributions among rural areas in the seven countries say something about structural transformation: In Sub-Saharan Africa, at the initial stages of economic transition, the overwhelming rural majority is poor and inequality is limited (with Gini indexes between 0.35 and 0.45). In Morocco and Nicaragua, which are moving quickly in the transition, average rural incomes are notably higher but with a strong inequality (Ginis between 0.6 and 0.7). This translates into wide differences between average and median incomes. Two of the regions in Mexico, which is the furthest advanced of the sample countries in the process of structural transformation, has the highest median rural incomes for two of the surveyed zones and lower Ginis (0.4).[13] In Mexico, the inequality question has changed and is now a rural versus urban issue. The marginalization of the countryside—*el campo*—has become a critical political concern.[14]

In Sub-Saharan Africa there is an apparent disconnect between household income (figure 3.2) and distance to market (figure 3.3). Income results do not seem to reflect proximity to markets, but they do seem to be correlated with a region's share of on-farm income as shown in figure 3.2. On the one hand, Mali and Madagascar are characterized by strong regional heterogeneity of access to markets and by the importance of their on-farm income shares. On the other hand, Senegal and Kenya have easier market access and more involvement in off-farm activities (which can account for up to 40 percent of earnings). Yet, rural areas are equally poor in all four countries. The three (relative) exceptions to this poverty among the 19 surveyed regions are Nakuru North in Kenya, Bas Delta in Senegal, and one Alaotra subregion in Madagascar. Nakuru and Bas Delta do not have better access to cities than the other surveyed regions (Bungoma and Nyando and the *bassin arachidier*, respectively). This observation is a reminder of an obvious fact: Time to urban markets is not the silver bullet, and the characteristics of urbanization (economic diversification, public goods, services, and levels of urban income) count.

Characterization and Classification of the Surveyed Regions. What do these results mean with regard to the ex ante classification of winning, losing, and intermediary regions used by the national teams to select the regional country cases? If one takes average household income aggregated at the regional level as a good proxy for regional characteristics in terms of rural wealth and rural dynamism, the survey results closely align with the ex ante estimate (see table 3.1). There are, however, some slight differences in ranking (reduced if medians are used) and a few challenging results, which will be discussed below.[15]

Figure 3.5 Median Annual Income per Capita in the Surveyed Regions

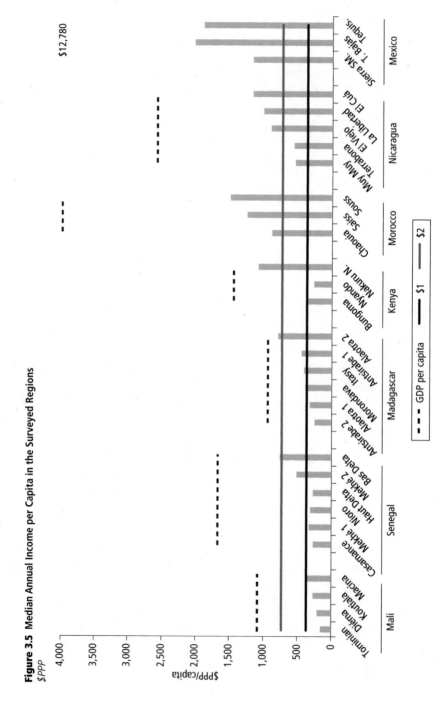

Sources: RuralStruc surveys for household incomes; WDI database for GDP data.
Note: Mexico's GDP per capita is $12,780.

In Mali, Koutiala, at the center of the cotton zone, was chosen as a winning region. It was supposed to illustrate the success of the "white revolution" of cotton in the savannah region. The disappointing income results reveal a crisis in the sector that affects all aspects of regional dynamism. The long-standing unfavorable international cotton price and uncertainties stemming from delayed reforms have resulted in a progressive reduction in cultivated area and led to a decrease in farm incomes. Additionally, large family sizes and migrations into the cotton zone from other parts of Mali (initially motivated by the high returns on cotton) explain the growing stress on resources and falling economic returns. The situation of Koutiala illustrates the famous paradox of Sikasso (named after the other major cotton-growing area in Mali), which expresses the contradiction between the success story of the cotton sector and the relatively low level of income per person in the cotton region (see box 3.3).

BOX 3.3

The Paradox of Sikasso . . . and Koutiala

In Mali, cotton is a strategic sector and is often considered to be the driver of development of the south of the country. The cotton sector directly involves 275,000 producers and nearly 3 million people. Called the "white gold of Mali," cotton fiber has been the country's primary export for several decades. The market has grown continuously since the 1960s, especially after the devaluation of the CFA franc in 1994. The few interruptions in this growth were related to crises in value-chain management; the most dramatic was the "cotton hold-up" of 2001, when cotton production shrank by half as a consequence of a sowing strike by farmers who were dissatisfied with the new prices. A public monopsony, the CMDT (Compagnie Malienne de Développement des Textiles), which engaged in a difficult (and still unachieved) privatization process, deeply shaped the sectors development. CMDT was in charge of providing inputs, extension, collecting, ginning, and marketing and of broader rural development in the cotton area (roads, capacity building of producer organizations, rural credit, technical support, training and literacy programs). The development of the sector allowed farmers to invest in equipment and livestock and to increase their assets, and all of this contributed to cotton's reputation as a powerful driver for poverty alleviation and regional development. However, the Malian Poverty Assessment (EMEP) survey (DNSI 2004) and other related studies showed that cotton production areas, such as Sikasso, have widespread poverty and among the highest child malnutrition rates in the country. The main characteristics of this paradox, according to Wodon et al. (2005) and Mesplé-Somps et al. (2008), are the following:

Poverty in the cotton-growing regions is globally less severe than in other regions.

(box continues on next page)

Household consumption is quite sensitive to cotton prices and volumes produced, and to other conditions that affect local agriculture, notably rainfall. The fact that the EMEP survey was implemented in 2001—the year of the sowing strike—directly affected the survey's results.

Malian cotton producers are clearly better equipped in durable goods (bicycles, motorcycles, radios, television sets) than farmers in other regions. This equipment spreads the benefits of cotton production over the long term, regardless of the circumstances of a particular year. It also reflects the preferential access to credit in the cotton sector.

The education level is generally better in cotton-growing areas, for both primary school attendance and level of adult literacy.

Owing to cotton's reputation in terms of monetary returns, Sikasso is the only region after the capital, Bamako, with a positive net migration flow. However, this migration has affected income per capita, making the region, in some ways, a victim of its success.

Although these indicators may cast the cotton-zone in a positive light, it is important to remember that welfare there is highly dependent on prices and somewhat fragile in the long run, given the context of degradation of natural resources.

The RuralStruc program's Phase 2 results reinforce these findings. The dependency ratio in Koutiala is the highest of the four study regions, reducing the positive effects of cotton production in terms of average income. While the price of cotton was low during the reference period of the survey (crop season 2006–07), the level of income in the cotton-growing region of Koutiala was comparable to that in the Diéma region, a remote rainfed area characterized by a high level of international emigration. However, the cotton producers of Koutiala are better off than those of the Tominian zone, the poorest of the surveyed zones. These disappointing income results mask an important issue: In the cotton areas, farmers are generally less vulnerable, because they are better equipped and better capitalized, particularly in terms of livestock, which plays a buffer role.

Sources: RS 2 Mali; communication with the RuralStruc Mali team 2009.

Regions' income levels are generally consistent with their ex ante classifications in Senegal, but it is worth mentioning the *bassin arachidier* and the Delta. A main observation in Senegal is the general lack of regional variation. Casamance is the poorest of the surveyed regions, but owing to a crisis in the groundnut sector, the *bassin arachidier* (historically the linchpin of the Senegalese economy) is no longer any better off. Mekhé 2 was able to obtain somewhat better economic returns only through crop diversification (cassava) and off-farm activities (handicrafts). The Haut Delta, despite its contract production of tomatoes, is similar to the other lagging regions and is much poorer than the Bas Delta.

In Kenya, Nyando and Bungoma were chosen to illustrate different situations. Bungoma, the intermediate region—endowed with better natural resources and engaged in more diversified agricultural activities, particularly coffee production—was supposed to have been better off. But the estimated incomes in the two regions are similarly sobering and do not differ significantly. They both show a high involvement in sugar cane production characterized by low returns and reliance on self-consumption. On the other hand, Nakuru North, where incomes are 3.5 times higher, confirms its status as a winning region and exemplifies the Kenyan success story. Located in the Rift Valley, with good natural conditions and benefiting from a dense and well-connected local urban network, the region is engaged in maize as well as high-value products in the dairy and horticulture industries. The city of Nakuru offers many off-farm opportunities, boosted by its strategic positioning on the Mombasa/Nairobi/Uganda corridor. Another specific characteristic of Nakuru North is its low dependency ratio (half that of the two other regions), which reveals higher productive capacities per household and consequently higher earning potentials.

The Antsirabe region in Madagascar is a highly diversified agricultural region (rice and temperate cereals, horticulture, dairy), that is well connected to markets and benefits from good infrastructure. Antsirabe, the third largest city in the country with about 200,000 inhabitants, is only 150 km from the capital, Antananarivo, with which it is connected by a paved road in good condition. The Antsirabe region was originally selected to illustrate a winning region. However, severe natural constraints (bad weather conditions and phytosanitary problems, specifically, potato disease) strongly affected yields and, consequently, farm incomes during the surveyed crop season. Additionally, the regional analysis showed that the region was quite heterogeneous, with remote areas facing marketing difficulties and turning more toward self-consumption activities that brought lower economic returns. These factors led to the Rural-Struc program's decision to distinguish between the two subregions.

In Nicaragua, the surprise comes from the two areas mainly dedicated to livestock production—Muy Muy and La Libertad—which were supposed to illustrate very different situations. Muy Muy (located in the "milky way" or dairy belt) was chosen as an intermediary region because of the development of integrated dairy value chains, but the income estimates revealed a harsher reality than expected, mainly because farmers do not benefit from higher milk prices that are captured downstream. On the other hand, La Libertad, selected as a losing region because of constraints such as its location in a remote mountain area with insufficient transport infrastructure and lack of public investments, appeared better off, partly owing to larger land holdings and a specific opportunity to produce and sell farm-processed cheese.

Finally, in Mexico, the aggregated results for the Sotavento region are, as expected, lower than for Tequisquiapan. However, and surprisingly, the average income of the Tierras Bajas subregion is higher than that of Tequisquiapan, the winning region, which proves that the returns from intensive maize produc-

Figure 3.6 Distribution of Households by Income Classes in SSA Surveyed Countries

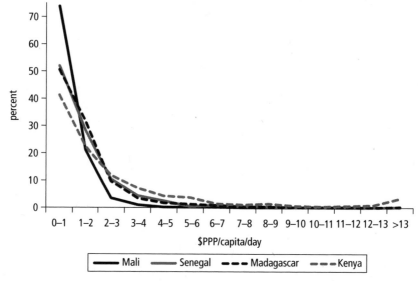

Source: RuralStruc surveys.

tion can be significant and more lucrative than a full specialization in off-farm activities (see below and box 5.5).

Distribution of Rural Incomes. A closer look at the distribution of incomes confirms the strong difference between SSA and non-SSA countries, as well as the importance of intraregional inequalities. When the survey results are aggregated at the national level and when income classes (defined as intervals of $1 PPP) are used, the difference in the shape of the curve is striking (figures 3.6 and 3.7).

In the sample, the reach of absolute poverty ($1/day/person) ranges from 3 percent of the population in the Mexican surveyed regions to 74 percent in the Malian regions. In the SSA surveyed regions, 90 percent to 95 percent of the households are captured in the first three classes (Kenya being slightly better off and Mali worse off). In Mexico, Nicaragua, and Morocco, the distribution is smoother, and the Mexican sample shows a markedly different pattern, peaking at the $3–$4 income class. In the three non-SSA countries, incomes per person per day above $13 are relatively common (between 5 percent and 15 percent of the sample).

To better characterize the regions and their income structures, the results have been split into household quintiles, each consisting of 20 percent of the household sample (see figures 3.8 and 3.9). This breakdown sheds new light on the rural reality of the surveyed regions.

Figure 3.7 Distribution of Households by Income Classes in Non-SSA Surveyed Countries

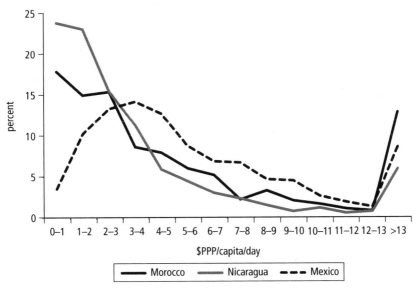

Source: RuralStruc surveys.

A major issue is the level of poverty in the first quintiles, which is dire. The worst incomes per capita are recorded in the poorest regions of Mali, Senegal, and Kenya, with a yearly average of $64 PPP (Tominian), $54 PPP (Casamance), and $51 and $61 in Nyando and Bungoma, respectively. This is only 15 percent of the value of the $1 a day absolute poverty line. The first quintiles in Madagascar are somewhat better: around $150. A major surprise comes from the poorest regions of Morocco and Nicaragua, which are just as poor as the regions surveyed in Madagascar. With the exception of Mexico, the first quintile always accounts for less than $1 a day.

Two common features can be seen in the quintile distributions:

The increase of the average global income per person from quintile 1 to 4 is relatively linear (the income of quintile *n* being from 1.3 to 2 times the income of quintile *n–1*), while a sharper jump is recorded for quintile 5 (the income of Q5 ranging from 2.7 to 5.4 times the income of Q4, in Diéma, Mali, and El Viejo, Nicaragua, respectively).

The profile of the fifth quintile differs from region to region, yet the income distribution of the richest quintile clearly indicates the same phenomenon in many regions: The average of the fifth quintile is pulled up by a handful of better-off households, benefiting from very specific social and economic conditions (for example, a one-off high receipt of a high level of remittances, rents

Figure 3.8 Incomes per Household Quintile by SSA Surveyed Regions
$PPP per capita

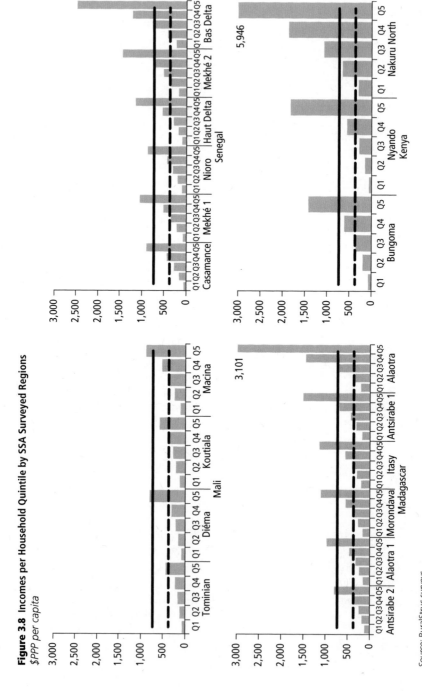

Source: RuralStruc surveys.
Note: $1 PPP poverty line (---); $2 PPP poverty line (⎯).

Figure 3.9 Incomes per Household Quintile by Non-SSA Surveyed Regions

$PPP per capita

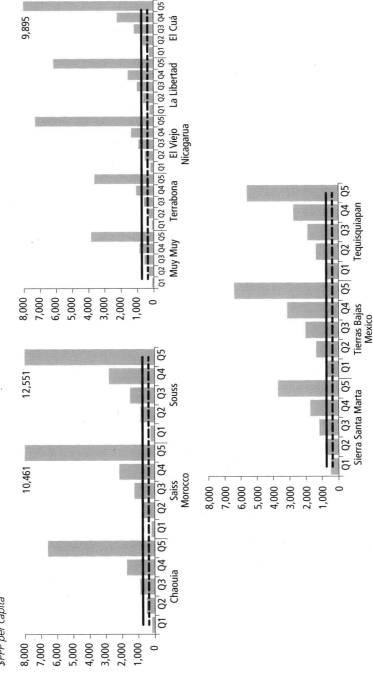

Source: RuralStruc surveys.
Note: $1 PPP poverty line (---); $2 PPP poverty line (___).

related to housing rentals, or an unusually good endowment in land and capital which translates into higher agricultural output).[16]

Fine-Tuning the Income Groups

To further investigate the economic reality of the surveyed households, the analysis is deepened by using adult equivalent ratios and by discussing food security through income conversion into kilocalories. The wealth status of farm households and female-headed households is also compared to the sample averages.

Improving Comparability by Using Adult Equivalent Ratios. Per capita ratios were used in the previous sections to compare the survey results with poverty lines and GDP per person, but it is more accurate to use an equivalent adult approach (EqA) to take into account the very significant differences that can exist among households, regions, and countries in terms of household structures. Adult equivalents are used in the following sections and chapters.

A substantial amount of literature exists on equivalence scales; the Rural-Struc program adopted a conversion based on nutritional needs per age and gender. This equivalence scale overemphasizes the role of food consumption and is consequently less accurate for higher income households. However, it corresponds to the structural reality of most of the surveyed households, in which food expenditures and self-consumption are central.[17]

Differences in household structures depend on demographic dynamics and are exacerbated by social structures and cultural patterns in a given country. Figure 3.10 shows major differences between West African countries, characterized by large households, and the other countries, which are more likely to have classic nuclear families. The large traditional family structures of Mali and Senegal—which aggregate several nuclear households under the authority of an elder, most often the head of lineage and the landlord—still play a central economic role.

The variations in size and structure translate into different dependency ratios, which directly affect the production capacity (the number of economically active household members/inactive members), the consumption pattern, and the available income in EqA. As shown in table 3.2, the higher dependency ratios in the SSA countries confirm the weight of young people and illustrate the unachieved demographic transition of the continent (see chapter 2).

The dependency ratio for the surveyed households is around 1.1 to 1.2 in Mali and Madagascar, 1.0 to 1.1 in Senegal, and reaches 1.3 in Kenya, with the exception of Nakuru, which has a very atypical situation.[18] The non-SSA countries are far ahead in the transition process and should have lower ratios; this is the case in Morocco and in two Mexican regions, but Nicaragua and Sotavento's Sierra de Santa Marta have different patterns.[19] These differences are important in terms of productive capacity and the looming challenges related

Figure 3.10 Size of Households
number of persons present

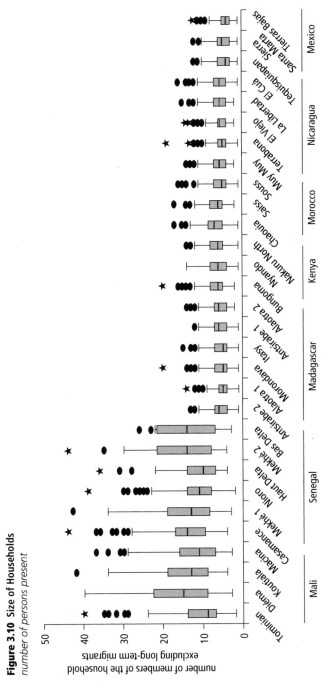

Source: RuralStruc surveys.
Note: Box plots show the distribution of the regional samples. The bottom of the boxes gives the first quartile, the top of the box the third quartile, and the horizontal line within the box is the median. The bottom end and the top end of the whiskers show the lowest and highest data within 1.5 interquartile range (IQR). Dots and stars are outliers. Extreme values are excluded from the figure.

Table 3.2 Household Structure and Income per Adult Equivalent

Country		Household size		Dependency ratio	Total income $PPP		Difference
		No. person	No. EqA		per capita	per EqA	%
Mali	Tominian	11.1	9.3	1.09	196	234	19
	Diéma	18.8	15.3	1.19	303	368	21
	Koutiala	14.8	12.1	1.25	301	368	22
	Macina	12.9	10.5	1.15	422	516	22
Senegal	Casamance	14.3	11.8	1.15	360	439	22
	Mekhé 1	14.7	12.2	0.99	436	527	21
	Nioro	11.8	9.5	1.15	376	484	29
	Haut Delta	12.1	10.1	0.85	443	524	18
	Mekhé 2	15.0	12.4	1.04	641	769	20
	Bas Delta	10.7	9.0	1.00	1,014	1,205	19
Madagascar	Antsirabe 2	5.8	4.8	1.19	340	409	20
	Alaotra 1	5.2	4.4	1.01	429	506	18
	Morondava	5.5	4.5	1.23	493	597	21
	Itasy	5.5	4.5	1.21	520	622	20
	Antsirabe 1	5.7	4.8	1.21	626	744	19
	Alaotra 2	6.0	5.1	0.90	1,181	1,346	14
Kenya	Bungoma	6.7	5.6	1.30	527	641	22
	Nyando	6.3	5.4	1.35	568	660	16
	Nakuru N.	6.5	5.7	0.61	1,973	2,258	14
Morocco	Chaouia	7.1	6.1	0.68	1,960	2,280	16
	Saiss	6.6	5.8	0.59	2,941	3,419	16
	Souss	5.8	5.1	0.57	3,583	4,131	15
Nicaragua	Muy Muy	5.8	4.7	1.02	1,140	1,417	24
	Terrabona	5.5	4.5	0.84	1,136	1,458	28
	El Viejo	5.6	4.5	0.94	2,038	2,575	26
	La Libertad	5.8	4.8	0.89	1,908	2,329	22
	El Cuá	6.0	4.9	1.00	2,835	3,610	27
Mexico	Sierra SM.	4.6	4.0	0.85	1,571	1,824	16
	Tierras Bajas	4.3	3.7	0.63	2,728	3,144	15
	Tequis.	4.6	3.9	0.61	2,486	2,879	16

Source: RuralStruc surveys.

to an increasing labor force. The conversion to adult equivalents increases the comparability between average incomes and results in the improvement of the regional income levels in a range of 14 percent to 28 percent.

Are Farm Households Better or Worse Off? The surveyed households were mostly farm households. What is their estimated wealth compared with that of nonfarm households? When the two types of households are compared, as in

Table 3.3 Household Incomes with and without a Farm

| | | Households with farm | | | | Households without farm | | | |
| | | Observations | | $PPP per EqA | | Observations | | $PPP per EqA | |
Country		No.	%	Mean	Median	No.	%	Mean	Median
Mali	Tominian	155	100	234	187	0	0	—	—
	Diéma	148	100	368	252	0	0	—	—
	Koutiala	153	100	368	318	0	0	—	—
	Macina	154	100	516	418	0	0	—	—
Senegal	Casamance	239	100	439	316	0	0	—	—
	Mekhe 1	110	99	531	394	1	1	120	120
	Nioro	240	95	460	358	12	5	972	585
	Haut Delta	58	95	525	307	3	5	489	527
	Mekhe 2	111	98	775	609	2	2	448	448
	Bas Delta	120	99	1,212	889	1	1	421	421
Madagascar	Antsirabe 2	303	100	409	296	0	0	—	—
	Alaotra 1	336	87	526	388	49	13	373	321
	Morondava	501	99	597	469	5	1	591	676
	Itasy	497	99	625	490	6	1	373	250
	Antsirabe 1	206	100	744	525	0	0	—	—
	Alaotra 2	103	90	1,455	1,052	12	10	405	369
Kenya	Bungoma	299	100	641	429	0	0	—	—
	Nyando	283	99	661	306	2	1	495	495
	Nakuru N.	289	100	2,258	1,213	0	0	—	—
Morocco	Chaouia	225	99	2,280	1,002	3	1	2,309	1,890
	Saiss	261	100	3,419	1,503	0	0	—	—
	Souss	181	75	4,758	2,122	59	25	2,208	1,157
Nicaragua	Muy Muy	290	97	1,436	670	9	3	803	734
	Terrabona	260	93	1,457	690	21	7	1,470	1,081
	El Viejo	264	92	2,678	1,176	24	8	1,440	1,279
	La Libertad	283	98	2,353	1,251	7	2	1,350	1,269
	El Cuá	299	100	3,619	1,428	1	0	995	995
Mexico	Sierra SM.	155	89	1,937	1,444	20	11	947	645
	T. Bajas	125	86	3,383	2,506	20	14	1,651	1,158
	Tequis.	101	28	3,697	2,873	263	72	2,565	2,055
		6,749				520			

Source: RuralStruc surveys.

table 3.3, the results are surprising. The "poor farmer" is a common characterization in rural areas of developing countries, and one might expect an income advantage for households entirely engaged in rural nonfarm activities. However, this is not the case. In the six regions where more than 10 percent of the surveyed households are without a farm, farm household income is, on average, twice that of households without a farm (with the exception of Tequisquiapan, where the difference is lower).

The situation is easily understandable in Madagascar, where families without land access in Alaotra are worse off and rely primarily on low-paying agricultural wages. The case of the Sierra de Santa Marta in the Mexican Sotavento is comparable: Nonfarm households have very few opportunities to sustain their livelihoods in this somewhat remote area. But the situations of Souss (Morocco) and Tierras Bajas and Tequisquiapan (Mexico) are paradoxical, because higher returns from nonfarm activities might have been expected. This surprising result from the survey tempers the common view about vibrant rural nonfarm activities. It is explored further in chapter 4.[20]

The Wealth Status of Female-Headed Households. With the exception of the two West African countries and Morocco, the share of female-headed households is around 10 percent of the sample. Significantly higher shares exist in Alaotra 1, El Viejo (20 percent), and Nyando (30 percent).[21]

These differences have multiple explanations related to the diverse ways different cultures handle certain life incidents (death, divorce) and to diverse migration patterns. In nuclear families, as in Nicaragua and Mexico (and to a lesser extent in Madagascar and Kenya), it is often the husband who leaves for long-term migration, while in West Africa it is mainly young dependents. The Nicaraguan civil war also left its footprint on these figures.

When a female heads a household, the household size is often smaller, which is logical in nuclear family contexts. The variation in the average income between male- and female-headed households is less important than one might expect (table 3.4): Incomes in female-headed households are generally about 10 percent lower, with a few exceptions (Macina, and again El Viejo and Nyando). On the other hand, in Tequisquiapan and the Sierra de Santa Marta in Mexico, average incomes of female-headed households are notably higher. Although the survey encountered difficulties in capturing the reality of migrations (see chapter 4), these results speak for themselves. While incomes reflect the role of remittances, household sizes are smaller and illustrate the consequences of long-term migrations (these households are in the early stages of their family cycle, and migrants are mainly men under 40 years of age who have left their wives in charge of the household).

Viability of Low-Income Households and Food Insecurity. The earlier breakdown of income results into household quintiles illustrated the dire situation of households in the first quintile in every surveyed region outside of Mexico. Their situations improve slightly when EqA is used (an increase of between 15 percent and 30 percent at the regional sample level—see table 3.2) but remain calamitous. How do the poorest households manage to survive, and how are they able to sustain their livelihoods with such low income levels?

Table 3.4 Share, Size, and Annual Income of Female-Headed Households

| Country | Region | Female-Headed HH | | HH size in EqA | | $PPP per EqA | |
		No.	%	Male HH	Female HH	Male HH	Female HH
Mali	Tominian	0	0.0	9.3	—	235	—
	Diéma	0	0.0	15.3	—	368	—
	Koutiala	1	0.7	12.1	4.4	367	495
	Macina	2	1.3	10.6	6.2	520	203
Senegal	Casamance	7	2.9	11.9	9.2	441	365
	Mekhé 1	3	2.7	12.4	6.3	519	799
	Nioro	13	5.2	9.6	7.7	473	698
	Haut Delta	5	8.2	10.5	5.8	499	794
	Mekhé 2	1	0.9	12.5	4.4	772	399
	Bas Delta	6	5.0	9.1	7.0	1,207	1,163
Madagascar	Antsirabe 2	25	8.3	4.9	3.6	409	406
	Alaotra 1	82	21.3	4.6	3.6	516	471
	Morondava	82	16.2	4.8	3.2	601	574
	Itasy	54	10.7	4.7	3.1	616	670
	Antsirabe 1	14	6.8	4.9	2.3	736	852
	Alaotra 2	11	9.6	5.3	3.6	1,362	1,188
Kenya	Bungoma	33	11.0	5.7	4.7	628	745
	Nyando	87	30.5	5.8	4.6	818	300
	Nakuru N.	48	16.6	5.9	4.4	2,255	2,272
Morocco	Chaouia	11	4.8	6.2	4.1	2,299	1,922
	Saiss	1	0.4	5.8	3.0	3,426	1,587
	Souss	4	1.7	5.1	3.8	4,175	1,521
Nicaragua	Muy Muy	35	11.7	4.8	4.3	1,472	1,000
	Terrabona	41	14.6	4.5	4.3	1,467	1,406
	El Viejo	65	22.6	4.4	4.9	2,891	1,491
	La Libertad	30	10.3	4.8	4.7	2,342	2,216
	El Cuá	42	14.0	4.9	4.7	3,670	3,241
Mexico	Sierra SM.	24	13.7	4.1	2.8	1,776	2,621
	T. Bajas	13	9.0	3.8	2.7	3,187	2,712
	Tequis.	50	13.7	4.1	2.8	2,820	3,247

Source: RuralStruc surveys.

The program used kilocalories (kcal) as a unit for income measurement to determine whether quintile 1 households were able to sustain their minimum food requirements with their existing incomes. This approach is a proxy—household needs cannot be reduced to food needs only, but it provides an estimate and helps refine the comparison among surveyed regions. Household incomes in EqA were transformed into kilocalories by using the local cost of households' main food staple. Incomes in kcal per EqA per day were then compared with the average individual's daily food needs, estimated by the World Health Organization (WHO) at 2,450 kcal per adult person per day.[22]

The cost of the kilocalorie varies from one country to the next and among regions in the same country (table 3.5): from $0.10 PPP to $0.49 PPP for 1,000

Table 3.5 First Quintile Total Income in $PPP and Kilocalories

| Country | Region | Price of 1,000 kcal in $PPP | Q1 Total income per EqA per day | | | | Kcal available/ daily needs | Main consumed staples |
| | | | in $PPP | | in kcal | | | |
			Mean	Index	Mean	Index		
Mali	Tominian	0.12	0.21	100	1,730	100	0.7	Millet sorghum
	Diéma	0.12	0.26	123	2,132	123	0.9	Millet sorghum
	Koutiala	0.11	0.39	188	3,557	206	1.5	Millet sorgham Maize
	Macina	0.19	0.36	171	1,870	108	0.8	Rice
Senegal	Casamance	0.15	0.18	86	1,197	69	0.5	Rice
	Mekhé 1	0.16	0.25	120	1,556	90	0.6	Rice
	Nioro	0.15	0.34	164	2,268	131	0.9	Rice
	Haut Delta	0.16	0.30	144	1,863	108	0.8	Rice
	Mekhé 2	0.15	0.56	271	3,755	217	1.5	Rice
	Bas Delta	0.15	0.72	349	4,825	279	2.0	Rice
Madagascar	Antsirabe 2	0.23	0.38	183	1,647	95	0.7	Rice
	Alaotra 1	0.21	0.49	235	2,319	134	0.9	Rice
	Morondava	0.20	0.53	253	2,626	152	1.1	Rice
	Itasy	0.25	0.64	309	2,564	148	1.0	Rice
	Antsirabe 1	0.23	0.57	274	2,471	143	1.0	Rice
	Alaotra 2	0.21	0.64	308	3,041	176	1.2	Rice
Kenya	Bungoma	0.44	0.20	98	462	27	0.2	Maize
	Nyando	0.49	0.16	78	329	19	0.1	Maize
	Nakuru N.	0.34	0.92	441	2,693	156	1.1	Maize
Morocco	Chaouia	0.18	0.58	281	3,241	187	1.3	Wheat
	Saiss	0.16	0.61	296	3,841	222	1.6	Wheat
	Souss	0.21	0.77	372	3,679	213	1.5	Wheat
Nicaragua	Muy Muy	0.18	0.36	176	2,026	117	0.8	Maize
	Terrabona	0.20	0.40	194	2,013	116	0.8	Maize
	El Viejo	0.20	0.64	311	3,222	186	1.3	Maize
	La Libertad	0.19	0.79	382	4,174	241	1.7	Maize
	El Cuá	0.18	0.88	426	4,912	284	2.0	Maize
Mexico	Sierra SM.	0.10	1.49	720	14,942	864	6.1	Maize
	T. Bajas	0.10	2.25	1,086	22,549	1,304	9.2	Maize
	Tequis.	0.10	2.18	1,050	21,795	1,260	8.9	Maize

Source: RuralStruc surveys.

kcal of corn in Mexico and in Nyando, Kenya, respectively. The cost of a kilo-calorie depends on the type of cereal cultivated in the region and the overall environment of the value chain. Mali's dry cereals (millet, sorghum, maize), mostly consumed in rainfed areas, are notably less expensive than rice ($0.11 PPP versus $0.19 for 1,000 kcal). But rice costs in Senegal are less than in other countries ($0.15 PPP), with little regional variation. These low costs are the result of strong market competition between imported broken rice and local rice. Similarly, Mexico's least expensive kilocalorie is the result of the permanent pressure of cheap imports from the United States and from government support for large commercial farmers (through credit mechanisms and technical assistance for the acquisition and use of technical packages); this support helps them compete against imported corn and leads to relatively good overall productivity at the national level.

Table 3.5 offers a new vision of the dire reality of the first quintile households and helps explain how poor rural households try to adapt to such low overall income levels in $PPP.[23]

Fourteen of the 27 surveyed zones in which the daily Q1 income is below the $1 PPP poverty line (that is, all countries except Mexico) would theoretically be able to satisfy their very basic food needs. In the other 13 zones, the situation of the poorest is most critical and confirms a strong food insecurity. All the poorest regions in every SSA surveyed country are characterized by a very high household vulnerability. The case of Bungoma and Nyando in Kenya is particularly awful and exacerbated by the high cost of maize in western Kenya. Muy Muy and Terrabona in Nicaragua also show high vulnerability. Moving back to the full sample (table 3.6), in 11 of the 19 SSA surveyed zones, 10 percent or more of the households are unable to reach the 2,450 kcal threshold; in three zones (Casamance, Antsirabe 2, and Nyando) more than 20 percent of households are in this position.

In conclusion, the kcal approach is a useful complement to the comparison on a monetary basis. It helps explain the apparent nonviability of low-income households and confirms the dire state of the poorest households. Food insecurity persists and is a major reality in several regions. This is confirmed by the perceptions of heads of households regarding their own food security situation: 23 percent to 40 percent of households in Mali, 15 percent to 43 percent in Senegal, and over 40 percent in some regions in Madagascar (Antsirabe) and Nicaragua (El Viejo) say their food security has deteriorated over the past five years, in quality as well as quantity (figure 3.11). This perception may have been exacerbated by the start of the food price crisis during the surveyed year (end of 2007–early 2008) and may have worsened in the following months. It corroborates the harsh reality of many rural households in numerous surveyed regions.

Table 3.6 Household Income Distribution Expressed in Kilocalories
percent

Country	Region	Classes of total income in kcal per EqA per day		
		< = 2,450	2,451–4,900	> = 4,900
Mali	Tominian	19	41	40
	Diéma	12	24	64
	Koutiala	5	10	86
	Macina	14	25	60
Senegal	Casamance	22	22	56
	Mekhé 1	17	15	68
	Nioro	12	25	63
	Haut Delta	13	31	56
	Mekhé 2	4	9	87
	Bas Delta	4	4	92
Madagascar	Antsirabe 2	29	41	31
	Alaotra 1	11	38	51
	Morondava	6	28	65
	Itasy	6	38	56
	Antsirabe 1	8	27	65
	Alaotra 2	3	19	77
Kenya	Bungoma	15	14	71
	Nyando	22	21	57
	Nakuru N.	1	1	97
Morocco	Chaouia	7	7	86
	Saiss	8	4	87
	Souss	8	5	87
Nicaragua	Muy Muy	12	13	75
	Terrabona	13	13	74
	El Viejo	8	6	85
	La Libertad	5	8	88
	El Cuá	3	8	89
Mexico	Sierra SM	0	0	100
	T Bajas	0	0	100
	Tequis.	1	1	98

Source: RuralStruc surveys.

Livelihood Strategies

In the face of such difficult situations in many of the surveyed regions, how do rural households choose livelihood strategies likely to help them meet their needs and build a future for their children?

Figure 3.11 Heads of Households' Perception of Their Food Security

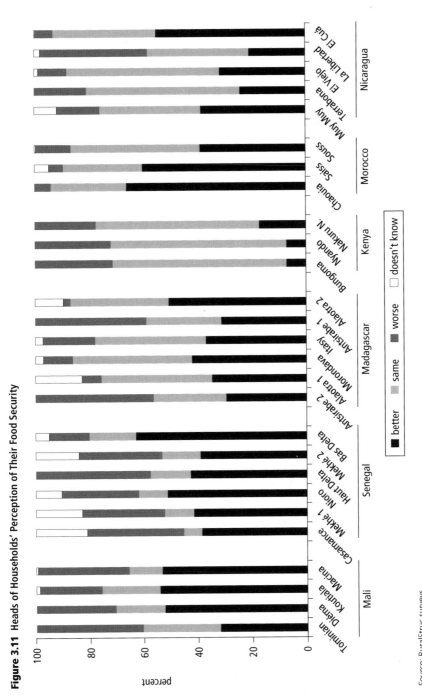

Source: RuralStruc surveys.
Note: Results not available for Mexico.

The WDR08, with its focus on exit pathways out of rural poverty, provides a helpful framework for discussion of the RuralStruc program's results. Using the approach developed by the RIGA project (see chapter 1), the WDR08 identifies four livelihood strategies among rural households (World Bank 2007, 75): (1) *farm-oriented* households derive most of their income from farming activities;[24] (2) *labor-oriented* households sustain their livelihoods from wage labor in agriculture, in the rural nonfarm economy, or from nonagricultural self-employment; (3) *migration-oriented* households choose to leave the rural sector entirely or depend on transfers from members who have migrated or on public transfers; and (4) *diversified* households combine income from the other three strategies.

Following the WDR08 Typology

Using these definitions,[25] table 3.7 and its companion figure (figure 3.12) display the survey results based on the WDR08 categories and provide an overview of how rural households are distributed among the four livelihood strategies. The large share of the farm-oriented category confirms the role of agriculture and on-farm incomes in the surveyed regions. In 18 of the 30 regions, on-farm income represents the major source of livelihood. In 12 regions it is the main strategy for more than 50 percent of the interviewed households; in 4 regions (Koutiala and Macina in Mali, Saïss in Morocco, and El Cuá in Nicaragua), it sustains 80 percent of households. In Kenya and Senegal, farm orientation does not appear as a generalized pattern, and Mexico is confirmed as a unique case.

As noted earlier, only one region is off-farm-oriented: Tequisquiapan is massively engaged in labor activities (80 percent), which corroborates the low number of households still engaged in on-farm activities. In the other regions, the off-farm orientation barely exceeds 30 percent, except for Mekhé 1 in Senegal, Nyando in Kenya, and El Viejo in Nicaragua, where a third of the households are labor-oriented. Migrations never appear as a strong pattern, even in countries such as Morocco, Nicaragua, and Mexico, where many households are traditionally engaged in migrations.[26] Few households are migration-oriented: Only Diéma in Mali, Chaouïa and Souss in Morocco, and Muy Muy and Terrabona in Nicaragua show migration of 7 percent to 8 percent.

Household specialization mainly occurs for farming. On the other extreme, the diversification category is well represented in all the surveyed zones and leads in 12 regions, with a maximum of 84 percent in Sotavento's Sierra (Mexico). However, the importance of diversification can be overstated; it is highly sensitive to the selected threshold of 75 percent of income, which tends to polarize the survey results. Additionally, Davis et al. (2007) consider this threshold as a specialization level rather than an orientation. To test the sensitivity of the threshold, the sample was broken down on the basis of a 60 percent limit (see table 3.7). The 15 percent difference strongly modifies the overall pattern: The

Figure 3.12 Livelihood Strategies in the Surveyed Regions Using WDR08 Typology

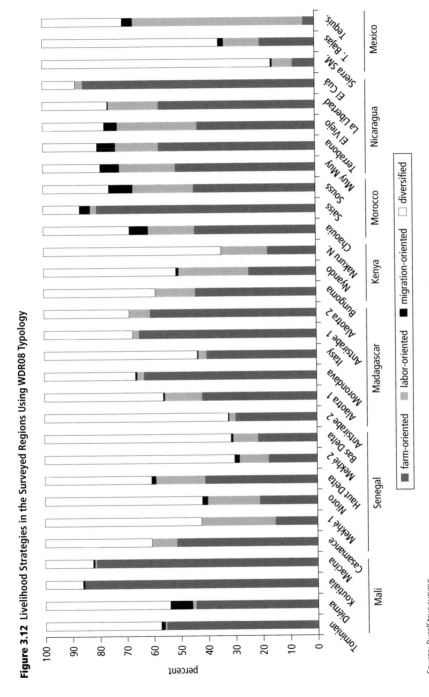

Source: RuralStruc surveys.
Note: Breakdown at the 75 percent threshold.

Table 3.7 Livelihood Strategies in the Surveyed Regions Using WDR08 Typology
percent

Country	Region	No.	Typology WDR08—threshold 75%				Typology WDR08—threshold 60%			
			Farm-oriented	Labor-oriented	Migration-oriented	Diversified	Farm-oriented	Labor-oriented	Migration-oriented	Diversified
Mali	Tominian	155	55.5	0.6	1.3	42.6	72.3	1.9	4.5	21.3
	Diéma	148	44.6	1.4	8.1	45.9	60.1	2.7	14.2	23.0
	Koutiala	153	85.6	0.0	0.7	13.7	92.8	1.3	0.7	5.2
	Macina	154	81.2	0.6	0.6	17.5	88.3	2.6	0.6	8.4
Senegal	Casamance	239	51.5	9.2	0.0	39.3	63.6	16.3	1.7	18.4
	Mekhe 1	111	15.3	27.0	0.0	57.7	25.2	46.8	3.6	24.3
	Nioro	252	21.0	19.0	2.0	57.9	33.3	37.7	2.8	26.2
	Haut Delta	61	41.0	18.0	1.6	39.3	52.5	26.2	3.3	18.0
	Mekhe 2	113	17.7	10.6	1.8	69.9	31.0	37.2	2.7	29.2
	Bas Delta	121	21.5	9.1	0.8	68.6	36.4	37.2	2.5	24.0
Madagascar	Antsirabe 2	303	29.7	2.3	0.3	67.7	61.4	11.6	0.3	26.7
	Alaotra 1	385	41.8	13.8	0.5	43.9	55.3	26.2	1.3	17.1
	Morondava	506	63.2	2.6	0.6	33.6	79.6	6.7	0.8	12.8
	Itasy	503	40.2	3.0	0.4	56.5	59.2	14.5	1.2	25.0
	Antsirabe 1	206	65.0	2.4	0.0	32.5	82.0	6.3	0.0	11.7
	Alaotra 2	115	60.9	7.8	0.0	31.3	67.0	19.1	3.5	10.4

Kenya	Bungoma	299	44.1	14.7	0.0	41.1	52.8	30.8	0.0	16.4
	Nyando	285	24.6	25.6	1.1	48.8	33.7	43.9	1.8	20.7
	Nakuru N.	289	17.6	17.0	0.0	65.4	29.8	46.0	0.3	23.9
Morocco	Chaouia	228	44.3	17.1	7.0	31.6	52.6	25.4	11.0	11.0
	Saiss	261	80.5	2.3	3.8	13.4	84.3	3.8	5.4	6.5
	Souss	240	44.6	22.5	8.8	24.2	50.0	28.8	10.4	10.8
Nicaragua	Muy Muy	299	51.2	20.7	7.0	21.1	55.5	28.8	8.7	7.0
	Terrabona	281	57.3	16.0	6.8	19.9	61.6	21.7	8.5	8.2
	El Viejo	288	43.1	29.5	4.9	22.6	45.1	37.8	5.9	11.1
	La Libertad	290	57.2	18.6	0.3	23.8	63.4	26.2	1.0	9.3
	El Cuá	300	85.3	2.7	0.0	12.0	90.3	4.7	0.0	5.0
Mexico	Sierra SM.	175	8.0	7.4	0.6	84.0	14.3	34.9	1.7	49.1
	T. Bajas	145	20.0	13.1	2.1	64.8	32.4	22.1	4.1	41.4
	Tequis.	364	4.1	62.6	3.8	29.4	5.2	86.3	5.2	3.3
		7,269								
Madagascar	1993 (*)	2,653	59.4	9.5	1.4	29.6				
Nicaragua	2001 (*)	1,839	18.9	48.2	0.9	32.0				

Sources: RuralStruc surveys, adapted from WDR08 (World Bank 2007); *RIGA results in Davis et al. 2007, 162.
Note: The primary strategy is shaded.

share of the diversified group is halved everywhere except in the Sotavento, which attests to the resilience of its diversified orientation. In some regions (Antsirabe 1, Alaotra 2, Chaouia, Muy Muy, Tequisquiapan), the category's importance is reduced threefold or more. The diversified category remains dominant only in the two Sotavento zones; the transfer of households mainly benefits the farm-oriented group (in Mali and Madagascar) and the labor-oriented group (Kenya and Senegal). The labor orientation of Tequisquiapan's households is strongly increased (86 percent).

If the program's results are compared with those of the RIGA project for Nicaragua and Madagascar—the only two common case studies (but with different years of reference, 2001 and 1993, respectively)—significant differences emerge, notably in Nicaragua (see table 3.7), where the share of labor-oriented households according to RIGA is 48 percent, instead of a maximum of 30 percent in the RuralStruc study. On the other hand, the share of farm-oriented households is much lower: 19 percent for RIGA compared with 43 percent to 85 percent for the RuralStruc surveys. The results are not so markedly different in the case of Madagascar, even though the reference period spans 15 years. One probable explanation for these differences is that RIGA's findings are based on aggregated national results, whereas RuralStruc data illustrate regional situations. Although the survey methodologies, level of analysis, and years of reference differ, these gaps illustrate the difficulty of establishing comparable measurements of income across countries, which was clearly indicated by the WDR08 (World Bank 2007, box 3.2).

Moving Forward

This typology of livelihood strategies helps explain the configuration of the studied regional economies. So far, it confirms the domination of farm-oriented households and the more limited role of alternative strategies based on off-farm activities or migration. It also serves as a reminder that the alternatives to farming are quite restricted and illustrates the limitations of local opportunities, which do not necessarily appear when data are aggregated at the national level.

As the WDR08 illustrates, it is difficult to ascertain the effectiveness of these livelihood strategies as pathways out of poverty. The lack of dynamic data, the high heterogeneity among households, and the small number of households per type of strategy at the regional level prevent any discussion of income levels per livelihood strategy.[27]

The application of the WDR typology to the wide range of situations in the RuralStruc program leads to two large groupings of households: One is strongly specialized in on-farm activities and the other is more diversified, without a significant specialization in any one of the off-farm activities. But, in fact, little is known about the characteristics of these activities. What constitutes "on-farm" and "off-farm" in the surveyed regions? Defining these characteristics is the objective of the next two chapters.

Notes

1. Annex 3 in the appendix posted at http://www.worldbank.org/afr/ruralstruc presents a brief overview of the main characteristics of these regions.

2. The program defines a farm household as a household directly engaged in agricultural activities in the broad sense and earning incomes, in cash or in kind, from these activities, whatever the level of productive assets and their ownership (for example, owned, rented, or lent land). See chapter 4 for the definition of household activities.

3. The valley of San Juan has four cities of 25,000–55,000 inhabitants, including Tequisquiapan (27,000).

4. The threshold of 50,000 inhabitants comes from the WDR09 agglomeration index and was used as one of the variables for the regression work based on the survey results (see annex 5 in the appendix posted at http://www.worldbank.org/afr/rural struc). It was not possible to generate equivalent maps for the three non-SSA countries, but their degree of urbanization and their infrastructure networks would have resulted in a dark-gray–black color for most of the surveyed regions.

5. This calculation is made on the full regional sample, including all the households (with farms and without farms), and is based on the share of the regional means corresponding to the regional structure of incomes (see chapter 6 for a discussion of the calculation of means). Off-farm activities are detailed in chapter 4; they include agricultural wage and nonagricultural wage employment, self-employment, public and private transfers, and rents.

6. In every country, regions have been sorted from left to right, from the poorest to the richest in relative terms. This pattern appears clearly in figure 3.4.

7. To allow for comparison, household incomes per capita aggregated at the regional level were converted from local currency units (LCUs) into international dollars at purchasing power parity ($PPP) for the year 2007, which is the year of reference of the collected information (see annex 1 in the appendix posted at http://www .worldbank.org/afr/ruralstruc). The same conversion into international dollars was applied to GDP per capita and domestic poverty lines initially expressed in LCUs.

8. The estimated total income per household is an aggregate of monetary incomes and incomes in kind (self-consumption) valued at the market price (see annex 1 in the appendix posted at http://www.worldbank.org/afr/ruralstruc).

9. This income gap is strengthened by the selection of the surveyed regions, as the southern part of the country is more broadly affected by rural poverty and characterized by smaller farm structures.

10. Annex 4 in the appendix posted at http://www.worldbank.org/afr/ruralstruc shows the domestic poverty lines for each country. However, national definitions of poverty are often influenced by political considerations, and the large variety of threshold types do not facilitate the overall discussion. Eleven of the 19 surveyed regions and subregions in Sub-Saharan Africa are below domestic poverty lines (the exceptions are Kenya and Madagascar, where the poverty thresholds are very low).

11. The figure recorded in Morocco is striking because the relative homogeneity among regions is in stark contrast with the huge heterogeneity within regions (among the highest of the seven countries) as expressed by the Gini indexes. The presence of some high-income households, whose earnings come mostly from rents (housing), obviously affects the sample's means and explains this pattern of apparent homogeneity, which is undermined by the income distribution (RS 2 Morocco,

151). The intraregional heterogeneity also results from the definition of the surveyed regions—particularly in Saïss and Souss—and from the national team decision to group plain and mountain localities. In Souss, the identification of a subregion for Taliouine in the mountain area could have been an option.

12. More broadly, and perhaps unsurprisingly, Gini indexes tend to be higher in the richest surveyed regions in every country except Mali, where the richest region—Macina—is internally equal, which reflects the homogeneity of land assets and production techniques in the irrigation scheme of Office du Niger, where the surveys were conducted.

13. This evolution has similarities with the debated Kuznets' curve, which has been contradicted by new evidence (see Bourguignon and Morrisson 1998; Deininger and Squire 1998). However, the discussion here is limited to rural areas and not overall country results, and this evolution in inequality sheds light on the process of rural transformation (see chapter 6).

14. Inequalities, rural poverty, and growing discontent about the consequences of NAFTA led to a strong social movement initiated in 2002 by rural producers organizations and named ¡El campo no aguanta mas! (The countryside can't stand it anymore!). See Sánchez Albarrán (2007) and Puricelli (2010).

15. Morocco is the only country where the ex ante classification is fully respected.

16. This feature is illustrated by the descriptive statistics of Q5 presented in annex 4 in the appendix posted at http://www.worldbank.org/afr/ruralstruc.

17. See annex 1 in the appendix posted at http://www.worldbank.org/afr/ruralstruc.

18. The mean dependency ratio observed in Nakuru North is consistent with other panel data, which also show ratios around 0.60 (RS 2 Kenya, 79), and it matches national statistics. A possible explanation is the demographic characteristics of the city of Nakuru, which is exceptionally youthful: 55 percent of the population is less than 20 years old and 75 percent is less than 30 years old (Republic of Kenya 2005). In addition, only 55 percent of Nakuru North households have children, which could be explained by the permanent migration of young people to host families in the city.

19. Population growth rates have fallen in Nicaragua since the mid-1990s. However, rural areas show a specific pattern related to the consequences of the civil war (fewer male adults) and long-term migration (long-term migrants are not counted in the household number of persons present on which the ratio is calculated). The latter is applicable to the Sierra de Santa Marta, which also has higher birth rates characteristic of indigenous populations.

20. In Nicaragua, although the share of households without a farm is smaller than in Souss and Mexico, the results of a comparison between farm and nonfarm households vary depending on the type of ratio (mean or median). The median incomes of nonfarm households are higher than those of farm households, but the average income for farm households is higher than that of nonfarm households. These distorted results mean that there are a small number of specialized and better-endowed farmers.

21. The case of Nyando appears exceptional. Panel data from the Tegemeo Institute confirm a rapid increase in female-headed families, 80 percent of whom are widows. AIDS is the most likely explanation.

22. The adopted methodology and conversion table are presented in annex 1 in the appendix posted at http://www.worldbank.org/afr/ruralstruc.

23. The table also shows new income gaps among regions. Using Tominian—the poorest region of the RuralStruc sample—as a baseline (index 100), the income conversion into kilocalories modifies the scale between the richest and poorest regions: Excluding the Mexican zones, where the kcal cost is very specific, the largest gap between rich and poor is nearly halved (2.8 to 1.0 instead of 4.4 to 1.0).

24. The WDR08 actually identifies five strategies. It splits the *farm-oriented* category into subsistence farming and market-oriented farming. The farm-oriented group is discussed further in chapter 5 with the program's results on market insertion.

25. The threshold for each group is 75 percent of total income. Farm-oriented households rely on farm production (all types); labor-oriented households rely on wages (all types) and nonfarm self-employment; and migration-oriented households earn their income from transfers (public and private) and other nonlabor sources, such as rents. In diversified households, none of these income sources contributes more than 75 percent of total income.

26. For a discussion of the difficulties of capturing remittances, see chapter 4.

27. "A household's income structure does not tell whether it is engaged in a successful income strategy. Each of the strategies can become a pathway out of poverty, but many households do not manage to improve their situation over time, reflecting the marked heterogeneity in each of the activities and the fact that income varies widely for each of the strategies" (World Bank 2007, 77).

Chapter **4**

Exploring Off-Farm Diversification and the Rural Nonfarm Economy

Not surprisingly, in the regions surveyed as part of the RuralStruc program, farming activities are extremely prevalent. However, each region is also home to a large amount of off-farm economic activity. This observation raises two questions. First, what are the characteristics of these rural off-farm activities? Second, what determines the extent and progression of their development? These questions serve as starting points for a discussion of the second hypothesis (H2) of the RuralStruc program, concerning the adaptation of rural households to challenges presented by their changing environment. Are these processes of adaptation new and have they led to a reshaping of rural areas? Or are they similar to historical paths of structural transformation? Above all, do they contribute to the improvement of rural livelihoods? In other words, is the much-praised rural nonfarm economy (RNFE) the best answer for dealing with recurring rural poverty?

The results obtained from the surveys provide a rather nuanced picture of the changes currently under way. They show very different types of diversification that are strongly related to the unique opportunities in each region. After reviewing the literature on diversification, this chapter addresses the various types of off-farm activities in which RuralStruc households engage: wage labor (agricultural and nonagricultural), self-employment, transfers, and rents.

The Question of Rural Diversification

It is necessary to review the existing debate on rural diversification before proposing a classification of rural activities and incomes. A careful definition of categories of activities is critical to avoid any misunderstanding or bias in the analyses.

A Brief Overview of Rural Diversification and the Related Debate
An important research trend has highlighted the observation that rural households in developing countries increasingly derive their incomes from nonagri-

cultural activities and transfers. A recent review of this literature (Haggblade, Hazell, and Reardon 2007) describes the multifaceted characteristics of the rural nonfarm economy. Haggblade (2007) stresses that the long-standing debate on RNFE involves four perspectives, all of which are rooted in development economics. The RNFE can be considered through the lens of agricultural growth linkages, its contribution to employment, its role in regional development, or its essential contribution to household income strategies. The RuralStruc program used the last perspective.

The increasing diversification at the rural household level results from both push (negative) and pull (positive) factors. On the pull side, a major driver is the new employment opportunities that derive from improved connections among rural areas, markets, and cities; a consequence of overall economic development and improvements in transportation and communication infrastructure as a whole (for example, cell phones and associated new services, such as cash transfer systems). But diversification also stems, on the push side, from more difficult farming conditions. These can be related to demographic growth, which can lead to growing pressure on natural resources (smaller landholdings and overused and degraded land) and can result in reduced agricultural incomes. They also stem from the many changes in institutional and economic environments related to liberalization policies and globalization that have occurred since the 1980s. New market opportunities have developed from these changes in the environment. However, the end of price regulation, the removal of subsidies (particularly for inputs), and the withdrawal of public-funded technical support have also created a more unstable and often more difficult environment for farm households. And the difficulties are exacerbated in remote areas, where market imperfections are more numerous (missing markets, high transaction costs) and provision of public goods is insufficient.

In the face of all these changes, along with the growing costs of many services (particularly education and health in Sub-Saharan Africa), many rural households are dealing with a need for more cash and more stable incomes. Under intense financial stress, they engage in risk management or coping strategies in which they seek additional income outside of agriculture.[1] As summarized by Barrett and Reardon, "diversification is the norm. Very few people collect all their income from any one source, hold all their wealth in the form of any single asset, or use their assets in just one activity" (2000, 1–2).

The importance of rural diversification is a strongly debated issue. The widely differing results in the literature arise from significant differences in the definition of activities, the objective of the study (for example, income versus employment estimates), and the type of data used (second or firsthand, and collection methods). The results also reflect the huge heterogeneity of income structures among countries, among regions within countries, and among households of the same region, as well as the scarcity of information on rural incomes. Compiling information from very diverse sources into aggregated data sets is a common feature of the literature on the RNFE (see chapter 1).

On the basis of many references, Haggblade, Hazell, and Reardon (2010) say that nonfarm activities account for about 30 percent of full-time rural employment in Asia and Latin America, 20 percent in West Asia and North Africa, and only 10 percent in Sub-Saharan Africa. However, when they refer to income data, which include revenues from seasonal and part-time activities, the estimated figures are significantly higher: 50 percent for Asia and Latin America, and 35 percent for Africa. All the data suggest that the old vision of rural economies focused solely on agriculture no longer fully reflects reality.[2]

How to Classify Rural Activities and Incomes

Discussion on the diversification of livelihoods is difficult because there are a number of parallel debates about the RNFE, not all of which take the household perpective (with reference to Haggblade's four perpectives). But even if one manages to keep all of these discussions straight, studying livelihood diversification is complicated by a lack of agreement on the definition of different types of activities and incomes.

Barrett and Reardon (2000) use a three-way classification for the economic activities of a rural household. They distinguish the sector (primary, secondary, tertiary), function (self- or wage employment), and location (local or elsewhere) of each activity. In this classification, the common definition of the RNFE includes all activities other than agricultural activities; that is, all secondary, tertiary, and nonagricultural primary activities, whatever the location and function.

To fine-tune the discussion, Davis et al. (2007) divided rural activities into six categories: (1) crop production, (2) livestock production, (3) agricultural wage employment, (4) nonagricultural wage employment, (5) nonagricultural self-employment, and (6) transfers (private and public). The first three categories are considered "agricultural" activities, while the last three are "nonagricultural" activities. Further, the first two categories are "on-farm" activities, while categories 4 and 5 are "nonfarm" activities. Agricultural wage labor is always considered an "off-farm" activity, but that term can be misleading: Sometimes it is used exclusively to apply to agricultural wage labor, and other times it is used to refer to all activities that are not conducted on a household's farm (activities 3 through 6).

Transfers are a separate category because they are not an income-generating activity but rather an income source. Money is transferred from household members who live elsewhere (typically in the form of remittances), from other households (donations), or from public or nongovernmental bodies (typically subsidies or social grants). The program also considered the specific case of rents, which are typically generated by rental revenues (from physical assets) or securities.

Figure 4.1 Classification of Activities and Incomes of Rural Households

Rural incomes

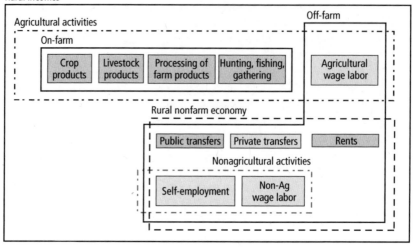

Source: Authors.

The RuralStruc program chose an income classification taxonomy that takes the perspective of the household rather than the activity, because its purpose and objectives are to identify patterns that express the complex livelihood strategies adopted by rural households. Consequently, the "off-farm" group includes all activities conducted and incomes generated away from the family farm, regardless of the sector or function. This includes agricultural wage employment and all other nonagricultural activities and incomes. The off-farm group is larger than the RNFE by the amount of agricultural wage labor.[3]

Thus, on-farm income includes crop and livestock production; on-farm processing of products;[4] and earnings from hunting, fishing, and gathering of natural resources.[5] Off-farm income corresponds to wage employment (agricultural and nonagricultural), self-employment, public and private transfers, and rents (figure 4.1).

A wide range of household strategies correspond to many possible combinations of these activities and incomes. Off-farm diversification does not mean the complete abandonment of crop and livestock production. The specific blend of activities in a household depends on existing assets and returns, and on the opportunities presented by the economic environment in terms of investment options and risk. Labor and capital can be reallocated locally to other activities when alternatives exist, or to other places when factor displacement is the only option.

The Reality of the Off-Farm Economy in the Surveyed Regions

The RuralStruc sample illustrates a large variety of livelihood strategies that combine different activities and sources of income. The importance of off-farm sources at the aggregate level will be discussed first, and an analysis of specific sources of income will follow.

Importance and Nature of Off-Farm Activities and Incomes

In the surveyed regions off-farm sources of income are widespread and share two main characteristics: their low returns and their failure to conform to patterns in terms of type or distribution.

Widespread Development but Low Returns. While agriculture remains the backbone of rural livelihoods in most of the surveyed regions (as shown in chapter 3), off-farm activities exist everywhere and provide a substantial complement to on-farm income or, in some cases, progressively replace it. Figure 4.2 shows the participation rates of surveyed rural households in off-farm activities by distinguishing among strictly farm households (with no off-farm activities

Figure 4.2 Participation in Off-Farm Activities in the Surveyed Regions *(% of households)*

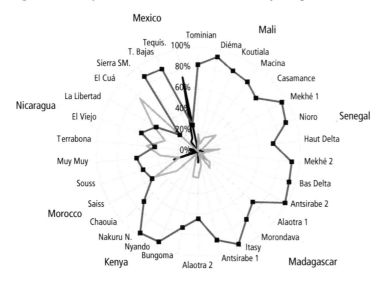

— % strictly nonfarm HH   — % strictly farm HH   ■ % of HH combining farm and off-farm

Source: RuralStruc surveys.

or income), farm households combining both types of incomes (on- and off-farm), and nonfarm households (those without a farm and therefore with no on-farm income).

In the SSA regions, the level of participation of rural households (almost all of which are farm households) in off-farm activities is extremely high (between 80 percent and 95 percent). In fact, it is higher than the levels observed in the non-SSA regions that have patterns of on-farm specialization. Specialization is particularly evident in Morocco and Nicaragua, where a significant share of households rely exclusively on farming activities (notably 50 percent in Saïss and Terrabona, and 75 percent in El Cuá). The three Mexican regions are unique. In Tequisquiapan, many households are no longer engaged in farming at all, while the Sotavento zones are still highly diversified.

Translated into earnings, off-farm activities' contribution to overall household incomes varies strongly by region, as shown in figure 4.3. Contrary to the results presented by Reardon et al. (2007), a work that compiled 40 studies in Africa and Latin America, the differences between SSA and non-SSA regions are less important than the differences observed within each group of countries, and SSA regions do not appear to be less diversified than non-SSA regions.

The paradox highlighted by this chart is the gap between the value of off-farm income and its share of overall household income. In the non-SSA regions, the value and the share follow the same trend, while in the SSA regions—with the exception of Nakuru North, Kenya—very low earnings from off-farm activities contribute a large share of total household income. This pattern, which is especially obvious in Senegal, relates to the high level of poverty discussed in chapter 3 and the limited availability of diversification strategies, a topic that will be explored further.

At the cross-national level, off-farm activities generate low incomes in SSA regions, where they provide the average household with less than $400 PPP per EqA per year (in Mali, Madagascar, and Casamance in Senegal, that number dips below $200 PPP). The exceptions to this pattern are the Bas Delta (Senegal) and Nakuru North (Kenya), where the value of off-farm incomes is higher and reflects more dynamic regional economies. This dynamism cannot be read simply as proximity to a city. In other regions in Kenya and Senegal, connection to a city is not enough to foster good returns from diversification; for example, Nyando in Kenya is quite close to Kisumu, which is larger than Nakuru (see figure 3.2 in chapter 3). In non-SSA countries, with the exception of agricultural-based regions, the value of off-farm incomes is higher (from $600 PPP to $1,600 PPP per EqA). Tequisquiapan ($2,600 PPP), where 70 percent of households do not engage in on-farm activities at all, is a unique case; it illustrates the situation of wealthier regions, where the role of agriculture has significantly diminished but the overall welfare of rural households is not necessarily better than in regions that are more focused on agriculture (see chapter 3).

Figure 4.3 Average Regional Value and Share of Off-Farm Income in the Surveyed Regions

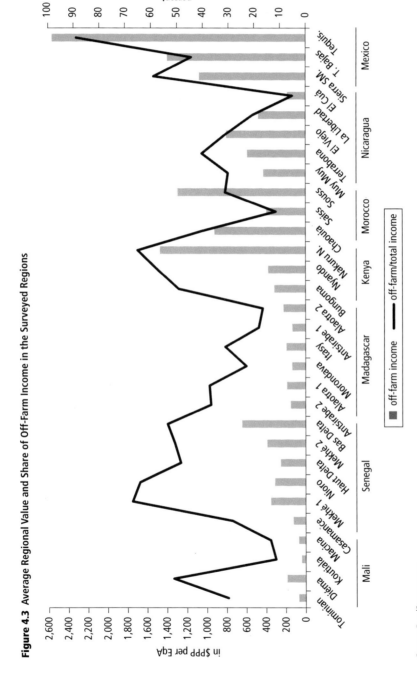

Source: RuralStruc surveys.

Heterogeneity of Off-Farm Sources. A significant dissimilarity appears among surveyed regions when off-farm income is further broken down into different sources. The breakdown reveals diverse situations and strategies, and highlights the opportunities and constraints of the local environment that shape economic alternatives. Table 4.1 shows the distribution of the surveyed house-

Table 4.1 Main Off-Farm Activities and Incomes

% of average off-farm income

Country	Region	Top off-farm	2nd off-farm	3rd off-farm
Mali	Tominian	Remit (48%)	Self Emp (37%)	Non Ag Wage (7%)
	Diéma	Remit (86%)	Self Emp (11%)	Ag Wage (3%)
	Koutiala	Self Emp (63%)	Remit (20%)	Non Ag Wage (7%)
	Macina	Self Emp (43%)	Remit (22%)	Ag Wage (17%)
Senegal	Casamance	Self Emp (69%)	Remit (20%)	Non Ag Wage (10%)
	Mekhé 1	Self Emp (69%)	Remit (19%)	Non Ag Wage (12%)
	Nioro	Self Emp (77%)	Remit (13%)	Non Ag Wage (8%)
	Haut Delta	Self Emp (76%)	Non Ag Wage (15%)	Remit (9%)
	Mekhé 2	Self Emp (68%)	Non Ag Wage (19%)	Remit (13%)
	Bas Delta	Self Emp (58%)	Non Ag Wage (22%)	Rents (13%)
Madagascar	Antsirabe 2	Self Emp (67%)	Ag Wage (21%)	Remit (7%)
	Alaotra 1	Self Emp (52%)	Rents (19%)	Ag Wage (18%)
	Morondava	Self Emp (50%)	Ag Wage (24%)	Non Ag Wage (16%)
	Itasy	Self Emp (53%)	Ag Wage (25%)	Non Ag Wage (12%)
	Antsirabe 1	Self Emp (62%)	Ag Wage (26%)	Non Ag Wage (6%)
	Alaotra 2	Self Emp (57%)	Rents (23%)	Ag Wage (16%)
Kenya	Bungoma	Non Ag Wage (54%)	Self Emp (38%)	Ag Wage (5%)
	Nyando	Non Ag Wage (56%)	Self Emp (31%)	Ag Wage (8%)
	Nakuru N.	Self Emp (72%)	Non Ag Wage (24%)	Rents (2%)
Morocco	Chaouia	Rents (30%)	Remit (23%)	Self Emp (22%)
	Saiss	Rents (47%)	Remit (15%)	Self Emp (15%)
	Souss	Rents (40%)	Self Emp (24%)	Non Ag Wage (14%)
Nicaragua	Muy Muy	Ag Wage (37%)	Remit (30%)	Non Age Wage (17%)
	Terrabona	Remit (32%)	Non Ag Wage (31%)	Self Emp (27%)
	El Viejo	Ag Wage (58%)	Remit (19%)	Non Ag Wage (17%)
	La Libertad	Ag Wage (67%)	Self Emp (20%)	Non Ag Wage (7%)
	El Cuá	Non Ag Wage (28%)	Ag Wage (26%)	Self Emp (23%)
Mexico	Sierra SM	Self Emp (38%)	Public Transfers (32%)	Ag Wage (15%)
	T. Bajas	Public Transfers (32%)	Self Emp (30%)	Ag Wage (15%)
	Tequis.	Non Ag Wage (47%)	Ag Wage (24%)	Self Emp (21%)

Source: RuralStruc surveys.

holds according to their main off-farm activities and the contribution of those activities to overall off-farm income. At the regional level, two major trends can be identified in terms of types and combinations of off-farm incomes.

The first trend is related to regional wealth levels: The diversity of off-farm incomes rises in richer regions. Households in non-SSA regions engage in a broader variety of off-farm activities. Their main off-farm income sources are more balanced, and the three largest sources generally contribute 75 percent to 80 percent of overall off-farm income (with a few exceptions). In SSA regions, however, the primary activity most often contributes the major share of off-farm income, with the three main sources frequently accounting for 90 percent to 95 percent of the total.

The other major trend is the importance of self-employment in SSA regions and the decreasing importance of this activity in richer regions. Self-employment is the top off-farm activity in 15 of 19 SSA regions but in only 1 of 11 non-SSA regions (2, if the specific case of rents in Morocco is excluded—see section on Other Off-Farm Incomes below). In most western African regions, a combination of self-employment and migration dominates off-farm strategies, while in Kenya and Madagascar, self-employment pairs with, respectively, nonagricultural and agricultural wage labor.

Characteristics of Off-Farm Activities

To explore the diversification options available to households, this section and the next will review the scope and importance of each category of off-farm income. While there is not enough evidence to draw conclusions about the absolute level of effectiveness of each type of activity as a pathway out of poverty, comparisons can be made between diversification patterns observed in different regions and intermediary conclusions can be drawn about the extent of opportunities for diversification out of agriculture.

The discussion centers on the level of development of each activity (the share of households involved) and the returns households earn from them (earnings per economically active person or EAP).[6] The survey was not sufficiently detailed to identify the specific economic activity of each EAP in the household; thus, for a given household, total earnings from each activity were divided by total number of EAPs. This approach likely understates the returns from each activity, so the indicator must be regarded as a proxy.[7]

Agricultural Wage Employment: A Common Activity but Rarely an Exit Option. A general discussion of the relationship between farm structures and the importance of wage labor is necessary before reviewing its characteristics in the surveyed regions.

Agricultural Wage Labor and Farm Structures. In developing countries, because of the high share of agriculture in employment, agricultural wage labor is a common feature and a well-developed option for rural households seeking additional income. The development of wage employment in agriculture, however, varies sharply according to local labor demand, which depends on the degree of differentiation among farm structures. The existence of larger farms that are unable to meet all their own labor needs is generally a prerequisite for the availability of agricultural wage employment. The cultivation of certain labor-intensive products, for which full mechanization is not an option (typically horticulture and tree crops), can also be a strong driver of labor demand.[8]

In the regions studied by RuralStruc, particularly those in SSA but also the surveyed regions of Morocco, Nicaragua, and Mexico, family farms dominate. The program defines family-based farming as "a form of production characterized by a particular kind of link between economic activity and family structure, one where this relationship influences the choice of activities, organization of family labor, management of the factors of production and transfer of property" (Bélières et al. 2002, p. 3). This definition makes it clear that within these family-based structures, most agricultural labor is provided by the members of the household who are not directly paid for their work. However, family farms can also make use of an external workforce when they are unable to meet all their own labor needs; for example, during peak activity periods. External labor can consist of both local mutual aid groups (relatives and other members of the community who work on a reciprocal basis without any monetary compensation) and paid workers—either casual laborers or permanent agricultural employees.[9]

Labor demand rises with the emergence of larger family farms or the development of managerial or large-scale entrepreneurial farms that rely on an external workforce. This type of farm differentiation is generally limited in Sub-Saharan African countries, where the majority of farms are small-scale units with few assets. It is more prevalent in other regions.

The RuralStruc sample shows different levels of farm differentiation. Farm sizes[10] are bigger in the two Latin American countries, mainly in Nicaragua, where the average farm operates on 15–20 hectares (Ha).[11] SSA countries show smaller acreages, particularly Kenya and Madagascar, where the means are around 1 Ha. Some surveyed regions of the highlands in Madagascar have even smaller farms, a consequence of the hilly landscape and, above all, of growing populations cultivating a limited amount of arable land.[12] The case of the two West African countries is unique. There, larger family farms have developed, but family structures are also bigger (as discussed in chapter 3) and tend to include several households on the same farm.[13] This is why figure 4.4 displays the distribution of plot sizes in the sample by hectare per family worker (EAP). Figures on average regional farm sizes would be misleading. Extremes are notably important in Nicaragua, where land inequalities are high. For example, in La Libertad, a remote livestock region in the agricultural frontier, 20 percent of the

Figure 4.4 Distribution of Farm Size per Family Worker (EAP)

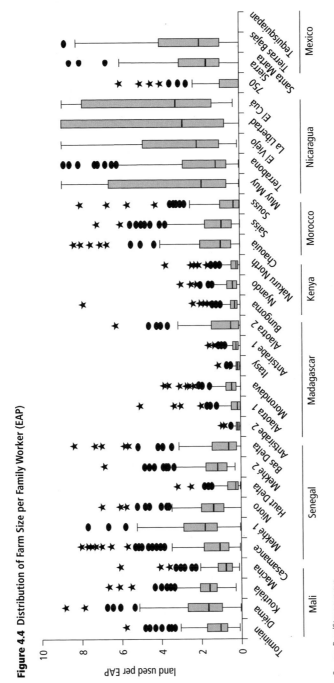

Source: RuralStruc surveys.
Note: See box plot definition in figure 3.10, page 99.

richest households own large-scale *latifundia* (agricultural estates)that account for 53 percent of the total land in the region. In El Viejo, a region in the Pacific plains that is known for unequal land distribution and land conflicts, as well as for being heavily engaged in the production of export crops such as sesame and sugar cane, 6 percent of the surveyed households are landless. A similar situation exists in Alaotra, in Madagascar, where 10 percent of surveyed households do not have access to land.[14] (They are mainly families that migrated to the region to benefit from agricultural labor opportunities.) In Morocco, land access can also be an issue, especially in regions with vast acreages of government agricultural development schemes. These very differentiated situations are not common in SSA, where land access is mainly based on customary land tenure rights.

However, whatever the farm structure, some demand for farm labor always exists, at least during the peak season (generally harvest but also transplanting in the case of irrigated rice).[15] The major constraint when farm differentiation is limited is that labor supply increases for all during the dry season, when labor demand is scarce, and labor shortages are frequent at harvest time. This situation explains the development of mutual aid groups and stimulates short-term migrations from other regions with different cropping seasons or different levels of available labor. Such is the case of migrations from the *bassin arachidier* to the Senegal River Delta in Senegal, and of similar migrations in Morocco for the wheat harvest and in El Cuá, Nicaragua, for the coffee harvest. More broadly, the cyclical imbalances between labor supply and demand reflect the prevalence of structural underemployment, which is characteristic of many rural areas in developing countries.

Extent and Characteristics of Agricultural Wage Labor. In the surveyed regions, agricultural wage labor is relatively common. A quarter of the interviewed households earn agricultural wages, and the proportion is almost 40 percent in the more fully differentiated regions of Mexico and Nicaragua. Malagasy households, many of which are landless poor, also are more heavily engaged in agricultural wage labor (46 percent of households).

There is, however, a bias related to the survey methodology. The focus on households prevents a full capture of the importance of agricultural wage labor: Wages earned in agriculture by households' members during short-term migrations in other regions are posted in the transfer category, and wages locally paid to migrants have to be counted on the migrant household's side. These limitations surely result in an underestimation of the local weight of agricultural wages.

Behind these overall figures are two major facts. The first, perhaps unsurprising, observation is that wage work in agriculture mainly engages the poorest households in each region, and its frequency decreases as overall income rises.[16] The inverse relationship between agricultural wage employment and overall household wealth is clearly illustrated by the share of agricultural wages in income per quintile.[17] Agricultural wages account for between 20 percent and 30 percent of overall income for households in the bottom two quintiles, then its weight decreases sharply. An exception is Nicaragua, where the shares remain high until quintile 4 (in Muy Muy, El Viejo, and La Libertad).[18]

Agricultural wage work is a major source of income for the poorest households of the first quintiles, notably in the regions where landless households exist.[19] In some extreme cases, households rent their land to larger and better-off farmers or agrobusinesses; because they lack the necessary means to develop their own plots, they end up as agricultural workers on their own land. This situation was observed particularly in Souss (RS 2 Morocco).

The second observation is the low level of earnings related to agricultural wages. Figure 4.5 illustrates the differences in labor prices between SSA and non-SSA surveyed regions. The official minimum wage is $3–$6 PPP per day in SSA and $8–$10 PPP in non-SSA countries.[20] The agricultural wages observed during the surveys, mainly paid informally, are lower, with a few exceptions in regions facing strong pressure (temporary or not) on the labor market. This is the case in regions with important demand peaks—like the rice-producing regions of Mali, Madagascar, and the Delta in Senegal—and of regions with a significant number of large-scale farms or agribusinesses in horticulture (Souss, El Viejo, Tequisquiapan) or livestock (La Libertad and Tequisquiapan).

The main issue is that in many regions, especially poorer ones, these local labor prices mainly refer to the peak season, when the available extra labor force of family farms is limited; during the off-season, there is no labor demand at all. Reported wages are daily prices for casual labor and cannot be converted to monthly or yearly rates.[21] Paradoxically, when interregional migrations exist—like those in the Delta region in Senegal and in El Cuá, Nicaragua—the benefits of this temporary labor demand are reaped by migrant workers coming from other regions. As a consequence, the average income earned from agricultural employment is very limited in the SSA surveyed regions (between $200 and $300 PPP per EAP per year) and even more insignificant in Mali. Incomes above $1,000 PPP (equivalent to $2.7 PPP per day) appear only in some of the previously mentioned regions of Morocco, Nicaragua, and Mexico, where more permanent labor opportunities exist.

These figures, as well as the small number of households engaged in agricultural labor, confirm the limited contribution of agricultural wages to income diversification and to poverty alleviation (Reardon et al. 2007). Even in Tequisquiapan, where the reported average daily agricultural wage is $18 PPP (thanks to the substantial development of agribusiness), returns averaged over the course of a year are low; in this case, around $6 PPP per EAP per day. Days in which an agricultural laborer could possibly earn $18 are severely limited in number.

Figure 4.5 Potential and Actual Returns from Agricultural Employment in the Surveyed Regions

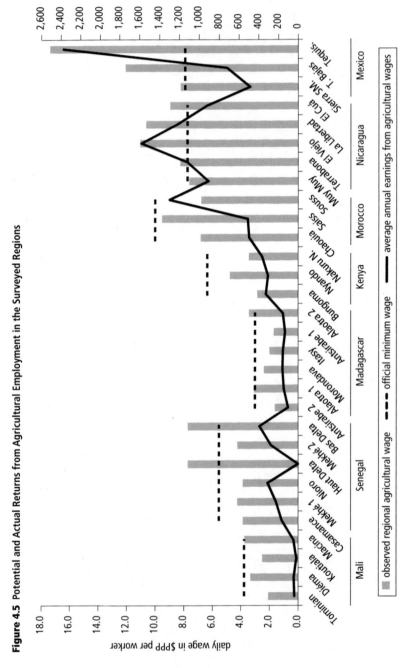

Sources: RuralStruc surveys; communication with RuralStruc teams; local regulations.

The main conclusion about agricultural employment is the lack of strong remunerative opportunities. Agricultural jobs are overwhelmingly temporary and, above all, provide a very limited return when averaged over a year. They are a limited complement for many rural households (a quarter of the sample), even though they are an imperative for the poorest, who have very few options. Only permanent jobs can make a difference and create an opportunity to escape poverty, but they are too scarce and too poorly paid to provide a sustainable solution for many.

Nonagricultural Wage Employment: Limited to Specific Regional Settings. The development of nonagricultural wage labor in general is a critical process in the standard model of structural transformation, and many developing countries that are engaged in economic transition show significant shares of waged activities in the production of nonagricultural goods and services. However, patterns of nonagricultural wage employment depend on national and regional economic characteristics, as well as the region's stage in the diversification process.

Here again it is worth mentioning methodological issues related to the characteristics of nonagricultural wage employment as a category. Its definition is quite vague, because it corresponds to all salaried activities that are not strictly related to the production stage of agriculture. This very broad definition includes extractive activities (mining, quarrying); off-farm processing activities in agribusinesses (cleaning, grading, industrial processing, and packaging); manufacturing (intermediate or final goods); construction; and all kind of services, public or private, in education, health, information, transportation, child care, security, and so on. All these activities include both skilled and unskilled jobs and can be developed with very different types of businesses in terms of size, capital, and management.

The breadth of the category, as well as the importance of the informal sector and small businesses in most developing countries, means that distinguishing self-employment from nonagricultural wage employment can be difficult. It raises questions about certain types of jobs, which, although nominally waged, are mostly carried out in small workshops or small businesses at the micro level—for example, taxi driving or apprenticeship—and are therefore difficult to analyze when included in the same group as formal office work or industrial work. The category is heterogeneous, and this must be kept in mind when comparing very diverse economic and institutional contexts.

In the RuralStruc regions, about 25 percent of the surveyed households were engaged in agricultural wage labor, but nonagricultural wage employment only involved 15 percent of them, and strong differences were observed among regions (figure 4.6).

In terms of participation, Kenya and Mexico stand out, with 40 percent of households involved in nonagricultural wage labor, while Madagascar and,

Figure 4.6 Participation in and Returns from Nonagricultural Wage Employment in the Surveyed Regions

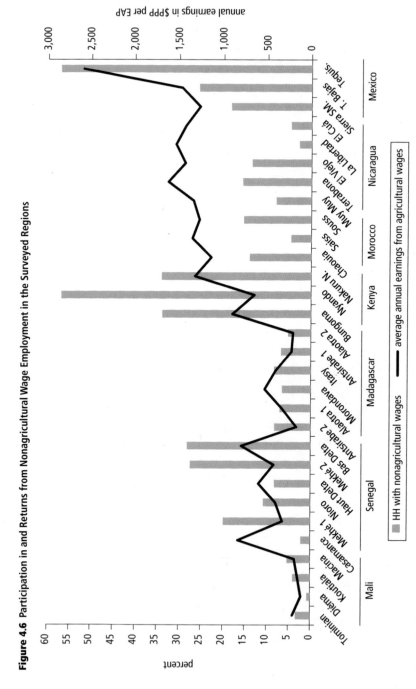

Source: RuralStruc surveys.

Table 4.2 Educational Level of the Surveyed Households
country average in %

		No education	Primary school started	Primary school finished	Secondary school started	Secondary school finished or university level
head of household	Mali	84	10	2	4	0
	Senegal	79	16	3	2	0
	Madagascar	18	56	7	18	1
	Kenya	0	68	14	8	9
	Morocco	50	15	22	10	3
	Nicaragua	39	4	52	5	1
	Mexico	24	38	22	1	15
highest level in the household	Mali	40	20	33	7	0
	Senegal	17	40	25	14	4
	Madagascar	6	34	8	28	24
	Kenya	0	26	28	26	20
	Morocco	7	4	42	39	9
	Nicaragua	0	0	8	56	36
	Mexico	n.a.	n.a.	n.a.	n.a.	n.a.

Source: RuralStruc surveys.

above all, Mali lag far behind. Even in Mexico and Kenya, disparities are important. In Tequisquiapan and Nyando, 57 percent of households participate in nonagricultural waged activities; in Bungoma and Nakuru, 34 percent; and in the two Sotavento subzones, only 21 percent. In Senegal, the Bas Delta and the north of the *bassin arachidier* (Mekhé) report figures of 20 percent and 25 percent, respectively. Souss, Terrabona, and El Viejo, in Morocco and Nicaragua, attain 15 percent, the sample average.

This situation is challenging and raises a question about the determinants of nonagricultural wage employment. As usual, there are micro- and meso/macro-levels of explanation for the observed differences among households. At the micro-level, as broadly reported in the literature,[22] the capability of households to seize local job opportunities mainly depends on their skills; this is shown by the positive and significant correlation between level of education and participation in nonagricultural wage labor.[23] Table 4.2 illustrates the vast differences among RuralStruc countries when it comes to education. Interestingly, a household's income quintile seems to have no effect on its participation in nonagricultural wage labor. Households in every income group engage in this type of labor, and the correlation between nonagricultural wage participation and total income level can even be negative.

BOX 4.1

Free Trade Zones and Nonagricultural Wage Labor in Nicaragua

In Nicaragua, the number of factories operating in free trade zones (FTZs) has increased considerably since the 1990s. The first industrial park, Las Mercedes, opened in 1976 with 11 factories. Today, the FTZ system consists of a dozen industrial parks with about 50 firms, mainly from Taiwan and the United States. The vast majority produce apparel for export, mostly to the United States. The sector has been very dynamic in terms of job creation: The number of jobs has increased from 1,003 in 1992 to 38,792 in 2001 to around 70,000 today. Fifteen thousand new jobs are expected in the next three to five years. It is estimated that 55 percent of the workers are young women with low education levels.

Factory work is highly concentrated in the Matagalpa and Managua zones, and benefits the nearby rural areas (Corral and Reardon 2001). In the RuralStruc surveys, it is mainly found in Terrabona, where the annual salaries generated by jobs in FTZs range from $2,500 to $4,500 PPP per capita. This is in line with estimates in other studies, which place monthly salaries at a maximum of US$500/month in 2009. In January 2010, the government of Nicaragua, labor unions, and the private sector signed an agreement that will set salary adjustments in the FTZ for the next three years. The objective is to protect jobs and offer predictability, so investors can develop financial plans for their firms. This agreement, known as the Social-Labor Consensus Agreement by the Free Zone's Tripartite Labor Commission, establishes minimum wage increases over the next three years of 8 percent, 9 percent, and 10 percent.

Sources: RuralStruc surveys; RS 2 Nicaragua.

At the meso- and macro-levels, beyond the few jobs related to education, health, and local administration (primary school teachers, medical assistants, civil servants), the opportunities for nonagricultural employment depend on regional dynamics. These dynamics encompass natural assets, population and population growth, the quality of infrastructure and provision of public goods, density and access to cities (illustrated in chapter 3 in the figure 3.3 maps), and the presence of leading economic sectors that enhance economic growth and generate labor demand. Local effects can be huge and can distort regional results if surveyed rural households are in the range of a factory that provides hundreds of jobs for its neighborhood.

In the RuralStruc surveys, manufacturing related to the apparel industry exists in Terrabona in Nicaragua as a result of the development of free trade zones (see box 4.1). But it is most prevalent in Tequisquiapan, Mexico, where a long tradition of *maquiladoras,* stimulated by NAFTA, has led to small production units spreading into the countryside (see box 4.2). The jobs provided by these factories are relatively well paid and have a strong impact on local wealth.

BOX 4.2

The *Maquilas* of the Textile Sector in La Fuente, Tequisquiapan, Mexico

The village of La Fuente in the *municipio* of Tequisquiapan is a good illustration of the process of "densification" and diversification of the rural economy in the south of the Querétaro state. With 3,884 inhabitants (2005 census), La Fuente is 18 km from Tequisquiapan (population 26,858) and 24 km from San Juan del Rio, a city of 210,000 that is connected by interstate highway to Querétaro and Mexico City. In spite of its urbanized environment, La Fuente remains significantly involved in agricultural activities, with 24.3 percent of the local value added coming from agriculture in 2000, while agriculture's share dropped to 3.5 percent in Tequisquiapan. Three *maquilas* operate in the village, with workforces of 150, 100, and 80. All workers are La Fuente residents or come from nearby villages. The large majority are women.

The two largest factories specialize in *ropa barata* (cheap clothing)—basic apparel for export—and have been suffering over the past years from intense competition with China. The third factory, Lecuria La Fuente, specializes in fine lingerie for the upper segment of the domestic market and sells its products under the Vanity brand to high-end boutiques like Liverpool and Palacio de Hierro. This market positioning and the higher skill tasks required have so far protected the company from foreign competitors. The business was founded by two people, including the director, a textile engineer who was born in the village. The land for the factory was bought from an *ejidatario*—a local resident who benefited from property rights associated with the *ejido* system (collective land distributed under agrarian reform).

The fabric is directly imported from South Korea and Japan, and is cut by laser before being sewn together into lingerie. This is highly specialized work (it takes 10 months to train a worker) and thus is well paid. Labor contracts are based on a price per minute and minutes per piece, and workers are paid according to their yield above or below the average time needed to sew a piece. The standard contract for a permanent worker provides a monthly wage of Mexican $2,400 ($330 PPP), plus social security and benefits. A good worker can earn 30 percent more: M$3,120 or $427 PPP; $5,130 PPP per year. Short-term (weekly) contracts are offered during peak production times. These contracts are offered to trained reserves and are better paid (+30 percent), at M$800 per week but without benefits. The wages can be compared with M$500/week for farm workers or, most often, M$120–$140/day ($16–$19 PPP) for casual work.

The RuralStruc program surveyed 49 households in La Fuente. Only 14 had a farm (see table below). Despite the availability of well-paid nonagricultural jobs, farm households earn more, on average, than nonfarm households ($13,645 PPP compared with $8,286 PPP). This is broadly explained by the multi-activity pattern of the farm households, in which members are also engaged in off-farm activities, mainly agricultural and nonagricultural wage labor (usually practiced by women). Half of the sample's households earn agricultural wages, and half receive nonagricultural wages; 15 percent earn both. Fifty-five percent of the households in La Fuente have an average annual income per EqA greater than $2,000 PPP; 10 percent have an income greater than $5,000 PPP.

(box continues on next page)

Box Table 4.2.1 Level and Structure of Income in La Fuente

Households	No.	Total income (mean in $PPP)		Means of share of total income (%)						
		HH	EqA	On-farm	Ag. wages	Non-Ag wages	Self-empl.	Public transfers	Remitt.	Rents
Without farm	35	8,286	2,542	0	34	39	20	2	4	1
With farm	14	13,645	3,800	28	22	25	6	7	0	13

Sources: RuralStruc interviews, January 2008; RuralStruc surveys; RS 2 Mexico.

In Souss, Morocco, the development of services related to the tourism industry in the nearby city of Agadir and the coastal resorts offers some limited opportunities. In the two other regions in Morocco, nonagricultural employment is still primarily related to processing and marketing agricultural products, and to construction and services.

In Senegal, Bas Delta benefits from a connection to the city of Saint-Louis, and the location of Mekhé on the major highway between Saint-Louis and Dakar helps explain the relatively higher participation of surveyed households there in nonagricultural wage employment. Nioro and, above all, Casamance are farther from the dense area of economic activity around the coast (even though they are close to population centers), and Casamance is on the other side of The Gambia. However, as noted in chapter 3, differences in opportunities and market access do not significantly affect overall household incomes.

Perhaps the most paradoxical situation is in Kenya, one of the most urbanized countries of Sub-Saharan Africa and a place where the urbanization process is still booming (see box 3.2). However, urban growth has not been accompanied by industrialization (the lack of which is a major feature of urbanization in SSA), so nonagricultural employment comes mainly from low-skill and often temporary jobs in the agroprocessing industry (sugar cane plants, canning), construction, and handicrafts, and in low-paid services (trade, transport, catering).

As a consequence of the various patterns among regions and countries, major differences are observed in households' participation in, and earnings from, nonagricultural employment. Income earned from these activities is limited in the surveyed regions, with a striking difference between SSA and non-SSA regions. In SSA regions, the average returns are in the range of $500 PPP per EAP per year; while in Morocco, Nicaragua, and Mexico, returns are near $1,500 PPP/EAP/year. Nakuru and Tequisquiapan deserve special attention. In Nakuru, returns average around $1,500 PPP, much closer to levels observed in Nicaragua and Morocco than to levels in the rest of Kenya. In Tequisquiapan, remuneration for nonagricultural wage labor can reach $2,500 PPP/EAP/year, well above any other opportunities observed in the RuralStruc surveys.

The two cases of Nakuru and Tequisquiapan—and, more broadly, Kenya and Mexico—illustrate the discussion on the importance of economic settings

Figure 4.7 Distribution of Households per Level of Nonagricultural Income, Kenya and Mexico

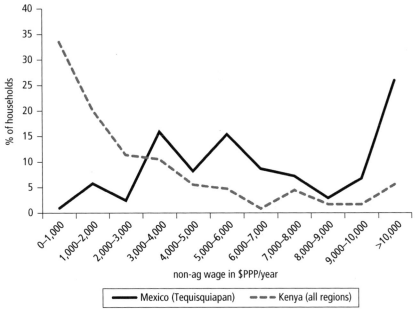

Source: RuralStruc surveys.

in identifying options for nonagricultural wage labor. In Nakuru North, where about 34 percent of households are engaged in nonagricultural wage labor, the proximity of the city and nearby local tourism assets (Nakuru national park) give some household members access to jobs in public administration, education (teachers), trade and transportation (the city is on the main Kenyan transport corridor), and the tourism industry. However, in Nyando, more than half the households are engaged in nonagricultural wage employment (20 percent more than in Nakuru), and their earnings are lower. Nyando's workers are employed in poorly paid jobs at sugar plants or in petty services. The difference in the type of nonagricultural wage labor available is decisive. In Mexico, the higher returns in Tequisquiapan are a direct result of the well-paid and sometimes highly specialized jobs available in the *maquilas*.

The difference in the type of employment available and the level of income obtained from this work is confirmed by the distribution of annual household earnings by level of income (figure 4.7). In Kenya, more than 50 percent of households earn less than $2,000 PPP, and only 5 percent make more than $10,000, because nonagricultural wage jobs are very low paying. In Tequisquiapan, households earn more money from nonagricultural wage labor. Twenty-five percent of households involved in these activities earn more than $10,000

PPP, which is possible with two household members working in a *maquiladora* (see box 4.2) or through participation in higher skilled jobs.

Overall, nonagricultural wage labor appears to be a limited option, its availability highly dependent on the characteristics of the regional economy. Opportunities, when they exist, most often come in the form of low-skilled and low-paying jobs; the rare exception is manufacturing jobs. Without a significant amount of further economic diversification (which is not necessarily related to urbanization, as exemplified by Kenya), this option is not available to the majority of households in either the short or medium term.

Self-Employment: A Prevalent Catch-All Strategy. As noted earlier in this chapter, self-employment is the most common off-farm income in most of the surveyed regions and the main diversification option in the poorest ones. In wage employment, the worker is a "labor taker"; with self-employment, the worker is a "labor maker," seizing opportunities to develop activities depending on his or her skills and capital.

As a consequence, self-employment covers a broad range of trade and handiwork activities, including those that rely on the transformation, transport, distribution, and sale of local natural and agricultural products (farm products, wood, forestry products, and charcoal); the transport and trade of manufactured goods for the local rural market (small hardware shops); handicrafts (pottery, basket making, jewelry, tailoring, shoemaking); and services (hairdressing, eateries, letter writing, or repairs to farm equipment, vehicles, TVs, and other appliances).

This diversity is illustrated in figure 4.8, which lists the activities engaged in by the surveyed households in Senegal. It shows the number of active persons (EAP) engaged in each of the main categories of self-employment by gender.

The returns from these self-employment activities are highly dependent on the purchasing power of customers, which directly relates to the regional level of wealth. Returns from self-employment activities are as diverse as the array of activities themselves. When the self-employment activity does not involve specialized equipment or a unique skill, returns tend to be close to the local labor price.

There is a strong heterogeneity among surveyed regions with regard to the share of households participating in self-employment. The survey also observed a high level of variance in the returns from self-employment at the household level. As shown in figure 4.9, these characteristics evolve in opposite directions and illustrate two kinds of situations.

The first situation occurs in regions with medium to high participation in self-employment (35 percent–80 percent) but low returns from these activities. This includes most of the SSA regions as well as those of the Sotavento in Mexico, where the level of engagement in self-employment is the highest in the survey. In these regions, the average annual return from self-employment is

Figure 4.8 Self-Employment Activities in Senegal

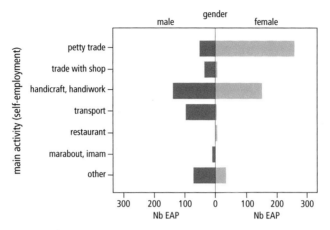

Source: RuralStruc surveys.

around $500 PPP/EAP; in the *bassin arachidier* and the Delta in Senegal, and in the Sotavento in Mexico, the return reaches $750 PPP/EAP/year.

The second situation occurs in regions with a low or very low level of participation in self-employment (5 percent–15 percent). This is the case in Morocco and Nicaragua, and to a certain extent in Tequisquiapan, where rural households are little engaged in self-employment because they have other opportunities, such as wage labor and migration. The returns from self-employment in these regions are much higher—on average, around $1,500 PPP/EAP/year. Souss and Tequisquiapan have even higher returns ($2,500–$3,000 PPP/EAP/ year), although these results mainly reflect their wealthier regional contexts. Nakuru in Kenya is a unique case, in which the levels of returns from self-employment rival those observed in Morocco and Nicaragua. However, Nakuru is widely stratified in terms of self-employment earnings: Although many households are engaged in this activity (77 percent), a limited number have very high returns, pulling up the regional average.[24]

Behind this diversity, two major patterns appear. The first corresponds to a sort of "positive diversification," in which self-employment contributes significantly to household income. It is generally a full-time activity—a microbusiness with some equipment—which explains why households with more or better assets—or the ability to make a significant initial investment owing to their financial, social, or human capital—are more likely to take advantage of opportunities shaped by the local market. Of the entire survey sample, 41 percent of households are engaged in self-employment but only 13 percent earn more than $5,000 PPP per year from this activity.[25] These households are not necessarily located in regions broadly engaged in self-employment:

Figure 4.9 Self-Employment Returns in the Surveyed Regions

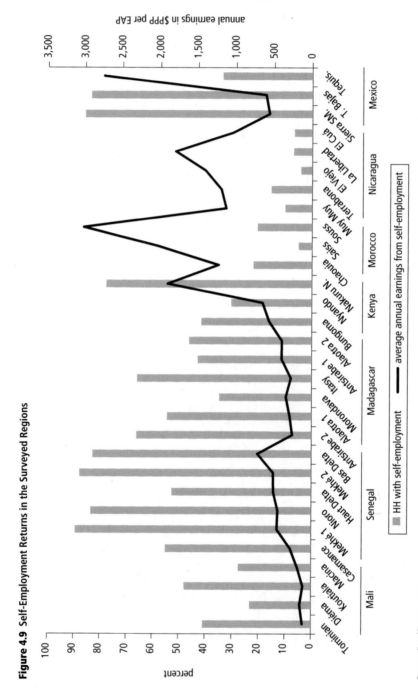

58 percent of Moroccan and 27 percent of Nicaraguan households that have self-employment activity are in this group, compared with 22 percent in Mexico and Kenya, and only 13 percent in Senegal.

The second pattern illustrates a more "neutral diversification," in which the poorest and most marginalized households develop coping or survival strategies by accessing minor self-employment activities with very low returns. These activities most often complement their on-farm incomes but pay far too little to serve as a viable poverty exit option. A full 51 percent of surveyed households engaged in self-employment earn less than $1,000 PPP per year, or $2.7 PPP per day.

A final result is that self-employment activities are not limited to places that offer no permanent waged activities outside agriculture (which is the conventional wisdom on the issue). The diversity of the regional situations shows that both coping strategies in poor rural areas with limited options and positive diversification strategies in richer and diversified regions are possible. Further, self-employment incomes benefit substantially from dynamic economic environments.

Other Off-Farm Income: A Substantial Complement

Off-farm income is not generated only through local activities implemented by the household members; it is also generated by activities implemented in distant locations by migrant workers who send a portion of their earnings home. These remittances play a very significant role in several surveyed regions. They constitute the major part of the "private transfers" income category, which can also include gifts or donations from other households, although these are much rarer.

Public transfers are another off-farm income group—they refer to subsidies from the central state or local government (support to economic activities or social groups), as well as grants from NGOs or other local communities. In the RuralStruc surveys, public transfers are mainly observed and only significant in Mexico.[26]

The other category of non-activity-generated off-farm income is rents. This includes rental revenues from physical assets (land, equipment, and housing), and would have included securities income if any had been observed. Between 5 percent and 10 percent of the surveyed households reported rental revenues, with the exception of households in Kenya, where the number is much higher (40 percent). But revenues from rentals are very low: 45 percent of households with rental revenues earn less than $100 PPP per year from them.[27]

Migrations: Different Patterns for Different Regions. Rural households have always developed livelihood strategies that combine fixed and mobile assets, where assets consist of both physical and human capital (Augustins 1989). Today, millions of people move every year to another region, to a city, or across borders and oceans, seeking to reduce the gap between their own position and that of others in wealthier places (Black, Natali, and Skinner 2005). Adopting a more structural and historical perspective, migration is frequently about the intersectoral movement of labor and results from differences in returns to labor among economic sectors, notably between agriculture and the rest of the economy (Larson and Mundlak 1997). These labor migrations have been one of the most powerful drivers of economic transformation (see chapter 2).

Often, migrations are not permanent or do not include the entire household, or both. This intermediate type of movement creates situations in which transfers of goods and cash between different geographical settings and between different household members are frequent. Thus, the development of temporary migrations (which can be long term), facilitated by improved conditions of transportation, has resulted in a significant increase in private transfers, especially international remittances, whose role in economic development has been much discussed over the past decade.

However, the global picture can be misleading. Not only do patterns of mobility differ broadly across regions—as illustrated by the RuralStruc countries (see box 4.3)—but the impact of remittances varies depending on whether

BOX 4.3

Patterns of International Migration in the RuralStruc Countries

Patterns of international migration depend on geography and national trajectories. Mexicans, Moroccans, and Nicaraguans have taken advantage of the geographic positions of their countries which border higher income neighbors; About 10 percent of the population of each country lives abroad. This option is less feasible in Sub-Saharan African countries, except in Mali, which has about 11 percent of its population living abroad. Kenya and Madagascar have extremely low rates of emigration.

Box Table 4.3.1 Importance of International Migrations among RuralStruc Countries

	Mali	Senegal	Madagascar	Kenya	Morocco	Nicaragua	Mexico
Stocks of emigrants in 2005 (millions)	1.2	0.5	0.2	0.4	2.7	0.7	11.5
Population in 2005 (millions)	11.4	11.7	17	33.4	29.9	5.6	104.3
Emigrants/Population (%)	10.6	4.0	0.9	1.3	9.1	12.2	11.0
Remittances in 2005 (millions $US)	175	511	16	494	4.724	600	21.802
Remittances (% GDP)	3.9	6.7	0.4	3.4	9.4	13.3	3.5
Remittances ($US/migrants)	144	1,103	106	1,156	1,738	878	1,895

Sources: Ratha and Shaw 2007; WDI.

The destination of migrants greatly affects the returns earned from migration. In Mexico and Morocco, where the overwhelming majority of migrants work in OECD countries, the average return per migrant is high (near $2,000). At the other extreme is Mali: The Kayes region in the west of the country near the Senegalese border has a long tradition of emigration to France, but 90 percent of Malian migrants stay in West Africa, mainly in Côte d'Ivoire, and their returns are less than 10 percent of those earned by Mexican and Moroccan migrants. Nicaragua and Senegal illustrate an intermediate position: About half of their migrants work in rich countries, while the other half work in neighboring countries (Costa Rica for Nicaragua, The Gambia and Mauritania for Senegal), with a proportional impact on the level of remittances sent. In Senegal, transfers have increased steadily since 2005.

Box Table 4.3.2 Destination of Migration Flows among RuralStruc Countries

| | | Migrants' country of origin (% in 2005) | | | | | | |
		Mali	Senegal	Madagascar	Kenya	Morocco	Nicaragua	Mexico
to developed countries	Canada	1		1	5	1	1	
	France	4	20	54		29		
	Israel					8		
	Italy		15	1		11	1	
	Netherlands					6		
	Réunion			17		0		
	Spain	1	5			25	1	
	United Kingdom			1	34	1		
	United States		3	1	11	2	36	90
	Others	1	3	3	7	9	1	2
	Subtotal	7	46	78	57	92	40	92
to developing countries	Burkina Faso	25						
	Comoros			14				
	Costa Rica						49	
	Gambia, The	1	27					
	Côte d'Ivoire	41						
	Mauritania	1	9					
	Nigeria	9	1					
	Tanzania				26			
	Uganda				8			
	Others	16	18	8	9	9	11	8
	Subtotal	93	55	22	43	9	60	8
Total		100	100	100	100	100	100	100

Sources: Ratha and Shaw 2007; WDI.

a micro- or macro-level analysis is undertaken. At the macro level, private transfers from abroad can weigh heavily on national accounts, but the impact of these monies at the regional or household level can be very different. This is particularly true in rural areas, where the role of migrations has often been overstated. As noted by Reardon et al. (2007), both the literature and the conventional wisdom among policy makers tend to emphasize the importance of migrant remittances, but many field studies suggest that the share of households involved in migrations is actually relatively low.

The discussion of the impact of migration is complicated by the difficulty of capturing the various characteristics of mobility; for example, domestic or international, short-term or long-term. The importance of different types of migration varies from country to country and results in different patterns of migration. It is also difficult to estimate the amount of remittances because of their irregularity, the fact that they arrive through many different channels,[28] and the fact that some respondents are reluctant to provide information about them.[29]

In the RuralStruc regions, all kinds of migrations are a common feature: domestic or international, long- or short-term.[30] Twenty-four percent of the surveyed households have experience in this area; the core range is 15 percent to 40 percent. The exceptions are Alaotra in Madagascar, La Libertad and El Cuá in Nicaragua, and the Sotavento in Mexico, where the number of households engaged in migration drop below 10 percent. On the opposite end, Tominian and Diéma in Mali and Nioro in Senegal exceed 60 percent (see figure 4.10).

The determinants of migration are many and relate to push-pull factors in individual regions. The economic situation of the household, lack of opportunities at the local or national level, visions of a distant Eldorado, and exogenous obstacles that limit possible migration routes combine to shape individual or collective decisions. Migration is often a choice at the household rather than individual level; sometimes, for international migrations, it is a decision of the community as a whole. Therefore, migration often relies on the ability of certain groups to create and maintain bonds of solidarity with diaspora members.

When it comes to international migration, the decision to migrate is often not enough. The voyage abroad can be long and costly, particularly when the destination is one of the rich countries, where regulations are increasingly adverse. Because of travel and other associated costs, households with members who engage in international migration are likely better off. Not only does it cost money to migrate, the family may have to wait for many months or years before the migrant is able to send his or her first remittance.

Households with international migrants are also likely to be more skilled and to have better social networks, both of which facilitate the success of migrations. Income and human and social capital—the key determinants of international migration—combine to present unique, customized opportunities to households. Any one determinant on its own does not show a clear relationship with successful migration—all three are important.

Remittances are the top off-farm income in only 3 of the 30 surveyed regions (Tominian and Diéma in Mali, Terrabona in Nicaragua). They are ranked as the second largest off-farm income source in nine others, including regions in

Figure 4.10 Importance of Migration per Surveyed Region

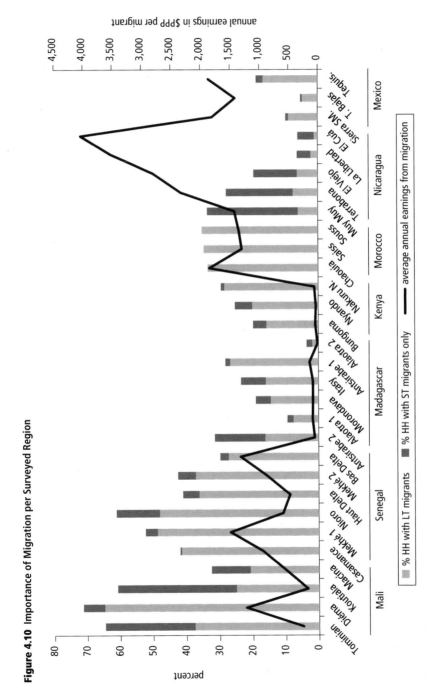

Source: RuralStruc surveys.

Figure 4.11 Migrants' Destination by Surveyed Region

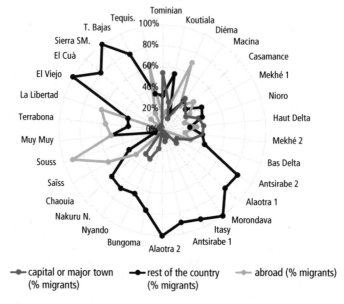

Source: RuralStruc surveys.

Senegal, Morocco, and Nicaragua (see table 4.1). However, even in regions where migration is important, earnings per migrant are very diverse (figure 4.10).

A core group of regions displays earnings between $1,000 PPP and $2,000 PPP (Diéma, Mekhé 1, and Bas Delta, all the surveyed zones in Morocco, and Mexico), while Kenya and Madagascar show evidence of very low transfers. The five surveyed regions of Nicaragua, where average returns are above $2,500 PPP, stand out.[31] In comparison, the earnings of Mexican migrants seem surprisingly low, given what is known about the development of migrations in that country.[32]

From this very diverse picture, three main patterns of migration can be identified based on the regional importance and duration of migrations, and the main destinations of migrants (figure 4.11). They correspond to 23 of the 30 surveyed regions, and their major characteristics are presented in table 4.3.

The first pattern corresponds to international long-term migrations, mostly toward OECD countries (Diéma, Souss, and Saïss, Tequisquiapan). The second pattern illustrates migrations to neighboring countries. It is exemplified by the specific case of Nicaragua, with short-term migrations to Costa Rica and El Salvador, where migrants are engaged in waged activities, mainly in agriculture (export crops) and services (especially construction, housecleaning, and security). One explanation for the higher returns observed in Nicaragua is that

Table 4.3 Main Migration Patterns among the Surveyed Regions

		% of households with migrants			
		>50	30–50	10–30	<10
>50% of migrants by destination	Abroad	Diema	Saïss	Terrabona	La Libertad
			Souss	Tequisquiapan	
			Muy Muy		
	Capital city	Tominian			
	Other regions	Koutiala	Chaouia	El Viejo	El Cuá
			Antsirabe 2	Kenya (all)	Tierras Bajas
				Madagascar (others)	Sierra SM
					Alaotra 1 & 2

Source: RuralStruc surveys.
Notes: ■ = >40% of migrants are short term.

migrants maintain closer links with their households because of the proximity of their destinations. Migrants often return home after several months and carry the main part of their income with them in cash, which is not the case for long-term migrants, who organize transfers on a more irregular basis. The third pattern corresponds to internal migrations—to the capital city or other major cities, or to other rural regions. These migrations are heavily weighted toward short-term work—as shown by Tominian and Koutiala in Mali and by Terrabona in Nicaragua—but they can also be long term. In the poorest regions and for the poorest households (for example, in Kenya, Madagascar, and Mali), these migrations do not just aim to generate income. They help decrease the number of mouths to feed during the intercrop season, when on-farm family labor is not needed and the labor surplus is massive (RS 2 Mali). Or, more durably, they are a radical way to reduce household expenses.[33] These migrants, who may work as servants or doing odd jobs, often earn very little money and simply find a way to sustain their most basic needs.

The seven remaining surveyed regions (the six Senegalese regions plus Macina) present a very mixed picture in terms of the destination of migrations (see figure 4.11). They illustrate strong combinations of all available migratory options. This situation is exemplified by the *bassin arachidier* in Senegal, where the migration pattern provides further evidence of a regional catch-all strategy in terms of activities and incomes. Good connections to Dakar, Thiès, and Saint-Louis offer multiple opportunities that help households cope with the deep crisis in the groundnut sector. Nevertheless, this strategy of engaging in multiple activities—characterized by the accumulation of *petits boulots* (odd jobs) in the village, in the nearby small town, in the capital city, or, for some households, abroad—offers only a partial answer and does not provide an exit option out of poverty, as evidenced by the low level of incomes in the region (see box 4.4).

BOX 4.4

Migrating to Dakar to Sell Phone Cards: An Illusory Pathway out of Poverty

A good example of the *petits boulots* in which many Senegalese households engage is the sale of mobile phone cards—a proliferating activity in all African cities. Many young people who have migrated from rural areas try their luck at Dakar's traffic lights for a couple of months.

Figures help explain the reality of this kind of work. These peddlers earn CFA75 (0.28 PPP) for every CFA1,000 phone card sold (a 7.5 percent margin), or CFA900 for a CFA10,000 phone card (9 percent). They can make CFA525 a day ($2) by selling seven CFA1,000 phone cards, knowing that selling a CFA10,000 card is a rare event. On this meager income, vendors must pay for meals and a place to sleep. The price of a basic place to spend the night is about CFA30,000 per month, so a worker must reach a sales target of 400 phone cards a month and the competition is harsh. These costs can be mitigated to a certain extent—sharing a room with many others or even sleeping in the street—but with this type of work, it is a challenge to cover one's costs, with little opportunity to bring any cash back to the village.

Source: RuralStruc interviews, October 2009.

Two primary conclusions emerge from this discussion of surveyed households' involvement in and earnings from migrations. The first is the overwhelming importance of geography. Places that are near high-income countries (Mexico, Morocco) or with easy access to dynamic middle-income countries (Nicaragua) have a clear advantage, because cost and difficulty of access are less of a constraint and workers can find better-paying jobs. Although it is not an absolute barrier (as illustrated by Senegal and Mali), distance complicates the picture, particularly when it is large and there is no ground transportation (the cases of Kenya and, above all, Madagascar are revealing).

The second conclusion refers to an emerging pattern that progressively reshapes many rural economies. Better transportation and communication everywhere have increased the opportunities for connections to a wide array of locations—nearby cities, regional and national capitals, locations outside the home country—which in turn lead to family networks connecting members of the same household who are working in these different places and for different periods of time. These networks correspond to new composite multilocalized systems, which redefine country-to-city links. In these "archipelago models," the household remains firmly based in the countryside and inserted in its rural environment (economically, socially, and culturally), with a decision center (the head of the household) that manages income streams from household members who live and work in different locations (like islands coordinated with their capital).[34] Although these family networks can facilitate permanent migration and exit from the countryside, they are most often a way of "leaving to stay."[35] By combining multiple livelihood strategies, households adjust to their evolving environments and maintain their affiliation with the local community, even if some members must leave to enable this to happen.

Public Transfers: Specific to Mexico. In the surveyed regions, public transfers are significant only in Mexico. As an upper-middle-income economy with a strong fiscal base, the Mexican state has implemented a well-developed public support system targeted toward rural areas (Léonard and Losch 2009). The transfer programs mainly focus on poverty alleviation, with social safety nets that target specific groups (for example, Oportunidades for the poorest) and subsidies to the agricultural sector through several programs (Procampo for production, Aserca for marketing, and Alianza for investment). Procampo benefits all farms, regardless of wealth level—the support a farm receives depends on the size of its area under cultivation. However, the other two programs are for large farms or agrobusinesses. These transfers have played a significant role, and their multiplier effect on incomes has been confirmed through research (Sadoulet, de Janvry, and Davis 2001). They have been complemented over the past few years by new programs related to decentralization (for example, Ramo 033 or "remote area" programs) and environmental protection, which mainly benefit local governments and communities.

More than 15 public programs were observed in the income structures of the surveyed households. Most of the farm households were involved in the Procampo program, which explains why 80 percent of households are involved with public transfers in the two Sotavento zones, while only 32 percent are involved in Tequisquiapan, where very few households have farms. However, these transfers may not be accurately targeted. In the Sotavento, they represent 12 percent to 20 percent of household income in all quintiles, which indicates a disconnect between the level of income and the allocation received (see box 4.5).

Off-Farm Diversification and Rural Transformation

Broadly, the literature suggests that diversification is the norm among developing countries' rural economies and that it leads to the emergence of vibrant rural nonfarm economies. However, the RuralStruc results provide a more nuanced picture. The survey results show that although diversification is present everywhere, its characteristics are dramatically different and vary significantly among regions.

Differences among and within regions reflect the strong heterogeneity of the studied situations. One major distinction between SSA and non-SSA

BOX 4.5

Unequal Access to Public Transfers in Mexico's Sotavento Region

In the Tierras Bajas and Sierra de Santa Marta surveyed zones of Mexico, respectively, public transfers are the first and second sources of off-farm incomes. They represent 32 percent of total off-farm income and constitute on average 15 percent of total income (RS 2 Mexico–Sotavento, 25).

As reflected in the figure below, one of the most striking survey results in these regions is the inequality of the distribution of public subsidies with regard to both social groups and geographic areas. The richest households benefit from a level of public transfers that is seven times higher than that received by the poorest households and 50 percent higher than the sum of the subsidies received by the households of the three lowest quintiles. This inequality has also a strong spatial dimension: In Tierras Bajas, where three-quarters of the richest households surveyed in the Sotavento are located, the average level of public transfers is regionally higher ($1,797 PPP) than in the mountain area ($1,329 PPP). Above all, subsidy levels are strongly correlated with incomes.

Instead of smoothing income inequalities and compensating for differences in asset provision, it appears that public transfers, in fact, contribute to accelerated differentiation with a "transition" toward a specialization in agriculture on bigger farms and attendant measures (safety nets) for other households.

Box Figure 4.5.1 Public Transfers by Surveyed Zone and Level of Household Income

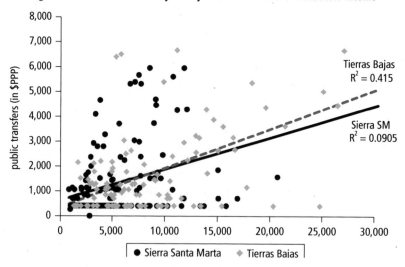

Source: Adapted from RS 2 Mexico.

countries reflects their different levels of economic development. This distinction does not refer to households' levels of participation in off-farm activities, which are quite similar; rather, it refers to the specifics of diversification—the type of activity and its economic returns.

Two types of diversification appear in the RuralStruc sample. In the Sub-Saharan African countries, diversification mainly represents coping strategies—a response to strong and persistent poverty. On-farm activities dominate and are accompanied by a structural underemployment that reflects the seasonality of agriculture, the lack of overall economic diversification, and limited job opportunities. Off-farm activities mainly correspond to low-return self-employment, while opportunities for waged labor (in agriculture and even more in other sectors) are scarce, low-paying (reflecting the situation of the labor market), and mostly temporary. As a result, off-farm incomes have a very low value and constitute only a partial response to poverty, even if they can contribute significantly to overall household income in regions facing difficult agricultural situations, such as the *bassin arachidier* in Senegal. Some households in every region obtain better returns: those that can find permanent nonagricultural jobs (for which an education is a strong asset) or that can develop specific types of self-employed activities (here, skills and existing income can make the difference). But these exceptions do not change the overall picture.

In non-SSA countries, where the level of wealth is higher and the economy more diversified, off-farm activities are more lucrative. They reflect a more positive diversification and often represent a full-time activity. This means that some households (or household members) specialize in off-farm activities while other households (or members) specialize in agriculture. This is clearly illustrated in the surveyed regions in Nicaragua and Morocco, and in Tequisquiapan, Mexico, where the number of households combining on-farm and off-farm activities is dramatically lower than in SSA.

The RuralStruc observations suggest that the characteristics of off-farm diversification to some extent mirror the process of economic transition as a whole: an incipient low-return diversification in the early stages of structural transformation and a more mature diversification at later stages that consolidates the process of change.

Three final interesting and cross-cutting outcomes deserve mention. The first is a result of the surveys that partially contradicts the conventional wisdom that says urbanization and demographic density can propel economic growth by themselves. The poor economic results obtained from the surveyed households in the dense coastal area of Senegal and in western Kenya show that although urbanization and density can facilitate and expedite the process of rural transformation, their characteristics (for example, the *quality* of densification) are important, as well as the characteristics of the economy as a whole, notably its diversification and productivity.

The second outcome relates to the difficulty of capturing the entire process of economic diversification. Because the surveys targeted rural households (households in areas defined as rural), they missed households that migrated into urban settings during the process of transformation. These new urban households were able to access better services and living conditions, engage in more off-farm activities, and in some cases even keep their farms—a situation observed in the Mexican survey. This methodological bias means that the distinction between rural boroughs and small cities is at least somewhat theoretical and that a major challenge for information systems is to capture the reality of the rural-urban continuum, which evolves through the process of densification. This issue also highlights the somewhat ephemeral nature of the rural nonfarm economy. The RNFE tends to grow and at the same time be dissolved into the urbanization process, as off-farm specializers migrate to urban areas and cities "move to the country"—a consequence of increasing demographic densities and the territorial development of cities related to the urban growth process.

The third outcome concerns what is learned from migrations. Although it is difficult to capture information on the amount of transfers, the surveys show that 24 percent of the households interviewed are engaged in migration, a level that is somewhat low but consistent with many rural studies. The surveys also show that the economic returns from migration are related to the destination of migrants, which is itself strongly influenced by geography, particularly by the proximity of high-income countries. In addition to the direct income benefit of migration in the form of remittances, a "network effect" can provide indirect returns. The survey results point to the development of archipelago systems, in which a household earns income from members in various locations. These workers can be spread along a geographic continuum from rural to peri-urban to urban, and can be located in other regions of the country or even abroad. But they all remain part of the same household. This type of organization, facilitated by improvements in transportation and communication infrastructure, allows for greater diversification and risk management, and improves the economic prospects of households.

If characteristics of the historical pathways of structural transformation are present, the development of these new kinds of links could modify the modalities of rural transformation by fostering additional opportunities. But they require access to services and adequate provision of public goods—in addition to infrastructure—to strengthen rural-urban linkages and create efficient density.

Notes

1. Ellis (1998) explains the common confusion between risk strategies and coping behavior: Risk management is an ex ante strategy to anticipate failure, while coping is the ex post response to a crisis. Ellis notes, however, that coping can also cor-

respond to the emergence of new livelihood patterns resulting from distress and crisis.

2. For a general approach, see Barrett and Swallow (2005), Ellis (2000, 2004), and Wiggins and Davis (2003); for regional issues, see Reardon, Berdegue, and Escobar (2001) on Latin America, and Barrett, Reardon, and Webb (2001) and Bryceson (1999, 2002) on Africa.

3. This is the definition of off-farm adopted by, among others, Barrett and Reardon (2000), Davis et al. (2007), and Haggblade, Hazell, and Reardon (2010).

4. Many authors include agroprocessing as a whole in rural nonfarm activities (see Haggblade, Hazell, and Reardon, 2010). The program considers that the on-farm processing of raw products should be included in on-farm activities, as in most cases it directly contributes to adding value to farm outputs. This is particularly true in SSA, where processing often concerns the products of the family farm itself. When products are processed by agro-industries or small-scale independent enterprises, labor earnings are obviously off-farm and considered as nonagricultural wage employment or self-employment.

5. Occasional hunting, fishing, and gathering are not agricultural activities per se but, as common rural practices based on the use of natural resources, they can be included in on-farm income.

6. Annex 4 in the appendix posted at http://www.worldbank.org/afr/ruralstruc shows these results by surveyed region.

7. The program chose to use this proxy rather than confining the analysis of off-farm activities to the household level, because it allows differences in the number of EAPs per household to be taken into account.

8. On agricultural wage labor related to horticulture, see McCulloch and Ota (2002) on Kenya and Maertens and Swinnen (2007) on Senegal.

9. Agricultural wages can be fully paid in cash or partly or fully in kind, for example, a quantity of the product, meals, and/or housing on the farm for permanent employees. Agricultural workers are often casual laborers, which complicates the estimation of annual values of agricultural wages.

10. The variable here is "land used"; that is, the farm area used by the household, whether owned or not, for crops and breeding, including fallow land (see annex 4 in the appendix posted at http://www.worldbank.org/afr/ruralstruc).

11. Farm structures in Mexico reflect the impact of the agrarian reform, even if strong disparities remain at the national level. The surveyed regions are, however, characterized by small to medium farms. The average size of the surveyed farms in the Sotavento region is around 10 Ha in the lowlands and 6 Ha in the mountains; in Tequisquiapan, they are smaller (2 Ha) and coexist with several agribusinesses that hire jornaleros (laborers).

12. In Madagascar, between the last two censuses (1985 and 2005), the national average size of farms dropped from 1.2 Ha to 0.86 Ha (RS 1 Madagascar).

13. The economically active population (EAP) per household is between six and nine persons in the surveyed regions of Mali and Senegal, which is two or three times as many persons as in other regions (see annex 4 in the appendix posted at http://www .worldbank.org/afr/ruralstruc).

14. In addition to Alaotra and El Viejo, other surveyed regions with significant landless households are Tequisquiapan (19 percent), Souss (10 percent), and Sotavento (7 percent). In the survey, landless households were defined as households engaged in agriculture through agricultural wage employment but without any access to farmland, regardless of the type of tenure.

15. Peaks of labor occur for all major regional productions: in the rice-growing regions of Madagascar (Alaotra, Itasy), Mali (Macina), and Senegal (Bas Delta); for horticulture in Madagascar (Itasy and Antsirabe) and Morocco (Souss and Saïss); for pineapple in the Tierras Bajas of Sotavento in Mexico (although maize is strongly mechanized); for cotton in Koutiala (Mali); for coffee in El Cuá (Nicaragua); and for sugar cane in El Viejo (Nicaragua) and Nyando and Bungoma (Kenya).

16. There is a negative correlation between the share of agricultural wages in the overall household income and the level of total income. The result is slightly negative for the overall sample (Pearson = −0,068) and higher for the non-SSA regions (Pearson = −0,24). Similarly, the level of agricultural wages decreases with farm size, which indicates better assets and possibly better-off households but also a better employment rate for family labor. The correlations between total farm size (land used) and the value of agricultural wages are significant: −0,114** in Madagascar; −0,096** in Kenya; −0,112** in Morocco; −0,059* in Nicaragua; and −0,059* in Mexico (*significant at the 0.05 level; **significant at the 0.01 level).

17. The shares of agricultural wage labor in the overall income are displayed per quintile and surveyed region in chapter 6, figure 6.1.

18. The cases of Mali and Senegal are again unique. Even if household members sometimes engage in agricultural wage labor, it is very occasional and the amounts earned are small (a few percent of the total income for all quintiles). This limited development of wage labor is explained by the importance of the family workforce, which limits the demand for external labor.

19. Agricultural wages of landless households account for about 50 percent of their overall income in Alaotra, 65 percent in Souss and Tequisquiapan, 75 percent in Sotavento, and more than 90 percent in Nicaragua.

20. The figures correspond to minimum national wages in Mali and Mexico, and to minimum rural wages in the other countries.

21. In the Senegal River Delta, Les Grands Moulins du Sénégal, a subsidiary of La Compagnie Fruitière, is one of the very few agribusinesses engaged in horticulture production for export (mainly production of cherry tomatoes in greenhouses). The company employs 1,200 temporary workers over a period of four months and 80 permanent workers. The wage for the temporary workers is FCFA 50,000 per month ($193 PPP), which is quite similar to the $8 PPP daily agricultural wage observed in the Bas Delta region (for a standard 22-day work month). But if the earnings of these lucky few, who accrue all their wages over the course of four months, were averaged over a year, the daily rate would be $2.1 PPP (RuralStruc interviews, March 2008).

22. See, for instance, Reardon, Berdegué, and Escobar (2001) and de Janvry and Sadoulet (2001).

23. The Pearson correlations between the level of education of the most educated member in each household and the level of nonagricultural wages is positively significant in every country, but particularly in the SSA countries: Mali (0,286**), Senegal

(0,225**), Madagascar (0,220**), Kenya (0,286**), Morocco (0,083*), Nicaragua (0,194**), and Mexico (0,194**) (*significant at the 0.05 level; **significant at the 0.01 level).

24. Forty percent of the households earn less than $500 PPP/EAP/year, a number closer to the other SSA averages (61 percent earn less than $1,000 PPP/EAP/year).

25. This threshold is somewhat arbitrary. It corresponds to $14 PPP per day. Twenty-two percent of the households earn more than $3,000, and 4 percent earn more than $10,000.

26. Other transfers were observed, mainly in Tominian, Mali (support from a religious charity to poor families), and in some villages of Madagascar. They are marginal.

27. The exception here is Morocco, where 19 households in the survey have rental revenues above $10,000 PPP per year, which mainly correspond to urban rentals in the regional cities. These outliers affect the regional averages and explain why rents appear as the first source of off-farm income in Morocco, which is a major distortion. The exclusion of these households from the sample was considered, but because they were part of the rural reality, it was decided that they should be included (RS 2 Morocco, 40).

28. Official banking and cash-transfer channels are an important vehicle, but significant flows are transferred from abroad through informal networks.

29. This is particularly the case in Mexico, where it is increasingly difficult to capture information about remittances, because many respondents refuse to answer. This reluctance is mainly related to illegal migration, which (even though it is overwhelmingly developed) is under official scrutiny and to fears linked to the criminalization of money transfers. RuralStruc surveyors encountered this problem.

30. For the survey, long-term migrants were defined as persons who are geographically distant from the household for more than six months in a year and who send (or do not send) remittances, whatever the amount.

31. The high returns in El Cuá and La Libertad (more than $4,000 PPP per migrant) must be put in perspective with the very small number of households involved (5 percent) and the migrants' destinations: mostly the United States and Spain.

32. Even though the Sotavento is not a traditional emigration zone, short- and long-term migrations to the irrigated perimeters of the Pacific coast have developed. The earnings declared during the survey were mainly related to long-term migration. Their limited amount is fully related to the difficulties presented above about survey conditions.

33. The Pearson correlations between the number of members of the household present and the total number of migrants are positively significant in Mali (0,390**), Senegal (0,144**), and Madagascar (0,168**). (**Correlation is significant at the 0.01 level.)

34. The archipelago model was initially developed in Andean studies in the 1970s to describe the multiple settlements of households across varied ecological landscapes related to the altitude (see Van Buren 1996). It has been applied to the new patterns of rural economies characterized by the importance of short- and long-term migrations, notably in Mexico. See Quesnel and Del Rey (2005), Léonard, Quesnel, and Del Rey (2004), Del Rey (2008), and Gastellu and Marchal (1997). At the same time, the concept was also used to qualify the spatial dynamics of globalization (Veltz 1996; Viard 1998).

35. This is the evocative title of Cortes's book (2000) on Bolivian peasant communities.

Chapter 5

Searching for New Patterns of On-Farm Specialization

A major finding of the RuralStruc surveys, discussed in chapter 3, was the persistent importance of on-farm activities in rural livelihoods. In almost all the regions surveyed, between 90 percent and 100 percent of rural households have a farm; the major exception is Tequisquiapan in Mexico. The share of households' on-farm incomes is significant in every region, although it varies according to the importance of the off-farm diversification processes described in chapter 4.

A core objective of the program, reflected in its first hypothesis (H1), was to investigate the extent to which the restructuring of agrifood markets linked to liberalization and globalization has led to the emergence of modern value chains and to assess the persistence of more traditional products and market organization patterns. A related question concerned the development of specialization in agriculture—one of the WDR08's possible exit pathways out of rural poverty—through increasing vertical integration.

The so-called "supermarket revolution" and new integration processes along globalized value chains have affected developing countries to very different degrees. These differences are directly related to the integration of national markets and their connection to the global economy, and thus to the overall process of economic transition. For this reason, upheaval in agrifood markets (often a focus in the literature) can be somewhat of a straw man. It tends to ignore the fact that large areas of the rural world remain unconnected, and it overemphasizes integration dynamics, which play out only gradually. Owing to the wide range of situations represented in the RuralStruc countries, significant variations were expected among them. However, the findings suggest that new integration patterns remain quite limited across the sample, and the program's investigation of on-farm activities became something of an elusive quest for a new agriculture. Of course, the selection of countries affects the results, and although the Mexican surveyed regions have clearly evolved significantly, the overall picture remains gray—marked everywhere by the extent and consequences of rural poverty.

After a brief overview of the general characteristics and consequences of the global restructuring of agrifood markets, this chapter focuses on the main features of on-farm activities in the surveyed regions, notably the importance of self-consumption and commercialization. It reviews the different patterns of crop specialization or diversification and finishes with an assessment of the ongoing processes of market integration.

The Big Restructuring[1]

The process of agricultural liberalization has been occurring over a long period and is not yet complete. Starting in the early 1980s, agriculture was subjected to the same process of state withdrawal that affected other economic sectors but at a slower pace, (owing to the fact that governments perceived it as a strategic sector).[2] This process continues today through the difficult and seemingly never-ending WTO Doha Round (see chapter 1). The liberalization of international markets is particularly difficult when it comes to the question of market access and public supports, but changes in domestic markets have been more radical. The dismantling of regulatory bodies and public companies and the subsequent wave of privatization have led to the entrance of new players (often with strong international connections) into the market, the gradual dissemination of new rules, progressive new balances of power, and the emergence of a new food regime.[3]

Ongoing Processes of Change

Changes in the market environment occur at both the national level and the international level. Changes at these two levels combine to create new rules of the game for local stakeholders that affect their room to maneuver.

Domestic Market Liberalization. At the national level, the main changes are related to state withdrawal and the privatization process, which was accompanied by the implementation of new regulations.

Before Liberalization. In all the RuralStruc countries, as in many developing countries, agricultural markets before liberalization were characterized by a dual system with asymmetric levels of state intervention. On the one hand, most domestic staple markets and commodity exports were controlled and highly regulated via marketing boards, state-run industries, administrative commodity pricing, and fixed wholesale and retail prices for many basic food products. Most of these public bodies were monopsonies, especially for major export products and sometimes for staples (with some cases of associated monopolies). The structures were initially created to (1) promote growth in the agriculture sector, because according to the development paradigm, capital accumulation in agriculture was the first stage in the development process; (2) stabilize producer prices (and incomes) over the course of a single crop season and reduce price variability between seasons, with the objective of reducing risks; (3) increase farm gate prices and improve farmers' investment incentives by reducing the number of intermediaries along the commodity chains; and (4) facilitate exports by managing the entirety of the national agricultural supply.

On the other hand, a few traditional nonstaple markets (mostly fresh products, such as fruit, vegetables, and dairy) were almost free, with little or no state intervention or price regulation. Spot transactions involving many small, nonspecialized, and unorganized buyers and sellers characterized these markets. Few, if any, grades or standards existed; poor market information systems prevailed; and informal contracts, largely enforced through social networks, were the norm (Fafchamps 2004).

Because of the weakness of the private sector, states also intervened in processing, mainly through parastatals. This often occurred in key industries in the traditional export sector, such as groundnuts, palm oil, tea, coffee, cocoa, and sugar. Many industrial crops were produced by public, vertically integrated firms aiming for economies of scale. State control was justified by the need to process quickly because of perishability and by stringent quality requirements for export products such as palm oil and tea.

Withdrawal of the State. In the 1980s and 1990s, market-oriented agricultural policy reforms were a centerpiece of liberalization in developing countries. They were often implemented in the context of structural adjustment programs designed to restore fiscal and current account balances, to reduce or eliminate price distortions, to facilitate efficient price transmission, and to stimulate investment and production (Akiyama et al. 2003; Barrett and Mutambatsere 2005). These reforms were justified by the fact that the state-run structures—such as marketing boards, development agencies, and public enterprises—were no longer meeting their original objectives and were perceived as symbols of state inefficiency. More broadly, state withdrawal was a prerequisite for moving toward full market liberalization. Thus, the first steps in reforming agricultural markets were the dismantling and privatization of these state-run structures, as well as the reduction of tariffs and export taxes, consumer subsidies, and producer price controls.

Tables 5.1 and 5.2 present some examples of the dismantling of former public bodies in RuralStruc countries.[4] These restructuring processes occurred over an extended period—from the end of the 1970s to the end of the 1990s. The starting point, scope, and pace of liberalization were country-specific, which explains the large variations among countries.

New Market Regulation. State withdrawal from agricultural markets and the dismantling of parastatals and regulatory systems generated a new economic

Table 5.1 Market Reforms in Non-Sub-Saharan RuralStruc Countries

	Before liberalization	After liberalization
Morocco		
ONICL *Office National Interprofessionnel des Céréales et Légumineuses*	*State marketing board:* full control on marketing of grains through fixed prices (especially wheat), and strictly controlled imports	1988–96: progressive liberalization of the grain market Quotas subsist for the "national flour"
OCE *Office de Commercialisation et d'Exportation*	*State marketing board:* monopoly on exports for citrus, horticultural products, canned foods etc.	1985: end of the monopoly and liberalization of exports
Nicaragua		
ENABAS *Empresa Nacional de Alimentos Básicos*	*State marketing agency:* monopoly on staples commercialization and export crops such as peanuts, sesame and soy	1984: elimination of price differential for basic grains 1990: full liberalization of staple commercialization
Mexico		
CONASUPO *Compañía Nacional de Subsistencias Populares*	*State-run enterprise:* monopoly on imports, supervision of exports, and domestic market supply for staples with controlled prices	1989: end of marketing monopoly on imports and on domestic market for all staples but maize and beans 1999: end of market intervention for maize and beans
INMECAFE *Instituto Mexicano del café*	*State marketing board:* support to farm production, processing and marketing, and monopoly on coffee exports	1993: dismantling of the board and liberalization

Source: RuralStruc country reports, Phases 1 and 2.

and institutional environment at the national level. These changes had several consequences that can be summarized by two related features. First, value chains rapidly became market driven and dependent on supply and demand variations. Many private actors emerged, but many were later eliminated in the intense competition that followed state withdrawal. One condition for survival was to increase alliances with foreign capital, a phenomenon that, in a context characterized by many fragmented producers and larger but fewer marketing agents or processors, exacerbated asymmetries and allowed the later groups to progressively control the value chains. The result was a process of concentration and the emergence of big players who greatly transformed market dynamics.

Second, as a result of the removal of regulations and price management, uncertainty and transaction costs increased for private actors in this increasingly competitive environment. Trade and processing companies responded by securing their supplies through the implementation of contracts with producers, producer organizations, and buying agents. Some of these companies engaged in even closer integration by buying local subsidiaries or organizing supply networks that in return offered specific support to producers. All of this changed the rules of the game.

Table 5.2 Market Reforms in Sub-Saharan RuralStruc Countries

	Before liberalization	After liberalization
Mali		
OPAM *Office des Produits Agricoles du Mali*	*State marketing board:* monopoly on commercialization of grains	1986: end of the monopoly 1989: liberalization of imports and domestic commercialization
Office du Niger	*Parastatal:* management of water, land, and irrigation infrastructure in the Office area; monopoly on marketing and processing of rice	1994: end of intervention on rice (except for extension)
CMDT *Compagnie Malienne de Développement des Textiles*	*Semipublic company* (40% to the French DAGRIS, now Geocoton): inputs supply, extension, marketing, and processing of cotton seed, supply of cotton fiber to the domestic public textile industry (COMATEX) and exports	On-going liberalization since 2004
Senegal		
ONCAD *Office national de commercialisation et d'assistance au développement*	*State marketing board:* monopoly on commercialization of domestic agricultural products (groundnut, grains) and imports, and supervision of producers' cooperatives	1979: liquidation 1991: liberalization of local market and imports of rice
SONACOS *Société nationale de commercialisation des oléagineux du Sénégal*	*State-run enterprise:* processor for groundnut oil	2006: privatization
Madagascar		
BCSR *Bureau de Commercialisation et de Stabilisation du Riz*	*State marketing board:* full monopoly on rice	1983–86: end of monopoly on domestic commercialization of rice 1990: privatization of imports 1991: end of the buffer stock
HASYMA *Hasy Malagasy*	*Semipublic company* (36% the French DAGRIS, now Geocoton): inputs supply, extension, marketing, and processing of cotton seed, supply of cotton fiber to the domestic public textile industry and exports	2004: privatization (90% of the capital held by DAGRIS)
Kenya		
NCPB *National Cereals and Produce Board*	*State marketing board:* monopoly on grain marketing (domestic market and exports)	1991–95: privatization and liberalization of marketing
KCC *Kenya Cooperative Creameries*	*Cooperative company:* monopoly on processing and sales of dairy products in all urban areas	1992: end of monopoly 1999: collapse as a consequence of new competition 2000: buyout and creation of KCC Holdings 2003: takeover by the government and "revitalization." Creation of new KCC

(table continues on next page)

Table 5.2 *(continued)*

CBK *The Coffee Board of Kenya*	*State marketing board:* monopoly on collection, processing, and exports of coffee	2001: end of monopoly. Now advisory role only.
TBK *The Tea Board of Kenya*	*State marketing board:* regulation of the tea industry (production, research, processing, trade, and promotion on domestic and international markets)	No change
KTDA *Kenya Tea Development Authority*	*Public development agency:* management of production through provision of inputs, extension, collection, processing, and marketing of tea	2000: privatization. Now Kenya Tea Development Authority with technical support to the industry.

Source: RuralStruc country reports, Phases 1 and 2.

The New Agrifood Markets. The major changes in the domestic markets took place in the context of other major restructuring processes in international agrifood markets. These processes are the result of the liberalization dynamics described above and of new patterns in food demand that emerged in response to globalization (see figure 5.1).

The main consequence of this evolution, which started in the 1980s, is a trend toward increasing levels of integration that feed and consolidate the ongoing restructuring of domestic markets. The main attributes of these processes of integration are the development of standards and closer relationships between producers and buyers. Of course, these changes develop at very different rates in different countries. The aim of the following section is to provide a frame of reference to understand the changes that are under way.

New Patterns in Agrifood Demand. The major trends on the demand side can be summarized as follows: (1) the world's population is becoming increasingly urban; (2) growing incomes result in quickly evolving diets, with more protein and high-value foods (meat and dairy, fruits and vegetables) instead of staples; (3) until the current period of increasing food prices, structurally decreasing prices stimulated agrifood market dynamics; and (4) an increasingly integrated world trade environment and improved transportation systems have spurred the convergence of dietary patterns and food preferences (FAO 2004).

As a consequence of these simultaneous changes, consumer-driven value chains (for fruits, vegetables, meat, dairy products, and fish and seafood products) grew rapidly. Telecommunications facilitated long-range commerce, and changes in shipping and storage technologies in the mid- to late 1980s allowed fresh produce (apples, strawberries, and asparagus, for example) to be shipped from Southern Hemisphere producers to Northern Hemisphere consumers. The expanding demand for and trade in perishable products and high-value foods brought about a need for more safety standards.[5] This change is evident

Figure 5.1 New Patterns and Trends in the Agrifood Systems Resulting from Liberalization and Globalization

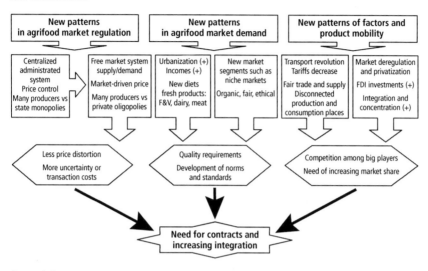

Source: Authors.

in the growing attention paid to the risks associated with agricultural inputs (residues from pesticides, veterinary medicines, and so on) and microbiological contamination. The implementation of stricter food safety and quality standards in the high-income countries has had a strong impact on the evolution of supply chains. Exporters and retailers, in particular, use new kinds of production and marketing contracts, and technical and financial assistance can be provided to strengthen the new linkages.

The shift of markets from supply driven to demand driven in a context of increasing incomes (at the aggregate level) has also transformed relationships among commodity chain stakeholders. Today, consumers in rich countries are increasingly looking for safety and for information on how products are grown and traded, to ensure socially fair and sustainable agricultural practices. This growth in consumer awareness has progressively supported a range of alternative initiatives in international, national, and local agrifood systems, and has fueled changes in retail patterns as fair trade, organic, and other alternative foods have entered mainstream venues. With the emergence of these niche markets, new standards and controls have been established parallel to the implementation of more generic certification structures. For instance, efforts are made to protect the integrity of organic standards to further differentiate organic foods and to promote different forms of short supply chains for local community development.[6]

Contracts, in their various forms and with varying degrees of obligation, usually reduce risks for the buyer and seller. They have appeared in response to the removal of the controlled marketing systems as a possible way to guarantee standards and requirements for the purchaser. For the producer, selling under contract arrangements is less risky if the requirements for the product are high and its characteristics are complex. Also, it is often the only way to access certain markets. For this reason, contracts have progressively spread to emerging fresh product chains and niche markets, where product attributes are clearly defined in terms of norms and standards, and where the final value of production allows for the coverage of specific costs of contracts (selection, negotiation, monitoring, and enforcement).

New Actors and New Patterns of Factor Mobility and Trade. Since the 1980s, increasing long-distance trade and foreign direct investment (FDI), facilitated by liberalization policies and the implementation of free trade agreements (FTAs), have broadly modified the scope of agricultural production and marketing. They are the consequence of a more open international economy resulting from economic liberalization and progress in technology: on the software side, the Internet for finance and information; on the hardware side, shipping, storage, and processing. These factors have all greatly increased the efficiency of international trade and domestic marketing, and have paved the way for major investments by new players everywhere, particularly in processing and retailing since the 1990s (Barrett and Mutambatsere 2005). A handful of vertically integrated transnational corporations and strategic alliances among major companies have increasingly gained control over specific national markets (box 5.1) and over global trade, processing, and retailing of food products (Vorley 2003). The "supermarket revolution" (box 5.2) is an example of the tremendous development of these processes.

The differences among countries can be explained by socioeconomic factors related to consumers' demand for supermarket services, product diversity, and quality. Among these factors are income level and urbanization, correlated with the opportunity cost of time (especially that of women); reduction in transaction costs through improvements in roads and transport; and development and ownership of refrigerators. These demand-side factors are necessary but not sufficient to explain the very rapid spread of supermarkets in the 1990s and 2000s in developing countries, most of which had a very small supermarket sector before 1990. Supply-side factors, combined with the overall objective of governments throughout the developing world to modernize the retail sector, were also extremely important, especially the influx of retail foreign investment (as countries liberalized the rules for FDI) and improvements in procurement systems. The RuralStruc countries are good examples of this evolution (see box 5.6).

BOX 5.1

Restructuring the Mexican Maize Industry

Mexico is a good example of a country in which extensive restructuring has occurred in the agricultural sector. It began at the end of the 1980s with the termination of a state-run company's monopoly on marketing (Conasupo—see table 5.1) (Yunes Naude 2003), price deregulation, and the implementation of NAFTA in 1993 (Appendini 2001). During this process, the maize sector received preferential treatment because of the crop's importance as the main component of Mexican diets; its weight in the agricultural sector; and its social, cultural, and political status. First, producers were offered transitional, nondistortive targeted support through a subsidy based on plot size (Procampo); this subsidy was set to expire in 2008. Second, the domestic value chain was protected from a surge of NAFTA-related imports through a transitional quota system. U.S. imports would be limited to an annual duty-free quota of 2.5 million tons, subject to a 3 percent annual increase. Imports beyond 2.5 million tons were to be taxed at a rate of 215 percent. This quota system was also planned to be progressively dismantled by 2008 (Lederman, Maloney, and Servén 2005).

These policy changes led to strong processes of concentration. Mexico's large commercial maize farms benefited from numerous public supports. One was the Procampo subsidy, which awarded more funds to farms with larger acreage under cultivation. Although this program was designed with a cap on subsidy amounts, it resulted in a situation in which Mexico's large maize farms (only 10 percent of the total) were capturing 53 percent of Procampo's resources by 2003. Large farms also benefited from programs designed to support their modernization and connection to markets. The Aserca and Alianza programs targeted farms with the best prospects for productivity growth with large subsidies for marketing and investment. Over time, the Ministry of Agriculture's budget shifted in favor of the latter programs. While Procampo represented 70 percent of its budget during President Zedillo's term (1995–2000), it fell to 50 percent under President Fox's administration (2001–06), with the difference going to fund Alianza and Aserca (Zahniser and Coyle 2004).

The concentration of production led to shifts in the geography of the sector (RS 2 Mexico, 36). Previously, Mexico's 2 million smallholders—mostly located in the central and southern regions—had dominated the national market. In the past 20 years, the 300,000 large commercial farms have grown to occupy 23 percent of the land under cultivation while supplying 35 percent of the market. Most are located in the northwest (especially Sinaloa), where irrigation is widespread and productivity can be up to 9.8 tons/Ha (compared with 1.4 tons/Ha for smallholders elsewhere). On the processing side, state withdrawal, privatization, the end of fixed tortilla prices, and supports to the industrial flour industry led to an erosion of the artisanal tortilla sector. A powerful oligopoly of industrial millers came to control 52 percent of the flour supply (SAGARPA 2007) and leveraged this control to vertically integrate tortilla producers through licensing systems (Léonard 2010). Today, two major groups supply the industrial flour market: Maseca (75 percent) and Minsa (15 percent).

(box continued on next page)

The dominant position of the industrial producers was strengthened by their involvement in importing yellow corn from the United States, and they benefited greatly from the government's decision to only sporadically enforce the quota restrictions and import duties described above (Wise 2009). Imports of maize increased from 1.3 million tons in 1992 to 8.8 million tons in 2008, well beyond the allowances created under the quota system. More than half of these maize imports (which are 95 percent–98 percent yellow corn) are controlled by seven companies (De Ita 2008). These include the two major millers—Maseca (in which ADM holds a 25 percent equity stake) and Minsa (associated with Corn Products International, which took control of the Arancia corn-refining company in 1998)—as well as Cargill-Continental; three major companies involved in the poultry and feed production industries (Bachoco, Pilgrim's Pride, and Purina); and Diconsa, a state-owned company spun off from the former Conasupo, which is still charged with supplying basic food products to marginalized rural communities.

The incorporation of yellow corn (traditionally used for feed) into flour production is a dramatic change that is modifying the structure of the Mexican maize market and consumption patterns (tortillas are traditionally produced with white maize). It is directly resulting in domestic producer prices that are well below the international reference price, while final tortilla prices have continued to rise (Appendini 2008).

BOX 5.2

The Supermarket Revolution

The penetration of modern food retailing varies among developing countries. Reardon and Timmer (2007) describe the process this way:

> Experiencing supermarket-sector "take-off" in developing countries in the early to mid-1990s, the first wave included much of South America, East Asia outside China, and South Africa—areas where the average share of supermarkets in food retail went from roughly only 10–20% circa 1990 to 50–60% on average by the early 2000s. The second wave includes parts of Southeast Asia, Central America, and Mexico, where the share went from circa 5–10% in 1990 to 30–50% by the early 2000s, with the take-off occurring in the mid- to late 1990s. The third wave includes countries where the supermarket revolution take-off started only in the late 1990s or early 2000s, reaching about 10–20% of national food retail by circa 2003; they include some of Africa and some countries in Central and South America (such as Nicaragua, Peru, and Bolivia), Southeast Asia, and China, India, and Russia. Sub-Saharan Africa presents a very diverse picture, with only South Africa firmly in the first wave of supermarket penetration but the rest either in the early phase of the third wave take-off of diffusion or in what may be a pending—but not yet started—take-off of supermarket diffusion. (p. 284)

Expected Consequences of Restructuring for Farming

All these changes in agrifood markets have upstream consequences at the producer level. However, questions remain about the strength, depth, and pace of this global restructuring for farming.

In theory, global markets present an opportunity for suppliers—valuable new consumers and products year round—as far as they are able to connect. Contractualization is often seen as a tool to facilitate smallholder integration into these new markets, increasing and stabilizing their incomes. The WDR08 supports this view and argues that contractualization and development of agricultural entrepreneurship is one way for smallholders in developing countries to escape from poverty. It is true that smallholders are constrained by capital and liquidity difficulties, as well as lack of access and capacity to adopt technological innovations. Contract farming with supermarkets, processors, or export agents could help them overcome these constraints. This perspective has fostered a renewed interest in the donor community in value-chain approaches, leading to an extensive literature as well as new programs and projects.[7]

However, as previously mentioned and noted by Reardon and Timmer (2007), among others, contractualization implies increasing requirements in terms of norms and standards, sometimes including specifications for how the product should be grown, harvested, transported, processed, and stored. Thus, contracts and the new markets with which they can connect farmers are an opportunity only for producers who can meet the requirements. For others, the increasing contractualization of supply chains carries a substantial risk of marginalization, particularly when the overall economic and institutional environment is not favorable for the large majority of producers—the situation in many countries, especially in Africa (Gibbon and Ponte 2005). This growing contractualization and associated marginalization will have a clear impact on farm structures. The core issue is to understand the development of these processes of differentiation and to be able to anticipate their positive and negative effects.

The Regoverning Markets research program (box 5.3) addressed these questions. The program found an initial increase in the participation of smallholders in modern value chains, frequently followed by their progressive marginalization as larger producers enter the market and are able to provide more supply with the required quality (Vorley, Fearne, and Ray 2007; Reardon and Huang 2008). This progressive differentiation among producers is exacerbated by the practices of major retailers and by supermarket procurement systems. As supermarkets and major retailers try to facilitate the adoption of their specifications and reduce their transaction costs, they often choose to work with a reduced number of suppliers that can provide high volumes and high quality.

BOX 5.3
_____

Regoverning Markets

Regoverning Markets was a multipartner collaborative research program (2005–07) that aimed to analyze the growing concentration in the processing and retail sectors of national and regional agrifood systems and its effects on rural livelihoods and communities in middle- and low-income countries. The goal of the program was to provide strategic advice and guidance to the public sector, agrifood chain actors, civil society organizations, and development agencies to help them anticipate and manage the effects of changes in local and regional markets.

The program focused on agrifood market restructuring to assess its upstream effects on the various segments of the value chain: retail (especially supermarkets), processing, wholesale, and farming. It compared country/product pairs at different stages of restructuring, using farm household surveys and commodity chain analyses. Household surveys were conducted with a focus on selected products in high-value chains, mainly fresh products such as fruits, vegetables, and dairy.

Source: http://www.regoverningmarkets.org.

Thanks to the Regoverning Markets program, more is known about the characteristics and modalities of value chain integration and contractualization development, but little is known about the extent of these processes. How far did these new forms of market integration trickle down in various developing countries in which the pace of change has differed? What numbers are at stake? How many farmers are engaged in these new value chains?

Agricultural and customs statistics provide data on high-value products and exports, but data are not available on the number of producers participating in the different types of value chains, which is a recurring obstacle in assessing these new developments. RuralStruc teams were unsuccessful in their attempts to collect accurate data on value chain participants during the Phase 1 sector reviews, but the few numbers gathered suggest that in every country thousands of farmers are engaged in these new value chains while hundreds of thousands (or even millions) remain involved in more traditional agriculture. The now-famous success story of the development of horticulture in Kenya is a good illustration of the potential and limitations of high-value exports (see box 5.4).

An Elusive New Agriculture

The processes of change under way in agrifood systems and their consequences in terms of the increasing integration of agriculture obviously occur at different

BOX 5.4

The Kenyan Success Story in Horticultural Exports:
How Many and Whom?

Over the past two decades, horticultural products (fruits, vegetables, and cut flowers) have become the largest category in world agricultural trade; they account for 20 percent of global agricultural exports. In SSA, horticulture exports have developed rapidly, but production remains localized in a few key regions. Kenya is a famous example. It is the second-largest horticultural exporter on the subcontinent after South Africa, the second-largest developing-country exporter of flowers after Colombia, and the second-largest supplier of vegetables to the EU after Morocco. Horticulture has become Kenya's second-largest commodity export sector, after tea (English, Jaffee, and Okello 2006).

This is an indisputable success story in terms of market share, export earnings, and growth, although some fears exist about its impact on water resources. It is useful to examine the development of these horticulture exports in the context of the structure of the Kenyan agricultural sector as a whole. Although information is scarce because there are no statistics, it is possible to build a generalized picture from targeted surveys and interviews with major stakeholders, notably exporters.

Several authors report that, in the early 1990s, the majority of horticulture exports were produced by smallholders (Harris 1992 and Jaffee 1994, among others). However, Dolan and Humphrey (2000) estimated that, by the late 1990s, when horticulture exports were much larger, 40 percent came from the exporters' own estates or leased land; 42 percent came from large commercial farms; and only 18 percent came from smallholders, who had difficulty meeting the safety and quality requirements of international buyers. Jaffee (2003) offered more optimistic figures on smallholder engagement, with small-holders' share of the export market at 27 percent for fresh vegetables and 85 percent for fresh fruit, for an overall sector share of 47 percent. These estimates reflect a situation in which the majority of export growth occurred outside smallholder agriculture.

Estimating the number of smallholders involved in the industry is equally difficult. According to the last national survey—the 1994 Welfare Monitoring Survey—the number of farms in the country was estimated at 3.4 million, and fewer than 20,000 small-holders were engaged in horticultural exports (Jaffee 1995; Asfaw, Mithofer, and Waibel 2007). English, Jaffee, and Okello (2006) estimated the total employment generated by the horticultural export industry in a range of 120,000–150,000 jobs in 2003, with a third in the cut flower industry, where smallholders are not involved. The other two-thirds are in fruits and vegetables, where employment is split among smallholder farms (40,000 jobs), processing plants (10,000), and the large estates and packhouses (50,000).

This analysis indicates that although the sector offers important macro-level returns and opportunities for tens of thousands of households (whom McCulloch and Ota showed to be richer than the average household in their area), one must keep in mind the size of the overall farming sector and the dynamics of the labor market. In 2010, there were 840,000 labor market entrants—650,000 in the rural sector alone

(box continues on next page)

(see chapter 2). Muendo and Tschirley (2004) showed that in Kenya, over 90 percent of smallholder farmers in nonarid regions produce horticultural products, mostly for domestic consumption, and that fruits and vegetables for the domestic market account for over 90 percent of total horticultural output by volume. This overall perspective is a useful reminder of the challenges that remain despite the impact of horticultural exports on Kenya's economy, as well as the potential for growth in other production sectors, which could also benefit from policy makers' attention and support.

---

speeds, depending on local and national characteristics. The RuralStruc countries are no exception, and the surveyed regions illustrate a large diversity of situations.

The most striking results of the fieldwork are the continued high share of staple crops in the farm production of surveyed households—even in regions that are involved in export crops—and the high proportion of self-consumption. The latter is not a surprise per se, as a large share of agricultural production in developing countries consists of self-consumed staple crops. However, in the ex ante "winning" regions of the survey, one could have expected results showing deeper levels of crop diversification and connection to markets. This is not the case: Even in the most integrated regions of the sample, agricultural production patterns are still relatively domestic-oriented and traditional.[8]

This section reviews the patterns of agricultural production observed and discusses the extent of crop diversification and conditions of market integration.

Characteristics of On-Farm Income

On-farm incomes are earned from a wide range of on-farm activities, the characteristics of which are related to agro-ecological conditions, the specific patterns of agrarian systems, and the local market environment.

Overview. On-farm income can be divided into four main types of rural incomes (see figure 4.1): crops; livestock; income from hunting, fishing, and gathering; and income from on-farm transformation processes, such as the transformation of milk into cheese. Figure 5.2 shows that crop production generates the main share of on-farm income and dominates regional output everywhere. Its dominance is challenged only in La Libertad in Nicaragua, Chaouia in Morocco, and Nakuru North in Kenya, where livestock accounts for around 50 percent of on-farm income.

The figure also shows that the surveyed farm households do not rely so much on natural resources for income generation.[9] The main activities in this category are fishing in the Office du Niger zone in Mali (Macina), in Lake Victoria in Kenya (Nyando), and along the Pacific coast in Nicaragua (El Viejo); and gathering fruits in Tominian and Koutiala (Mali). Processing of on-farm products remains surprisingly limited. Where it does occur, processing concerns

Figure 5.2 Overall Structure of On-Farm Income
% per surveyed region

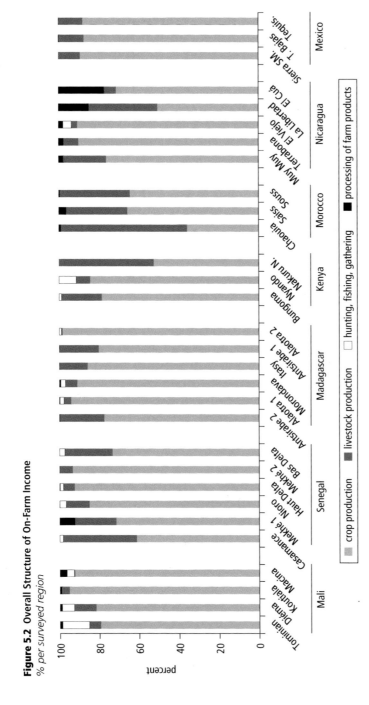

Source: RuralStruc surveys.

Table 5.3 Categories of Products Used for Data Analysis

Staples	Rice, maize, wheat and durum, other cereals (millet, sorghum, fonio, barley), cassava, potato, other staples (peas and beans—niebe, voandzou, chick peas, lentils, etc.), soy
Traditional commodities	Cotton, groundnut, sesame, coffee, sugar cane
Fruits and vegetables	Olive, citrus, other fruits, green beans, tomato, onion, other vegetables
Livestock products	Milk, other livestock products (butter, meat, etc.), live animals
Others	Forage, others (coconut, herbs and spices, etc.), other subproducts (sweet potato, cassava, groundnut leaves, etc.)

Source: RuralStruc surveys.

livestock products (mostly low-quality cheese production) and initial processing of coffee in Nicaragua, cheese and olive oil in Morocco (Saïss), and groundnut paste in Senegal.

To further analyze agricultural production, five main categories of products (see table 5.3) were designed by summarizing more than 30 products identified during the surveys. This kind of grouping exercise is always complicated, especially when it includes different regions and their different consumption patterns, as the use of products varies.[10]

Figure 5.3 displays the overall structure of households' gross farm product across the regions.[11] The striking result is the large share of staple food crops. Ninety percent of the farm households in the sample are engaged in staple production (98 percent in SSA and 76 percent in non-SSA regions). In 18 of the 30 surveyed zones, staple production is more than 50 percent of the gross farm product; it sometimes reaches 80 percent. The main exceptions are Morocco and, partially, Kenya and Senegal. Generally, staple production concerns one main type of product, usually cereals. The term refers to rice throughout Madagascar, in Macina (Mali), and in Senegal's Delta and Casamance; millet and sorghum in the three other regions of Mali and in the *bassin arachidier* in Senegal; wheat in Morocco; and maize in Kenya, Mexico, and Nicaragua. Cereal production is mainly rainfed, but in some cases farmers have developed irrigated rice (Madagascar, Senegal, and Mali) and maize (Mexico).[12]

Beans are the second staple crop in Nicaragua; in Antsirabe (Madagascar), potatoes are an important share of staple food production. Although the potato value chain originally developed in response to urban demand, the product has progressively transformed local consumption patterns and is now widely self-consumed as well as sold. Roots, tubers, and plantains are grown in most regions, except in Morocco. In Senegal, cassava developed in the *bassin arachidier* and is one of the major diversification options in response to the deterioration of the groundnut sector.

Livestock are present in all the surveyed regions, and commercialization of live animals is the rule. This is particularly true in Mali, one of the main cattle

Figure 5.3 Main Farm Products per Surveyed Region

% of gross farm product

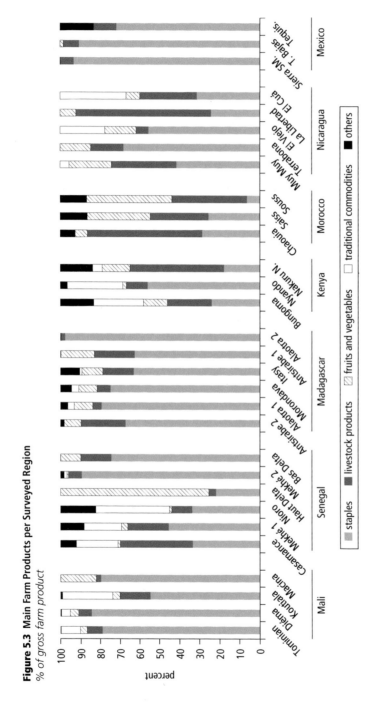

providers for the coastal countries of the Gulf of Guinea. Some regional specialization in livestock products exists, particularly in dairy. Nicaragua's "milky way" (Muy Muy) produces fresh milk and dairy products, and La Libertad has a traditional on-farm, low-quality processed cheese industry (industrial processing units are not used owing to infrastructure constraints). Nakuru North in Kenya, Antsirabe in Madagascar, and the Saïss region in Morocco have dairy belts that have led to the development of agro-industries. Casamance in Senegal also engages in some processing and trades these products locally. Marketing patterns for livestock products and the development of agro-industry can be explained by the quality of infrastructure available in each region. This determines what can be sold (for example, fresh refrigerated milk for processors and supermarkets that supply cities versus homemade low-quality cheese for local rural markets in Nicaragua), as well as the strength of reachable local demand (proximity and access to cities).

Livestock income, in absolute and relative terms, can be affected by specific conditions. This was the case of Chaouia in Morocco, where a very bad crop season deeply affected cereal yields and obliged many farmers to sell off their live cattle and small ruminants.[13] Similarly, the significance of livestock in the cotton zone of Mali (Koutiala) results from the low price of cotton that affected the growers in 2007. Many of the farmers decapitalized and sold their livestock to maintain their purchasing power. The good crop season in Macina led to the opposite effect: increased investment in livestock. In Mali, and generally in all of Sub-Saharan Africa, livestock can be a patrimonial asset—providing draft force and supplying manure for crop production—as well as the embodiment of financial savings that are stored to use in difficult times.

Horticulture is a common activity—vegetables are grown everywhere for domestic consumption. In many of the surveyed regions, however, specialization in horticulture has occurred, encouraged by favorable natural conditions and stimulated by urban development, which led to specific private investments. This is especially the case in Saiss and Souss in Morocco, where production of fruits and vegetables for export or for the agro-industry (mainly fruits and tomatoes) has become a major industry over the past two decades, and where processing and exporting companies are fostering development through contractual arrangements. The same phenomenon has occurred in Nakuru North. Even though the surveyed zone is not located in the region's famous flower production area, households are involved in tomato production and selling to a canning company. Fruits and other vegetables are also dynamic sectors. In the Senegal River valley (Haut Delta), tomato production developed in response to the presence of a processing plant that provides the local market with tomato paste. The fact that many of the surveyed households are located in the collection area of the factory explains the high share of horticulture in their gross product. The production of fresh foods for cities has developed in

Antsirabe and Itasy (Madagascar), where temperate fruits and vegetables (for example, peaches, apples, and carrots) can be grown.[14] Onion production has flourished in Saiss (Morocco) and in Office du Niger (Macina, Mali); it supplies the domestic and regional markets, and constitutes nearly 20 percent of the region's gross farm product. In Terrabona (Nicaragua), the richest households engage in irrigated horticulture production that is mainly sold domestically through traditional spot markets but also through more integrated value chains (supermarket procurement systems).

The importance of traditional commodities is linked to region-specific circumstances. Their development is mainly related to regional history and results from both natural advantages and specific interventions by the state or the private sector, most often during colonization—a time when foreign powers were organizing their own supply from their colonies. Where traditional commodities are produced, they have generally played a major role in shaping the region's agricultural complexion, owing to their long-standing economic and sometimes political importance, even if this importance has faded over time. This is the case for cotton in Koutiala and Casamance, groundnut in the *bassin arachidier*, coffee in El Cuá and Bungoma, and sugar cane in El Viejo, Nyando, and Bungoma.

Self-Consumption versus Sales. Despite very different regional contexts in terms of agro-ecological, agrarian, historical, and institutional conditions, the main characteristic of on-farm incomes in the RuralStruc sample is the importance of self-consumption.[15] It accounts for a large share of gross farm product, and variations among regions reflect differences in market connections. However, even when self-consumption is important, it does not necessarily imply disconnection from markets. Households have different patterns of market engagement: Even if they cannot sell much of their farm output, they can sell their labor (see chapter 4) and they are also consumers, buying goods (including food) and services. Taking the example of Mali (see table 5.4), even in regions with very significant levels of self-consumption, a large percentage of households participate in food markets as consumers.[16]

Nevertheless, as shown in figure 5.4, self-consumption levels stay high in many surveyed regions—higher than anticipated considering the methodology used to select the regions. The major exception is Mexico (see box 5.5).

Table 5.4 Malian Households' Participation in Food Markets

Region	HHs with food purchases	HHs with staple sales
Tominian	60%	8%
Diéma	64%	53%
Koutiala	58%	77%
Macina	71%	89%

Source: RuralStruc Surveys.

Figure 5.4 Share of Self-Consumption

% of gross farm product per household quintile

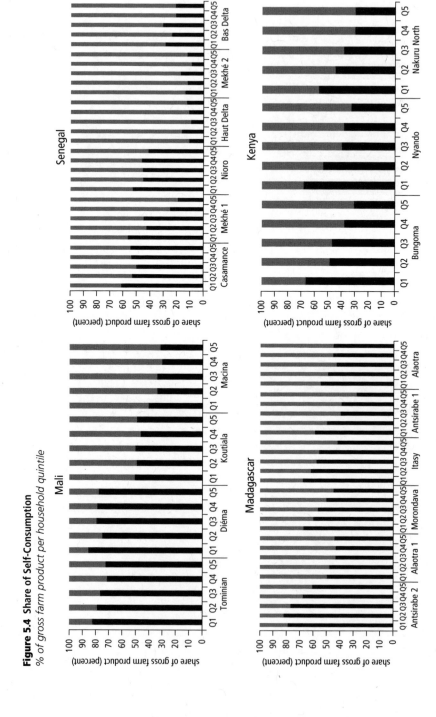

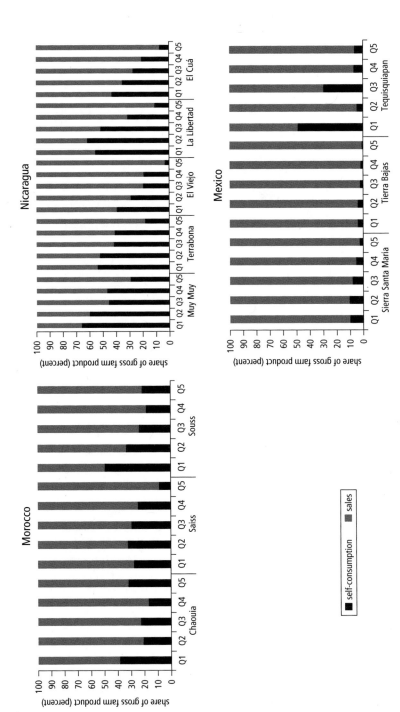

The RuralStruc sample also reflects significant differences among countries and regions, and among income levels.

In richer countries and richer regions, households apparently self-consume a smaller share of their output, while the poorest households are more oriented toward self-consumption. The differences among quintiles seem to be strongest in Madagascar, Kenya, and Nicaragua, although they are present almost everywhere.[17]

The two main drivers of self-consumption are demand and risk. Demand depends mostly on distance to markets and possibilities for integration through specific value chains. As examples of the demand effect, self-consumption is lower in Koutiala because a strong demand for cotton provides opportunities to move away from subsistence farming; the same occurs with tomatoes and cassava in Haut Delta and Mekhé 2, respectively.

On the other hand, households that consume much of their own output often do so because there is little demand for their products, usually because they lack a good connection to markets.[18] When demand exists, either through proximity to a large market or through the presence of a specific buyer, self-consumption decreases. Demand effects are more likely to appear at the regional level because market access does not vary strongly within a region, although differences can occur at the subregional level (this is notably the case in remote areas of Chaouia or Souss in Morocco, and was the reason for the distinction between Antsirabe 1 and 2).

The second driver is related to risk and level of income. Households with very weak incomes face food security challenges (see chapter 3) and adopt risk-management practices, so they can control their own food supply by producing it themselves. This can be called a supply effect. Because of a heightened level of risk, households are unwilling to sell their output on the market and consequently self-consume a large portion of it. Supply effects are more likely to arise among income quintiles in the same region.

Nicaragua is a good example of a country where differences among household quintiles dominate the pattern of self-consumption. In low-income quintiles, self-consumption rates often reach 60 percent, and a number of households (20 percent to 40 percent) are completely uninvolved with agricultural markets (that is, their self-consumption rate is 100 percent). Only one region, La Libertad, is characterized by physical seclusion and therefore faces transportation problems, which means that infrastructure is not the major explanation.

Risk-management strategies seem to be a primary reason for the limited connection to agricultural markets. However, middlemen might have little interest in incurring the expenses of collecting the limited quantities produced by very small farmers when they can access larger quantities from large farmers—a clear argument for collective action on the part of small producers. Specific local conditions can also shape household strategies. For example, in Terrabona, alternative off-farm options (wage labor in agriculture and *maquiladoras*) allow a dual strategy of self-consumption of farm products and insertion into labor markets. Households prefer to grow food for family consumption and earn cash from wage labor to meet needs such as schooling, health, and consumer goods.

Regional Patterns of Product Diversification

The previous section discussed types of farm products and the importance of self-consumption in the surveyed regions, but what is the degree of specialization or diversification of farm production?

Figure 5.5 shows the overall structure of households' gross farm product across regions. It focuses on the main products in each region, showing the share of farm output self-consumed and the share of on-farm income that comes from selling the two most important products.

The analysis of commercialized products confirms the strong persistence of staples, which are sold by households at all income levels in all regions. Staples make up over 25 percent of farm output in every region except those in Morocco, where the importance of wheat was masked by a bad crop season and the subsequent sale of livestock assets. The survey shows that staples are often one of the best options available to farm households, even the richest, and suggests a generally low level of opportunity for specialization in higher value crops.

The analysis confirms the importance of self-consumption at the aggregated regional level, especially in poorer regions; however, it also illustrates patterns of on-farm diversification. In Sub-Saharan Africa, households in 13 of 19 surveyed regions earn, on average, more than 70 percent of their on-farm income through self-consumption alone or through self-consumption plus the sale of only one type of product. This is the case in just 2 of the 11 non-SSA regions and subregions: the two Sotavento zones in Mexico, where a very specific process of deep specialization in maize production has developed (box 5.5). Generally, as wealth increases (moving from the poorest regions on the left to the richest regions on the right), the share of self-consumption falls and the share of "other products sold" rises.

On-farm diversification varies not only between poorer and richer regions but also between poorer and richer households within regions. In 20 of the 30 surveyed zones, households in the fifth household quintile are more diversified than those in the bottom quintile: Sales of their top three products make up a smaller portion of their on-farm income (on average, about 8 percentage points less, although the difference can reach 16 percent). The increase in on-farm diversification between the poorest and richest quintiles is seen in 10 of 11 non-SSA zones but only 10 of 19 SSA zones, consistent with the previous observation that diversification is less widespread in SSA in general.

On-farm diversification among households within regions is often characterized by the addition of new sales crops rather than by dropping one type of production in favor of others. In fact, in 20 of the 30 zones surveyed, the top sales crop of households in the fifth quintile is the same as the top sales crop

Figure 5.5 Farm Output Breakdown: Self-Consumption and Main Sales

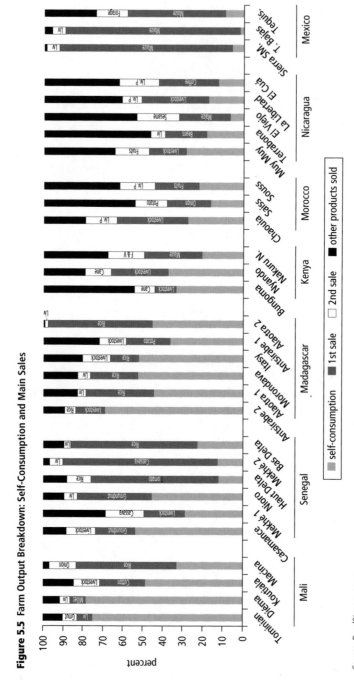

Source: RuralStruc surveys.
Note: Liv = livestock; Liv.P = livestock products

BOX 5.5

The Sotavento Exception: On-Farm Specialization and the Collapse of Self-Consumption

In the RuralStruc survey, Sotavento in the state of Veracruz is unique—characterized by specialization in maize production, increased integration into marketing channels, and dramatic reduction in self-consumption.

The significant development of maize in the 2000s occurred in spite of an adverse economic environment. Between 1994 and 2007, real prices of maize fell by 60 percent as a consequence of the major restructuring of the sector—while input prices grew by about the same proportion (Léonard and Palma 2002; Zahniser and Coyle 2004; RS 2 Mexico). Despite these unfavorable circumstances, maize acreage increased in the two surveyed Sotavento zones (Tierras Bajas and Sierra de Santa Marta). The increase in production was most pronounced in the lowlands—30 percent—while in the mountain areas it grew by 6 percent. In Veracruz state as a whole, maize acreage fell by 18 percent over the same period.

This trend has two explanations (RS 2 Mexico—Sotavento). In the lowlands, large floodplains offered high fertility and allowed economies of scale through mechanization. Large farms developed, but small producers were able to participate in this restructured market through producer organizations that gave them access to mechanization services, contracts (mostly informal) with buyers or large farms, and the incentives offered to the commercial sector by the Aserca and Alianza programs (Brun 2008). In the Sierra, remoteness restricted opportunities for diversification—both on-farm and off-farm—and the Procampo program ensured that maize remained the best agricultural option. Thus, in both zones, on-farm specialization increased and other farm products were abandoned, for example, rice in the lowlands and even beans in the Sierra, where they were traditionally intercropped with maize.

The specialization in maize production was accompanied by a collapse in self-consumption, notably in Tierras Bajas, where it is now nearly nonexistent. The situation is far removed from the traditional food system based on homegrown maize, with small plots (la milpa) where local varieties of maize and beans are grown for family consumption. Four factors explain it. First, to access public credit and technical support via the large enterprises, producers were required to sell all their output to the private firms. Second, farmers welcomed the opportunity to sell all their output rather than store it, because the new hybrid maize varieties were highly vulnerable to rodents after harvest. Third, in the Sotavento lowlands, the maize harvest was completely mechanized through services provided by the firms. And fourth, in the lowlands, women were increasingly engaged in off-farm activities and no longer able to dedicate time to making tortillas from farm-grown maize. Thus, in a rapid restructuring of the "maize-tortilla complex," farmers sell their hybrid corn and buy industrial maize flour or prepared tortillas at local markets (Appendini and Gómez, forthcoming).

The Sotavento exception among the surveyed regions is significant, as it shows the potentially strong effect of new marketing channels supported by a combination of drivers of change. It also illustrates how quickly production-consumption patterns can be radically modified. Finally, it emphasizes the impact of public support programs on households' processes of adaptation.

of households in the first quintile. It does not seem to be the case that the poor are restricted to selling staples while the rich are able to sell commodities or high-value products. Of the 20 zones where rich and poor households have the same top sales crop, that crop is a staple in 11 cases. Not only is it common to see richer households primarily selling staples, it is common to see households in the bottom quintile selling livestock or traditional commodities (coffee in El Cuá, groundnut in Senegal, cotton in Koutiala).

The same pattern is observed among regions. Contrary to expectations, the richest region in a country is not primarily selling a high-value product, while poorer regions primarily sell a low-value staple. The possible exceptions are Morocco and Nicaragua, where richer regions are more specialized in fruit and coffee, respectively.

The types of products grown depend on the unique situation in each region in terms of natural resources, public goods, private investments, and the presence or absence of buyers. When large shifts into sales of different products occur, they seem to encompass all households in the region. The differences between richer and poorer households tend to be in the diversification of their on-farm income sources: Richer households tend to have more on-farm income sources, with each source making up a smaller share of total income. A defining characteristic of these diversification patterns is heterogeneity. Farmers use their individual asset endowments to respond to opportunities arising from the natural and economic environments of their region. Staples and certain commodities seem to be within reach of all farmers in a given region. But richer households, with more assets, can take advantage of more of these opportunities to increase their levels of diversification.

Even in areas of crop specialization, such as Mexico, the same mechanisms are at play. Richer households with better asset endowments can take advantage of the opportunities presented by their environment; but in this specific case, because of unique conditions, it makes more sense to specialize in maize than to diversify into other products (box 5.5). However, specialization is an exception in the RuralStruc surveyed regions—most rich households operate in an environment that prompts them to diversify rather than specialize.

Regional Patterns of Market Integration

The farm production patterns described here reflect a high prevalence of traditional forms of commercialization and market integration in the surveyed regions. High-value exports, which were supposed to introduce new types of marketing arrangements through connection with foreign buyers in higher income countries and highly competitive markets, are extremely limited.

Although the RuralStruc countries are at different stages in their penetration of modern food retailing systems, they are (with the possible exception of Mexico) very far from the supermarket revolution (see box 5.6). And even

BOX 5.6

Contrasted Development of Modern Food Retailing in the RuralStruc Countries

According to the Regoverning Markets program (Reardon and Huang 2008), the Rural-Struc countries can be classified into three levels of modern food industry development: (1) advanced stage countries where more than 40 percent of overall food sales are in supermarkets (Mexico); (2) intermediate stage countries where the supermarket's share is between 10 percent and 40 percent of food sales (Nicaragua, Kenya, and Morocco); and (3) initial stage countries where supermarkets make up less than 10 percent of sales (Madagascar, Mali, and Senegal).

Mexico: The development of modern food retailing occurred in three stages. Before 1980, the development of supermarkets focused on large cities in the north and center of the country, and was mainly based on domestic capital, although some chains were set up with U.S. capital. In the 1980s, supermarkets began to move from their regional bases and started their consolidation through alliances with both domestic and foreign capital in a context of intense competition. Beginning in 1990, very rapid expansion occurred, impelled by the entry of giant chains from the United States (Walmart) and France (Carrefour) (Schwentesius and Gomez 2002). Today, supermarkets make up 55 percent of modern food retailing; however, the country's overall average masks strong regional disparities and a significant urban-rural divide.

Nicaragua: Supermarkets began developing in the 1990s. Initially only Nicaraguan enterprises were involved, then Costa Rican enterprises established a competitive supermarket chain and regional enterprises like Hortifruti engaged in wholesaling. In the 2000s, Walmart bought up regional supermarkets and intermediary companies such as Pali, La Union, Paiz, and Hortifruti. Supermarkets deal today with about 20 percent of the consumer demand for high-value products (RS 1 Nicaragua, 43–45).

Morocco: Following limited initial development in Casablanca and Rabat in the early 1960s with Monoprix (France), supermarkets started to grow in the 1990s, led by several Moroccan-owned chains, notably Marjane, Label'Vie, and Aswak Assalam. The first major foreign investment was made in 2001 when Auchan (France) entered into a joint venture with ONA (Omnium Nord Africain), Morocco's largest consortium of private companies, and took control of Marjane and then Acima in 2002 (Codron et al. 2004). ONA holds 51 percent of the joint venture, and Auchan holds 49 percent. The number of hypermarkets grew from 6 stores in 1993 to 19 in 2007 (RS 1 Morocco, 104).

Kenya: Supermarkets have developed from a tiny niche market only 15 years ago to 20 percent–30 percent of urban food retail today, and continue to gain prominence quickly. The first store outside Nairobi was built by Uchumi in Nakuru in 1993, starting a national competition. The rivalry between the two leading chains—Uchumi and Nakumatt—became an important growth driver as a new strategy by one chain forced imitation or a counterstrategy by the other (Neven and Reardon 2004). In 2003, there were 225 large-format stores in Kenya: 209 supermarkets and 16 hypermarkets.

(box continues on next page)

Madagascar: The share of supermarkets in retailing remains limited, but supermarkets have developed in the main cities of the country through three foreign companies. Before the recent political crisis of early 2009, which particularly affected the modern retail sector (looting), the situation was as follows: The South African chain Shoprite, operating in Madagascar since 1992, when it bought out local assets of the French company Champion, has seven stores (five in Antananarivo, one in Antsirabe, and one in Toamasina); Leaderprice (France) has three stores in Antananarivo; and Score (bought by the Vindemia group, now a subsidiary of the French Casino) has three hypermarkets in Antananarivo and two supermarkets in the other provinces (RS 1 Madagascar, 63).

Senegal: Modern food retail is very limited in the country, with only three supermarkets in Dakar. Initially created by SCOA (France) under the brand name Score, they have been franchised with Casino (France) since 2007.

Mali: There is no significant modern food retail in Mali.

Sources: RS country reports and other references cited.

---

where a significant degree of supermarket penetration has occurred, the effects on the average family farmer remain limited. The Regoverning Markets research project showed that (1) a gap exists between the overall level of penetration of supermarkets and the level of penetration into high-value segments of the food chain (estimated at only 25 percent in Mexico), and (2) supermarkets tend to source the majority of their products from wholesale markets, and sometimes from large-scale companies under contract.

Outside of Mexico, the surveyed regions of the RuralStruc countries show a more classical picture shaped by long-standing trade systems, mainly based on informal arrangements. This occurs for all types of products and stakeholders. However, several value chains have specific market structures that lead to specific organization.

Traditional Marketing Prevails. "Traditional marketing" refers to the range of middlemen and rural intermediaries who connect the countryside with national, regional, and international markets (that is, retail systems and exporters). They include wholesalers and the agents or brokers[19] who work for them, as well as independent buyers. This type of marketing gives farmers two options, often with imprecise scopes. First, they can sell "spot," either directly at the farm gate or in the village market to a broker or a wholesaler agent. Or they can sell on a routine basis to a wholesaler, although this option may not include a formal arrangement and may not guarantee a specific sales quantity or a better price than what could be earned on the spot market. However, the second option does reflect a certain formalization of the commercial transaction over time.

In the surveyed regions, traditional marketing is dominant. Figure 5.6 classifies the existing methods of commercialization into four main categories: spot

Figure 5.6 Types of Commercialization in the Surveyed Zones
% of the value of sales

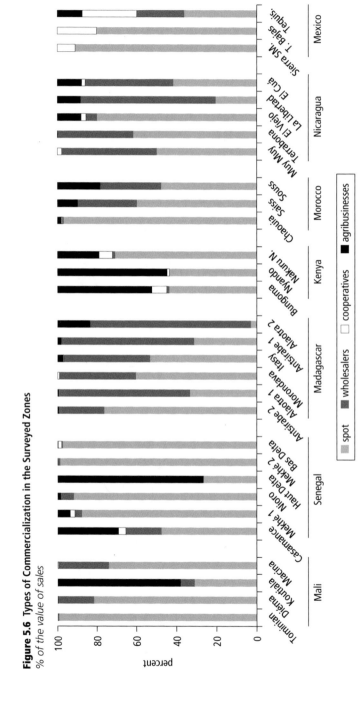

Source: RuralStruc surveys.

and wholesaler sales (the two types of traditional marketing), and sales to cooperatives and agribusinesses.[20] The first two categories account for a large majority of the total value of sales, with very few exceptions. Spot sales at the farm gate or the village market account for 100 percent of sales in Tominian, Mali, and 95 percent in the *bassin arachidier* (Senegal) and in Chaouia (Morocco). However, commercialization with wholesalers is also significant, particularly in Madagascar for rice (Alaotra, where wholesalers are based) and horticulture products (Antsirabe 1, in the vicinity of the city of Antsirabe), and in Nicaragua.

Surprisingly, outside of Mexico, the share sold to cooperatives (a topic on which many previous agricultural policies focused) is nonexistent in the large majority of the surveyed localities and is anecdotal in the others. In Sotavento, new producers' organizations were created to support the development of maize production, but these organizations were assembled primarily as a way to access public subsidies (see box 5.5). In Tequisquiapan, farmers sell maize or forage to producers' organizations, which are often under contractual arrangements with large cattle enterprises.

Sales to agribusinesses are more significant in many places, although their strength varies from one region to another. Logically, this variability is related to the presence or absence of a processor (and, of course, to the production of crops that require processing). Thus, the highest shares of sales to agribusinesses are found in Koutiala, Mali, where all cotton is sold to the ginning company CMDT (Compagnie Malienne pour le Développement des Textiles). High levels of sales to agribusiness are also observed in the Haut Delta, Senegal, where tomatoes are processed by SOCAS (Société de Conserves Alimentaires du Sénégal), and in Kenya, where sugar cane is sold to several factories.[21] In other regions, the importance of commercialization through agribusinesses is lower and generally accounts for less than 20 percent of sales. This is the case with tomatoes, citrus, and olives in Saïss and Souss (Morocco); tomatoes and dairy products in Nakuru North (Kenya); coffee in El Cuá (Nicaragua); rice to rice mills in Alaotra 2; and green beans for export in Itasy (Madagascar).

Underdeveloped Contractualization. The development of contracts is often seen as an indicator of increasing integration among economic agents in a value chain, so the RuralStruc survey was designed to identify these contractual arrangements. However, three caveats are necessary in presenting the survey results. First, the program teams selected regions and localities for the survey that would illustrate different situations and different stages of integration. Consequently, no conclusions can be drawn from the observed differences in the number of contracts between regions and subregions. Second, the analysis of contractualization cannot accommodate imprecision. The definition of types of contracts is a core issue, and while formal contracts are usually written contracts, informal contracts can correspond to a wide range of situations in which trust between buyer and seller is the main component. Third, to make a statement about contractualization, one must analyze the level of contracts along the entire length of the value chain. This was not possible in the methodology of the RuralStruc fieldwork.

But even with these caveats, it is obvious that contractualization at the producer level is low almost everywhere in the selected regions. Only 539 of the households surveyed (7.4 percent of the sample) reported being engaged in at least one contractual arrangement (table 5.5).[22]

This low level of contractualization—especially the lack of formal contracts—is significant. It reflects the low intensity of the integration processes in the surveyed regions and the limited development of high-value chains, in which product requirements justify contracts. This situation is not totally surprising, even though several "winning" regions had been selected with the aim of identifying market dynamics related to higher value products or agro-industries.

In some of these regions, contracts with agribusinesses are almost nonexistent. This is particularly true in two regions of Nicaragua (Terrabona and Muy Muy), where only a few farmers are directly connected to fruit and vegetable integrated value chains (domestic supermarkets such as Walmart/La Union-Palí or La Colonia) and to dairy chains (supermarkets and processors such as Parmalat or Eskimo). However, these cases illustrate an important finding: In many situations, contractualization is not occurring at the producer-level segment of the value chain; rather, it is downstream, between the wholesaler or cooperative and the processing firm or procurement service.

Three types of contractual arrangements and relationships between economic agents are generally identifiable in the survey: (1) an informal contract resulting from long-standing relationships, mainly with wholesalers; (2) a supply contract with an agroprocessor; and (3) direct integration into high-value chains.

Informal Contracts. Growing urban demand for fresh products has led to the development of value chains that are structured by wholesalers and supplied by producers with informal agreements. This is especially common if the competition among middlemen is high and the product is perishable.

For example, the fruit and vegetable sectors in Antsirabe are integrated on the basis of informal agreements between individual producers' or farmers' organizations and brokers who supply urban wholesalers. The producers who benefit from these agreements are generally the biggest producers with the best factor endowments (correlations are statistically significant), which allow them to reach a surplus. In the *bassin arachidier* (mainly Mekhé 2, Senegal), cassava producers have developed informal contractual agreements with middlemen based on transaction routine and reputation. These contracts guarantee the flow of supply to urban areas, although production is widely dispersed throughout the region.

Table 5.5 Formal and Informal Contractual Arrangements in Surveyed Regions

Country	Region	HH with contract No.	HH with contract %	Type	Type of industry and contracting agents
Mali	Tominian	1	0.6		
	Diéma	0	0.0		
	Koutiala	0	0.0	df	Cotton industry (CMDT)
	Macina	16	10.4	I	Rice industry
Senegal	Casamance	11	4.6		
	Mekhé 1	26	23.4	I	Cassava wholesalers
	Nioro	1	0.4		
	Haut Delta	54	88.5	F	Tomato processor (SOCAS)
	Mekhé 2	33	29.2	I	Cassava wholesalers
	Bas Detla	12	9.9	I	Rice industry
Madagascar	Antsirabe 2	16	5.3	I	Vegetables collectors
	Alaotra 1	2	0.5		
	Morondava	15	3.0	I	
	Itasy	50	9.9	F	Green beans processor (Lecofruit) and tobacco
	Antsirabe 1	46	22.3	F/I	Milk industry (Tiko) and vegetables collectors
	Alaotra 2	8	7.0	I	Rice industry
Kenya	Bungoma	75	25.1	F	Sugar industry
	Nyando	7	2.5	F	Sugar industry
	Nakuru North	16	5.5	F/I	Milk industry and tomato processing
Morocco	Chaouia	1	0.4		
	Saiss	20	7.7	F	Milk Industry
	Souss	1	0.4		
Nicaragua	Muy Muy	9	3.0	I	Milk industry (Parmalat and Eskimo)
	Terrabona	4	1.4		
	El Viejo	13	4.5	F/I	Sesame and sorghum industry
	La Libertad	20	6.9	I	Milk collectors
	El Cua	47	15.7	I	Coffee Industry
Mexico	Sierra S. M.	0	0.0	df	Producers' organizations
	Tierras Bajas	6	4.0	F/df	Maize Industry and Producers' organizations
	Tequis.	29	8.0	F	Producers' organizations
		539	7.4		

Source: RuralStruc surveys.
Note: F = formal; I = informal; df = de facto.

Similarly, in Nicaragua, in response to growing urban demand and the development of supermarkets, wholesalers have recently expanded their collection
area. In some villages in La Libertad, verbal agreements are used to satisfy this
demand. These agreements provide many advantages for farmers; in particular, they enjoy the insurance of selling milk daily instead of selling on-farm

processed cheese once a week. They also incur lower costs. Usually, the house-holds that access these informal agreements are those with more land and big-ger herds (hence, they are capable of producing more milk). On average, they own 2.3 times more land and 3 times more cattle (correlations are statistically significant).

In the Sotavento region, informal contracts have developed between farmers' and producers' organizations for the purpose of accessing public transfers and offering technical assistance and inputs in exchange for the commercialization of products. Although farmers did not report being engaged in contracts, mem-bership in producers' organizations often means de facto contracts.

Supply Contracts with Agroprocessors. These contracts are a very old practice, initially developed to guarantee supply (and thus profitability) to industrial investments. Several examples exist in the surveyed regions, especially in the dairy industry. In Madagascar, privatization of the parastatal monopoly did not significantly change the configuration of the value chain, which is largely controlled by Tiko, a private firm that plays (or played, until the recent political crisis) a central role in the Malagasy dairy industry. Tiko was collecting more than 90 percent of the milk marketed in the main production region (Antsir-abe) and processing most of the dairy products in the country. With Tiko, con-tracted producers delivered milk to collection centers, where it was required to meet quality criteria stipulated in a formal contract. In return, the agro-industry provided inputs and sometimes cash advances. Producers with larger herds are more involved in these integration strategies. Similar patterns exist in Saïss and Souss, Morocco, and in Nakuru North, Kenya.

Comparable formal supply contracts also exist with sugar factories in Kenya (Bungoma) and with the tomato industry in both Haut Delta (Senegal) and Nakuru. This market configuration—one agroprocessor and many suppliers—can include situations of monopsony. In these cases, there are no contracts but a tacit contractualization resulting from the fact that the producers do not have any options other than to sell to the monopsonist. Cotton is a good example: 75 percent of the family farms in the Koutiala region grow cotton; they have a de facto contract with CMDT, even if nothing is actually written. The sector is vertically integrated, with the provision of inputs through producers' organiza-tions; a system of credit secured by cotton sales; extension services and technical support; and fixed prices, which are negotiated to a certain extent.[23]

Contracts Related to High-Value Exports. Contracts with high-value export companies are the typical contract cases cited in the literature. However, the RuralStruc survey found only two cases of this type of arrangement. The first case is Lecofruit in Ifanja, Itasy (Madagascar), a famous example in the litera-ture, where farmers grow green beans for export (see box 5.7). The other is in the coffee region of El Cuá, Nicaragua. In this region, organic coffee is mainly

BOX 5.7

Lecofruit: Malagasy Smallholders Selling on European Markets

Lecofruit (Légumes Condiments et Fruits de Madagascar SA) was established in Madagascar in 1989, when free zones were implemented and promoted by the Malagasy state through tax exemptions and other fiscal advantages. Initially, Lecofruit processed pickles in partnership with approximately 100 farmers. To develop its export markets, the firm associated with the French company Segma Maille, which guaranteed regular outlets for its products in Europe. Lecofruit began to diversify its production, with green beans, snow peas, cucumbers, asparagus, and baby vegetables for export to the European market. Currently, Lecofruit focuses on production of extra-fine green beans: The company exported 3,000 tons of products during the 2004–05 season, of which 70 percent were green beans. Approximately 90 percent were processed and canned ·in the company factory in Antananarivo and sent to Europe by sea. The remaining 10 percent were fresh green beans and snow peas shipped by air.

In 2007–08, the company branched out to involve 10,000 farmers under contract in the production of green beans. Producers are located in the highlands of Madagascar, which has a long tradition of fruit and vegetable production. To optimize the costs of transporting products to the processing plant in Antananarivo, the company targets the growing areas connected to major roads.

Farmers cultivate their own land, which helps overcome the problems of land availability in the highlands. Production contracts are standardized and individual, although producers must belong to a producers' organization. A contract is limited to an area of approximately 1,000m² to ensure that producers will be able to comply with all stages of the production until harvest, as production is labor-intensive. Other commitments relate to specific technical recommendations (preparation of compost, plowing, seeding, and so on) and the need for daily harvest to meet the extra-fine size requirement.

Producers receive cash advances and free seeds; costs of fertilizer and pesticides are deducted from the final payment when the green beans are delivered. Lecofruit provides a "package" of seeds, mineral fertilizers, and pesticides to ensure compliance with standards for maximum residue limits in agricultural products exported to the European Union. Some sanitary conditions are also stipulated in the contracts, such as washing hands with nonperfumed soap before harvesting the beans. Finally, producers are required to sell only to Lecofruit. Payment is periodic. The price is set in advance by the company and remains unchanged during the season: 630 Ariary/kg for green beans in 2007–08 ($0.83 PPP).

Despite the balance of power that favors the processing firm, the number of farmers involved in contract farming with Lecofruit has never declined, which indicates that they are satisfied with the terms. Farmers can generate income and earn cash to finance their other agricultural activities or meet their needs.

Source: RS 2 Madagascar, 84–85.

promoted by COMANUR-RL (Cooperativa Multisectorial Alfonso Núñez Rodríguez), which sells conventional and organic coffees. Farmers produce organic coffee under strict specifications for the cooperative at a predetermined price, and the cooperative provides technical assistance to its members, including access to coffee management and plant materials (new varieties of coffee), agricultural inputs (fertilizers and other agrochemicals), and expensive equipment or infrastructure.

Because of the very limited information and the few cases gathered by the surveys, it is difficult to draw conclusions about the consequences of contractualization on household incomes. Moreover, there is a reverse causality issue: In general, a low level of household production is one of the biggest barriers to participation in contractual agreements. To lower their transaction costs, procurement systems and agro-industries prefer to work with large suppliers. Thus—with the exception of Madagascar's green bean producers, whose plot areas are restricted by the contracting company—the households that engage in contracts tend to be those with the best factor endowments.[24]

Nevertheless, on the basis of the RuralStruc case studies, one can assume that returns to contractualization are limited, with a few exceptions. The survey shows that income differences between households with and without contracts are most often minimal. The maximum average earned from green bean production under contract in Itasy, Madagascar, is very low: $43 PPP per household per year. Similarly, the tomato producers under contract with SOCAS in the Haut Delta in Senegal are not significantly better off than other Senegalese households. In many of the surveyed regions, the main advantages of contractualization are related to access to technical packages, credit, and a secure marketing channel.

On-Farm Specialization and Rural Transformation

On-farm specialization is one of the three exit pathways out of rural poverty. Households surveyed by the RuralStruc program are broadly specialized in agriculture—on-farm incomes constitute a high proportion of total income—but they remain poor. This contradictory assessment, discussed in chapter 3, justified a close examination of the characteristics of rural incomes in general and of the observed on-farm specialization.

Although nearly all of SSA households are engaged in farming, most are diversified and as such also engage in off-farm activities as a general coping strategy. Therefore, total on-farm specialization is rare, although it does occur in several regions in Nicaragua and Morocco, where more robust value chains can offer secure returns.

On average, on-farm incomes are characterized by high levels of self-consumption, the importance of staples, and heterogeneous patterns of product diversification that develop in response to region-specific opportunities. This picture is quite far from the "new agriculture" that has been widely discussed in the literature, and does not reflect the increasing processes of integration, new players, and new rules that the literature predicts.

In the surveyed regions, self-consumption is still very significant in response to both supply and demand effects. The supply effect corresponds to risk-management strategies households employ to retain control over their food supply—a direct response to incomplete and imperfect markets. The demand effect expresses the weak demand for their products owing to poor access to and integration with markets. Limited infrastructure can be a major obstacle and can be reinforced by weak marketing systems in which middlemen do not have incentives to collect limited quantities of low-value products (a consequence of low productivity of staple crops), especially in low-density areas where collection costs are high.

Most private collecting agents operating in the RuralStruc surveyed areas rely on informal relationship-based strategies to obtain output from small farmers, while agribusinesses generally employ traditional contract farming practices. The extent of contractualization is very limited, even among farms that are solidly integrated into markets through ongoing relationships with wholesalers and other buyers. Furthermore, contractualization rarely occurs at the producer level: It is often downstream, between the wholesaler or collection unit and the processing firm or procurement service.

The share of self-consumption decreases with wealth at both the regional and household levels, and the surveyed regions in Sub-Saharan Africa are less advanced in this process. The richest SSA households are less diversified than their non-SSA counterparts, mainly owing to market environments that offer Sub-Saharan Africa fewer opportunities to engage in new value chains. This lack of opportunity also explains the persistently high share of staple products in households' production baskets, even when they move away from self-consumption and even when they become richer. Staples are not only the prerogative of poor farmers; the development of on-farm product diversification (its extent and the types of products involved) depends on a process that encompasses a region as a whole. The result tends to be that all households can participate in new value chains, with their level of participation determined by their assets (production factors, human and social capital). The famous high-value chains focused on exports are few and far between. They employ a very small share of the farmers surveyed, and their development depends on existing operators (processors, exporters) and their capacity to develop contracts with foreign markets.

Despite the numerous changes that have occurred in many developing countries' agricultural sectors in the past few decades, old agricultural patterns persist. Full on-farm specialization is limited, and on-farm activities in general are characterized by a trend toward product diversification—a way to seize opportunities and share risks in economic environments that are uncertain.

Notes

1. The objective here is not to provide an extensive review of the abundant literature on global restructuring but to offer a brief summary of the major developments of the past three decades.
2. Whatever the political regime, agriculture has always been a "state affair" (Coulomb et al. 1990). As a last resort, the sector provides for the basic needs of the population and government constituents.
3. For a "genealogy" of food regimes, see Friedmann and McMichael (1989) and McMichael (2009). McMichael suggests the progressive consolidation of a new "corporate food regime."
4. These tables provide only a few examples per country, although dozens of parastatals existed in most countries. See the RuralStruc country reports for more details.
5. An expanding trade in agricultural products (notably, exports of meat products) has also developed between OECD countries and many low- and middle-income countries; it is often associated with less stringent concerns for health and food safety.
6. An example of this trend is the emergence of the International Federation of Organic Agriculture Movements (IFOAM), which bases certification on issues of health, ecology, fairness, and the principle of precaution.
7. See World Bank (2007). A good description of the applications of these new approaches is presented in Webber and Labaste (2010).
8. As mentioned in chapter 1, the selected countries and regions do not include major tropical export commodities areas in which a long-standing connection to markets has deeply affected the pattern of the rural economy over an extended period. However, several surveyed regions are engaged in these export commodities as well as in high-value crops. "Traditional" here refers to crops that are not involved in new integrated value chains.
9. Estimating incomes generated by gathering activities is difficult because they involve small amounts of products that are gathered throughout the year and are often self-consumed. However, wild fruits, animals, and fish often play a core role in the food security of rural households.
10. This is the case for potatoes, a horticultural product that is self-consumed and can be considered a staple in Madagascar, one of only two places in the surveyed regions where it is significantly grown (the other is Saiss, Morocco). This is also the case for groundnuts, the traditional export of Senegal, which is considered an export even though it is increasingly consumed locally as a consequence of the adverse evolution of the value chain. Sugar cane is a traditional export commodity, but in Kenya the production is mainly sold on the domestic market and is insufficient to meet local demand.
11. In this chapter, dedicated to on-farm production and commercialization, the survey results are displayed as absolute and relative gross farm product per household (total value of sales and self-consumption of crops and livestock productions) rather than as income. This option reflects the methodological choices of the program: The

breakdown of costs by type of product was impossible in the survey framework—total costs were applied, respectively, to gross crop product and gross livestock product to calculate crop and livestock incomes and then total farm income.

12. Although traditional irrigated production systems existed in Madagascar, irrigation development has benefited from public infrastructure through irrigation schemes in other countries, notably Senegal and Mali. Irrigated maize in Mexico is mainly on large commercial farms. The situation of Sotavento's Tierras Bajas zone, with its natural floodplains, is unique.

13. After a severe drought, the Moroccan production of cereals dropped by 73 percent in 2007; it affected most of the regions, notably Chaouia (RS 2 Morocco, 145), and livestock sales increased significantly in absolute and relative terms.

14. A small (and now famous, because of frequent citation in the literature) green-bean-production-for-export market has developed in Itasy, closely linked to the presence of Lecofruit, an export-oriented processing firm (see box 5.7).

15. Self-consumption includes gifts to family and to social and religious networks. It also includes food reserves (see annex 1 in the appendix posted at http://www.world bank.org/afr/ruralstruc).

16. The case of Tominian is amazing: 30 percent to 40 percent of households do not participate in food markets at all, either as buyers or sellers.

17. In Mali, very small differences exist among quintiles. This can be explained by the low level of income, even for the richest households, and a preference for maintaining grain reserves because a high level of stocks is a sign that households are better off. Also, the 2004–05 crop season was very bad, and many households were still replenishing their stocks when the survey was conducted in 2007.

18. The connection of rural *producers* to agricultural markets is frequently discussed; however, the connection of rural *consumers* to markets for goods and services can also be a stumbling block. When there is little or nothing to buy, there is no incentive to sell or to increase output. This "reverse side" of markets is generally ignored in the policy debate.

19. A wholesaler takes possession of the product; a broker does not.

20. This category refers to agro-industries that transform raw agricultural products to semiprocessed products (for example, cotton to cotton fiber) or processed products (for example, tomatoes to tomato paste or canned tomatoes). It also refers to businesses that clean, grade, and package high-value products, like fruits and vegetables, mainly for the export market.

21. Sales to agroprocessors can sometimes occur through farmers' organizations or so-called "cooperatives" (actually creations of the agro-industry, which is their sole buyer). This is the case with SOCAS in Senegal and CMDT in Mali.

22. Contractual arrangements listed in table 5.5 include formal written contracts as well as informal contracts perceived by the producer as effective.

23. For a long time, public and semipublic monopsonies such as CMDT were obliged to buy all producers' outputs. After years of negotiation, CMDT was privatized in 2010; however, it will not fundamentally change the market pattern and the company will be replaced by regional monopsonies.

24. This seems to be especially the case for land. However, the small number of households with formal contracts does not allow any conclusion. In Antsirabe 1, where the number of contracts in the sample is sufficient, the T test is significant.

Chapter 6

From Regional Patterns of Rural Transformation to Policy Guidelines

The previous three chapters provided a detailed analysis of the level of income and the characteristics of on-farm and off-farm activities in the surveyed regions. The goal was to answer the following questions, which refer to the program's hypotheses. How do farm households adapt to their evolving environment? Do they specialize in agriculture as they become more deeply inserted into markets (H1)? How do rural households combine activities to create more diversified sources of income (H2)? An important question remains, however, regarding the links among these specialization and diversification patterns, and the level of total income. What does this relationship say about the viability of different pathways out of poverty, the overall process of rural transformation, and the identification of possible risks of transition dead ends (H3)?

Chapter 6 explores this relationship. It begins with a review of the determinants of total income, which were not directly addressed in chapter 3. The chapter then analyzes regional patterns of income diversification and discusses the relationship between income levels and income structures, leading to an investigation of regional specialization and diversification. Finally, the chapter groups households according to their income-based room to maneuver and draws conclusions about the significance of observed rural realities for policy making. It concludes with policy options for facilitating rural transformation in this context.

Regional Patterns of Income Diversification and Specialization

A quantitative analysis of the survey data using regression techniques helps to better understand the determinants of rural income and highlights their important heterogeneity in terms of asset combinations and environmental conditions. However, a more detailed investigation of the regional patterns of income structures leads to the identification of significant regularities. There is a close relationship between income, specialization, and diversification, which relates to the dynamics of structural transformation. A better understanding of these dynamics provides evidence of poverty traps for most of the regions in Sub-Saharan Africa.

Understanding the Regional Level of Income

A household's level of income per capita depends on an array of factors, including the type of economic activities in which it is engaged, the returns from those economic activities, the assets available to the household, the size and demographic structure of the household, and its economic environment. Chapters 4 and 5 explored the types of activities in which households are engaged and found a strong heterogeneity among households and regions, with no evidence that any one type of activity was the best option in every case. Thus, the investigation of income determinants presented below does not test the usefulness of particular activities. Rather, it focuses on determinants that allow a household to take advantage of regional opportunities.

The analysis of the determinants of total income unfolds along four lines of inquiry: household characteristics and human capital, assets related to farm productivity, environment and market access, and off-farm diversification. To pursue this investigation, the RuralStruc program engaged in a series of regression analyses. A brief overview of their motivation and a summary of key results are presented below.[1]

The regression work primarily took place at the regional level and was conducted in all 30 RuralStruc surveyed zones. The analysis includes only households with a farm, as including households without a farm would have reduced the explanatory power of variables related to farm assets. In each regression, the dependent variable is the log of household income per equivalent adult (EqA).[2]

The program also engaged in regression work at an aggregated level. For these specifications, all surveyed households in each country were used as observations in one catch-all regression, and regional affiliations were not considered. This additional regression work has the benefit of capturing the effects on wealth of assets or environmental conditions whose distribution varies significantly among regions (for example, irrigated land in Mali, where Macina is very well endowed while other regions are not) but not within them (all households in a region are likely to face the same transportation hurdles, but households in other regions will face different problems). Tables 6.1 and 6.2 give an overview of the results of the analysis and display the significant variables.

Table 6.1 shows many results with many possible interpretations. The regressions have more explanatory power in certain regions, while in others they do little to explain the variance in incomes. In general, the regression does better in regions with higher shares of on-farm income; for example, the importance of self-employment in Senegal is probably why the regression, laden down with variables related to farming, has limited explanatory power. The main results by category of variable are discussed below; the diversification index is discussed in the next section.

Demographic and Human Capital Variables. The total number of people in a household (persons present) is significant in 18 of the 30 regions and is therefore one of the most broadly significant variables in the regression. In almost every case it is significant with a negative coefficient. This implies that in most households, an additional household member "costs" more to maintain than he or she is able to earn. This is the case everywhere except Koutiala in Mali, where the relationship between persons present and income is positive. This implies that families in Koutiala may not have enough labor, which makes sense in light of the labor requirements of cotton farming.

Given the prevalence of surplus labor in households (discussed in chapter 4 and illustrated by the regression results), it is surprising that migrations are significant determinants of income in only five regions. This phenomenon has two possible causes. First, as was shown in chapter 4, returns to migration depend strongly on the destination of the migrant, which varies significantly among countries but less so within them, meaning that an effect is unlikely to be captured in within-region or within-country regressions. Second, migrations are less common than expected in the survey.[3] Long-term migrants are present in only 20 percent of the entire sample of farm households. Short-term migrants are even less common, appearing in 10 percent of the sample. The regression work reflects the discussion in chapter 4 about strong barriers to migration that make it a nonviable option for many households.

Conclusions from the education variables are less clear. The educational level of the head of the household is less frequently associated with income in the countries of North and West Africa (Senegal, Mali, and Morocco) and in Mexico. In North and West Africa, this is explained by the overall low levels of education (see chapter 4). In Mali, for example, 84 percent of surveyed household heads have no formal education, although this is changing. The surveys show that the most educated person in the household is often not the household head. Children are becoming better educated than their parents, implying that these regions will benefit from increased education in years to come.[4]

Household Assets Related to Productivity. Three important findings relate to household assets. The first is the continued supreme importance of land; specifically, how much land is available to the farmer. This is significant in 22 of the 30 regions, making it the most commonly significant variable in the survey. In seven regions it has the largest coefficient of any variable in the regression. It is the second largest in five additional regions. The implication of this finding is that, despite all the efforts of the development community over the past decades to improve the output of a fixed-sized plot, the best way for a farmer to improve his or her income is to acquire more land. This confirms a main find-

Table 6.1 Regional Regression Results

		Mali				Senegal					
		Tominian	Diema	Koutiala	Macina	Casamance	Mekhé 1	Nioro	Haut Delta	Mekhé 2	Bas Delta
Demographics and human capital	Number of persons in HH (Nb_PersonsPres_hh)			P							
	Dependency ratio										
	Number of long-term migrants / HH										
	Number of short-term migrants / HH		N								
	HH head has at least some primary education (binary)										
	HH head has at least completed primary education (binary)										
	HH head has at least some secondary education (binary)							N			
	HH head has at least completed secondary education (binary)										
Household assets related to productivity	Hectares of land used by HH, per EqA (land owned in Nic.)										
	Hectares of irrigated land by HH, per EqA										
	HH uses technical package (improved seeds/fertilizer) (binary)										N
	HH uses manure (binary)										
	Number of livestock units (weighted avg) (no. of cattle in Mexico)										
	HH uses animal draft (binary)										
	HH uses tiller for draft (binary)										
	HH uses tractor for draft (binary)										
Market integration	Transportation is easy only part of the year (binary)										P
	Transportation is difficult (qualitative binary)										P
	Transportation difficulty is unknown (binary)										P
	c_50,000 (c_ports in Kenya, Sub-Regions in Morocco)										
	Contract (binary)										
	Diversification index										

■ Significant at the 5% level   □ Included but not significant
▨ Not Included in the regression   N The coefficient is negative
▢ Significant at the 10% level   P The coefficient is positive

ing of chapter 5, that the differentiation processes related to farming that were anticipated with increased economic integration have yet to be broadly realized.

Further confirmation is provided by the second important finding: the comparatively broad insignificance of the technical package variable.[5] It is only significant in eight regions, and in two of those regions it enters negatively (farmers with the technical package are worse off than those without it). Per-

Madagascar						Kenya			Morocco			Nicaragua					Mexico			No. of regions significant	
Antsirabe 2	Alaotra 1	Morondava	Itasy	Antsirabe 1	Alaotra 2	Bungoma	Nyando	Nakuru N.	Chaouia	Saiss	Souss	Muy Muy	Terrabona	El Viejo	La Libertad	El Cua	Sierra SM.	T. Bajas	Tequis.	at 5% level	at 10% level
																				17	1
																				1	4
																				4	0
											N									2	0
	N																		N	4	2
						N							N					N		5	3
					N															6	4
																				2	0
																				19	3
							N													4	0
										N										5	3
						N														1	0
																				19	1
																				4	1
																				2	1
																				4	3
P		P														P		P		7	1
																				4	3
																				1	1
																				4	1
																				5	1
																				17	1

haps more surprisingly, it is only significant among regions in two of the seven RuralStruc countries (Madagascar and Kenya). The third important finding is that the number of livestock owned is broadly and significantly associated with income. However, livestock can be an output, a productive asset, a method of saving, or a social attribute—these diverse roles complicate the interpretation of the livestock variable.

Market Access Variables. Even with the caveat that insertion and integration into markets are difficult to measure, a main finding of the regression work is

Table 6.2 Nationally Aggregated Regression Results

		Mali	Senegal	Mada-gascar	Kenya	Morocco	Nicaragua	Mexico	No. significant at 5% level	No. significant at 10% level
Demographics and human capital	Number of persons in HH (Nb_PersonsPres_hh)								6	0
	Dependency ratio								4	0
	Number of long-term migrants from HH								1	1
	Number of short-term migrants from HH	N		N					2	0
	HH head has at least some primary education (binary)								2	0
	HH head has at least completed primary education (binary)	N							1	1
	HH head has at least some secondary education (binary)								2	1
	HH head has at least completed secondary education (binary)						N		2	1

Household assets related to productivity

- Hectares of land used by HH, per EqA (land owned in Nic.)
- Hectares of irrigated land by HH, per EqA
- HH uses technical package (improved seeds/fertilizer) (binary)
- HH uses manure (binary)
- Number of livestock units (weighted avg) (no. of cattle in Mexico)
- HH uses animal draft (binary)
- HH uses tiller for draft (binary)
- HH uses tractor for draft (binary)

Market integration

- Transportation is easy only part of the year (qualitative binary)
- Transportation is difficult (qualitative binary)
- Transportation difficulty is unknown (qualitative binary)
- c_50,000 (c_ports in Kenya, Sub-Regions in Morocco)
- Contract (binary)
- Diversification index

Legend:

■ Significant at the 5% level.
▨ Included but not significant.
▦ Not included in the regression.
□ Significant at the 10% level.
N The coefficient is negative.
P The coefficient is positive.

that market integration does not necessarily mean improved incomes: Whether it does or does not is context-specific. The regression suggests this conclusion by examining connections to markets along two axes: (1) distance to markets (including a qualitative assessment of transportation quality), and (2) level of integration into value chains through the number of households with contracts (what constitutes a contract is discussed in chapter 5).

The variable on travel time to markets (c_50,000) produced little in the way of patterns to be discerned. Further, the variable about transportation quality is significant in the anticipated direction (poor quality associated with lower incomes) in only six regions, spread out relatively evenly across RuralStruc countries. However, in almost as many regions (five), a negative assessment of transportation quality is significantly associated with higher incomes.[6]

The regression shows that contracts are significantly associated with income in Kenya and Nicaragua. This has nothing to do with the prevalence of contracts: Some farmers in all countries are engaged in contract agriculture, and Kenya and Nicaragua are not particularly well endowed. The difference is in where the contracts are concentrated on the income spectrum. For instance, in the Haut Delta region of Senegal, where over 90 percent of farmers have contracts with the local tomato processor, SOCAS, the few households without a contract are actually richer. Those with contracts are heavily dependent on the processor. Through this arrangement they receive preferential access to farm inputs they can use for other crops, but this is generally not enough to alleviate poverty and furthers their dependence on the factory. Whether a contract allows farmers to increase their incomes or prevents them from taking advantage of more lucrative opportunities depends on the regional context.

Main Conclusions. The conclusions from the regression work so far can be summarized under two main results. The first is the persistence of old patterns of wealth. In regions where agriculture plays a major role, income still responds as it did hundreds of years ago throughout the world. Accessing land and increasing the amount of land under cultivation are the best ways to improve farm incomes. In addition, depending on economic alternatives and local constraints (availability of natural resources and access to resources), population dynamics are decisive. As a household's size increases, income per head falls.

The second result suggests that changes are occurring, but sporadically and in a way that does not follow a set pattern. Individual households are responding to their environments with their asset endowments in the best way they can to improve their incomes. Because environment and asset endowments differ significantly from region to region, so too do households' strategies. The effectiveness of specific strategies in terms of income generation also varies extensively among regions. This is clear in the regression results. Education is significantly associated with incomes in some areas and not in others, without seeming to follow any set pattern. So is the type of draft force used and the quality of transportation available.

A good illustration of this heterogeneity is provided in table 6.3, which lists the three variables most strongly associated with income in each region. The top variable is the one with the largest coefficient (in absolute value) that is significant at least at the 5 percent level. If fewer than three variables are significant at the 5 percent level, the variable with the largest coefficient that is significant at the 10 percent level is used.

The table is straightforward: "Hectares of land used" is a top driver of income in half of the RuralStruc regions. This result is driven by the share of poor regions (the case of Madagascar is clear) but is also significant in Morocco and Mexico. After "Hectares of land used," no single variable appears as a main determinant of income in more than six regions. Additional patterns of significance in the chart are indiscernible.

Fine-Tuning the Regional Patterns

After discussing the consolidated household income structure in the surveyed regions using a quintile approach, a diversification index is proposed, the utilization of which helps to investigate the income-diversification relationship.

First Overview. The final line of inquiry into determinants of income in the regression involved diversification. But before analyzing the relationship between diversification and income, it is useful to look at the overall picture of household income sources. Figure 6.1 builds on the analyses in chapters 4 and 5 and shows income structures by quintile and region.[7] This is the first step to understanding diversification patterns. The charts show regional income patterns per quintile using on-farm income as a whole and the six types of off-farm income discussed in chapter 4: agricultural wages, nonagricultural wages, self-employment, public transfers, private transfers, and rents.

This overall picture confirms the important place of on-farm activities in regional income structures but also illustrates differences among regions. The share of on-farm income is high for most of the quintiles in Mali, Madagascar, Nicaragua, Casamance in Senegal, and Saïss in Morocco. In a number of regions, on-farm activities are the dominant income source of the richest households. On the other hand, off-farm incomes are very significant in Senegal, Kenya, Mexico, and in Chaouia and Souss in Morocco. Furthermore, the configuration of off-farm incomes varies: Self-employment is a key activity in Senegal; nonagricultural wages and self-employment are important in Kenya; agricultural wages play a large role in Nicaragua; and Mexico is more broadly diversified.

The analysis shows an array of situations and illustrates the heterogeneous nature of household diversification patterns among the regions. Even if it is

Table 6.3 Variables Most Strongly Associated with Income, by Region

		Mali				Senegal					
		Tominian	Diema	Koutiala	Macina	Casamance	Mekhé 1	Nioro	Haut Delta	Mekhé 2	Bas Delta
Demographics and human capital	Nb_PersonsPres_hh			P		N			N		
	Dependency ratio									▢	
	Number of long-term migrants from HH										
	Number of short-term migrants from HH		N								
	HH head has at least some primary education										
	HH head has at least completed primary education								■		▣
	HH head has at least some secondary education	■								■	
	HH head has at least completed secondary education										
Household assets related to productivity	Hectares of land used by HH, per EqA (land owned in Nic.)	▢	■			▢					
	Hectares of irrigated land by HH, per EqA				■				▣		
	Technical package	▣				■					N
	Manure										
	Number of livestock units (weighted avg)							▣		■	
	HH uses animal draft										
	HH uses tiller for draft										
	HH uses tractor for draft										
Market integration	Transportation is easy only part of the year										
	Transportation is difficult		■						▢		
	Transportation difficulty is unknown										
	c_50,000 (c_ports in Kenya, Regions in Morocco)										
	Contract								■		
	Diversification index			P	P	P	▢				

■ Most strongly associated variable.   N The coefficient is negative.
▣ 2nd most strongly associated variable.   P The coefficient is positive.
▢ 3rd most strongly associated variable.

possible to broadly suggest why some regions diversify and others do not (for example, comparative advantages, access to markets, urbanization, institutions) and why, within each region, some households diversify and others do not (assets), the mechanisms that contribute to the many combinations of income sources remain unclear.

Characterizing the Trends. To shed more light on this subject, the RuralStruc program created an index of household diversification based on the well-known

| Madagascar | | | | | | Kenya | | | Morocco | | | Nicaragua | | | | | Mexico | | | Significance scores | | | |
Antsirabe 2	Alaotra 1	Morondava	Itasy	Antsirabe 1	Alaotra 2	Bungoma	Nyando	Nakuru N.	Chaouia	Saiss	Souss	Muy Muy	Terrabona	El Viejo	La Libertad	El Cua	Sierra SM.	T. Bajas	Tequis.	No. of 1st	No. of 2nd	No. of 3rd	total
			N													N		N		0	4	2	6
																				0	0	1	1
																				1	0	1	2
												N								0	0	2	2
								N											N	1	1	3	5
														N						1	3	0	4
						N														4	1	1	6
																				1	1	0	2
																				7	5	3	15
																				2	1	0	3
												N								2	1	1	4
							N													0	0	1	1
																				2	3	1	6
																				1	0	2	3
																				1	1	0	2
																				2	1	0	3
P				P													P			0	3	3	6
																				1	0	1	2
																				0	1	0	1
									N	N	N									2	1	0	3
																				2	0	2	4
																P		P		0	1	5	6

Herfindahl-Hirschman index (HHi).[8] The index is set between 0 and 1, and returns higher values as a household becomes more heavily involved in more kinds of activities. Higher values on the diversification index mean more diversification, while lower values mean more specialization.

Figure 6.2, which was constructed using the overall sample, shows the average level of the diversification index by region and household quintile; in this figure, trends emerge on three levels: among countries, among regions in the same country (regional effects), and among income quintiles in the same region (quintile effects).

Country Level. At the country level, there is a significant drop in the diversification index moving from SSA into non-SSA regions. In Morocco, Nicaragua, and

Figure 6.1 Income Structure by Quintile in the Surveyed Regions
% of $PPP/EqA

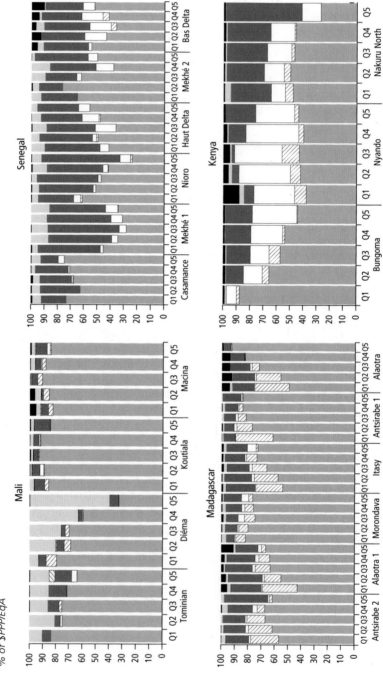

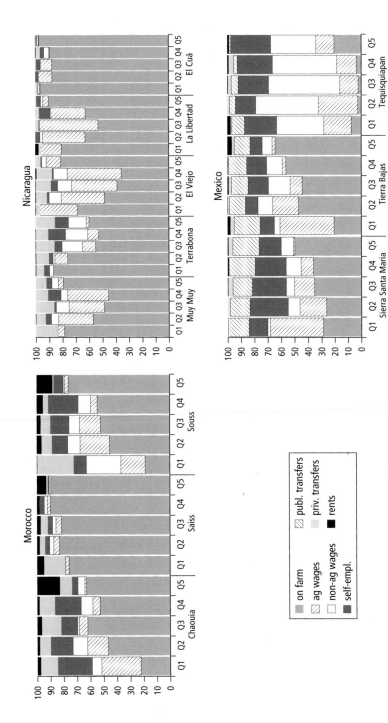

Source: RuralStruc surveys.

Figure 6.2 Diversification Index (1-HHi) per Region and Quintile

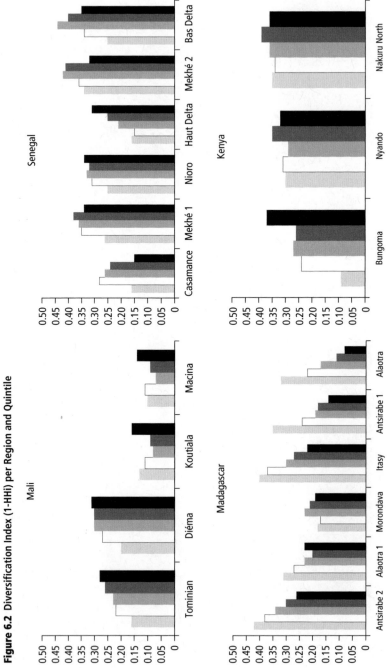

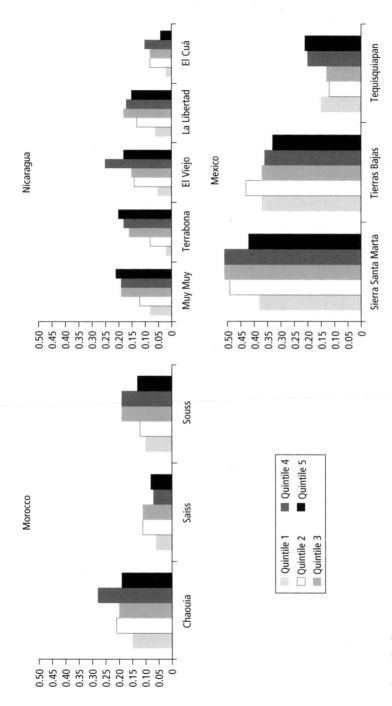

Source: RuralStruc surveys.

Tequisquiapan, the average value of the index hovers in the vicinity of 0.15 to 0.2. In most of the other survey regions (including 16 of the 19 SSA regions), diversification indexes are around 0.3.

The exceptions are few and noteworthy. The lower level of household diversification is observed in Sub-Saharan Africa, in Koutiala and Macina (Mali) and Morondava (Madagascar). These low levels are the result of specific regional situations that will be discussed further. The higher level of diversification is observed outside Sub-Saharan Africa in the two zones of the Mexican Sotavento (Tierras Bajas and Sierra Santa Marta), and is largely a result of the way the index is constructed.[9] Even with the presence of these exceptions, household diversification tends to fall as country incomes increase.

Regional Level. Patterns also emerge among regions in the same country, although these regional effects do not follow any specific trend. Some regions tend toward diversification with rising incomes: In Senegal, the Bas Delta is significantly more diversified than Casamance; and in Kenya, Nakuru North is more diversified than Nyando. But the opposite situation also exists, as exemplified by Mali and Mexico.

Local characteristics are fully at play. For example, the higher household specialization in the two richer regions of Mali (Koutiala and Macina) reflects long-standing government attention to the cotton industry in Koutiala and to rice in the Office du Niger irrigation scheme in Macina. In Mexico, Sierra Santa Marta households have a significantly higher diversification score than those in Tierras Bajas and Tequisquiapan. In the Sierra, households are unable to specialize in maize (like their neighbors in the lowlands) or in off-farm activities (like households in Tequisquiapan) (see figure 6.1). This situation stems partly from isolation, agro-ecological characteristics (mountains versus floodplains), and lack of access to technical packages and large maize buyers, but also from smaller plot sizes and the lower land productivity of mountainous terrain.

Household Level. However, regional effects are less pronounced than intraregional quintile effects. Although richer quintiles are more diversified in some regions and more specialized in others, in most regions the change from quintile to quintile is important. Clearly, a strong relationship exists between income and diversification.

First, the direction of the quintile effect (that is, whether richer households tend to be more specialized or more diversified) appears to be the same for regions in the same country (with a few notable exceptions, such as Morondava in Madagascar, Casamance in Senegal, and El Cuá in Nicaragua). Second, a preliminary attempt to classify regions by the nature of the relationship between diversification levels and household quintiles yields additional results. Although these relationships are diverse, 11 regions exhibit a pattern that could roughly be described as an inverted U (this is the most common pattern). These regions are characterized by a situation in which at lower income levels (quintiles 1–3), as households become richer they also become more diversified, but above quintile 3 or 4 they begin to specialize again.[10]

The Diversification-Income Relationship. A closer look at the relationship between diversification and income requires the consideration of the full distribution of households, masked in the previous analysis by the quintile averages. These averages are particularly distorted by the large jump in income that characterizes the gap between the 4th and 5th quintiles in every region (see chapter 3).

Plotting all households in a region on a graph with axes representing income and diversification and conducting second order polynomial regressions confirm and strengthen the classification identified above: 22 of the 30 surveyed regions display an inverted U pattern.[11] Among the 8 regions challenging the inverted U, 7 show a U shape and one has a downward slope (box 6.1).

The persistence of the inverted U pattern suggests that households prefer to specialize. This is, after all, what those with the most resources choose to do. If households prefer to specialize but at poorer levels do not do so, it must mean that they cannot. Thus, the implication of an inverted U pattern is that poor households diversify as a way of earning more money to meet their basic needs and mitigate their very high levels of risk, but beyond a certain income threshold they begin to specialize (figure 6.3).

The regression work presented in tables 6.1 and 6.2 provides further evidence of a strong relationship between diversification and income. The diversification variable is significantly associated with income among surveyed regions in every country (that is, at the nationally aggregated level). Within regions,

Figure 6.3 Stylized Representation of the Inverted U Pattern

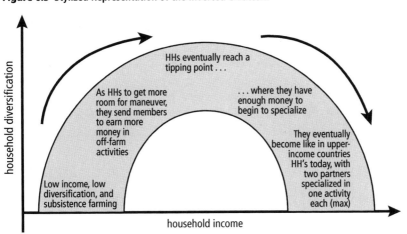

Source: Authors.

BOX 6.1

Challenging the Inverted U Pattern

The surveyed regions in Madagascar challenge the inverted U pattern: five of the eight regions whose distributions do not follow this shape are found here. Except for Morondava, they follow a U shape, which means that poor households are already diversified, then engage in specialization, and finally tend to diversify.

Households in poorer quintiles in Madagascar are more diversified than in other surveyed regions, because some households do not have the resources to survive on subsistence agriculture alone. High population densities have resulted in very small farm sizes (less than half a hectare) and a sizable group of landless peasants. Consequently, the very poorest must seek off-farm work and find it in agricultural wage labor supporting the rice industry (see figure 6.1). This is one of the most poorly paid activities in the entire survey. Households obviously try to exit this situation and reach a point at which they can survive on subsistence farming (on-farm activities) alone, which is equivalent to a specialization. The situation in Morondava, which is the exception among the Malagasy surveyed regions and follows the inverted U shape, is explained by lower population density and larger farms. There, the poorest households can survive on subsistence farming. Also, the region is less specialized in rice, so fewer opportunities for agricultural wage labor exist. In this region, income improvement means accessing additional sources of income and diversification before a possible specialization in fewer activities.

The two other surveyed regions that do not follow the inverted U pattern are Koutiala in Mali and El Cuá in Nicaragua. Koutiala, like the regions in Madagascar, displays a U shape. Here, the cause is the presence of a cash crop with a guaranteed buyer. For poor households, deeper involvement in cotton is the best option, because it benefits from a somewhat secure environment. However, the paradoxical limitations in the development of the cotton-growing areas (decreasing land availability and fertility— see box 3.3) mean that cotton can only earn a household so much. Richer households are those that engage in diversification activities.

El Cuá is the only region to display a full downward slope, meaning a trend toward specialization across all income levels. The driving force here is also a cash crop with easy access to markets. However, returns to coffee farming are much higher than returns to cotton farming, so the need to supplement incomes is not as strong.

---

diversification is also widely significant (17 of the 30 regions, making it the third most common significant variable in the regression).

Moreover, at the regional level, the direction of significance of the diversification variable (the sign on the regression coefficient) tends to match that of the nationally aggregated level.[12] The two countries in which diversification is negatively associated with income at the nationally aggregated level are Madagascar and Mexico, which are, respectively, among the poorest and the richest subsets of the sample. In Madagascar, this relationship stems from the already highly diversified structure of poor households' incomes (see box 6.1); in Mexico, it has to do with farm households' specialization in maize.

To conclude, the evidence from the investigation of income structures and the regression work indicates that the diversification-income relationship is mainly governed by an inverted U pattern, whereby poorer households diversify to mitigate risks while more well-off households tend to specialize. The next section introduces an additional perspective that advances the idea of the inverted U pattern and relates this observation to broader issues of structural transformation.

Household Specialization, Regional Diversification, and Structural Transformation

Literature about rural diversification tends to focus on its development and how it affects the reshaping of the rural economy. The progressive erosion of on-farm activities and the development of new activities feed the process of structural transformation (Hazell, Haggblade, and Reardon 2007). However, little is said about the difference between diversification/specialization patterns at the household level and at the regional level, a comparison that highlights important transformation dynamics.

To illustrate the difference between these patterns and how it is related to the household's inverted U shape, consider a hypothetical country in which no structural transformation has occurred, with the following stylized historical sequencing. At the beginning of the transformation process, all citizens of this country are subsistence farmers, and no one is involved in any other type of activity. The first tentative steps will involve some people doing things other than farming, but it is unlikely that these "early diversifiers" will risk their food supply or give up their plots. Consequently, the diversification observed at this first stage of transformation will be largely within the household. As the country continues to transition and markets become more reliable, early diversifiers may get to the point where they are well established in a nonfarm activity and can rely on other sources of income for their food supply. At this point, they may stop farming altogether and dedicate most of their time to the new activity (small business or waged labor). When this switch and progressive specialization in off-farm activities begin to occur, diversification within households starts to fall across the country, but diversification among households, which are now specialized in different activities, continues to grow at the regional and national levels. The end result is a country in which many households are specialized and earn income from only one or a limited number of activities, while the regions and the country as a whole have diversified.

This story makes it clear that a discussion of income levels and diversification/specialization patterns must be more nuanced. Rather than speaking only of

Figure 6.4 Diversification within and between Households and the Inverted U Pattern

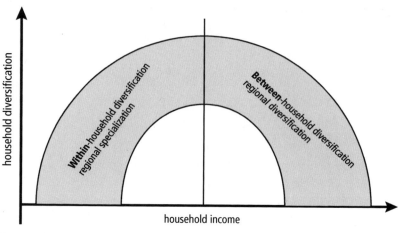

Source: Authors.

absolute diversification or specialization, one must consider the patterns of change both within and between households.

At the beginning of the transformation process, "within households" diversification will be the major trend as households try to diversify from their on-farm base and the region as a whole remains characterized by the weight of agriculture (overall specialization in farming). As the transformation continues, patterns of specialization begin to emerge and then dominate at the individual household level. Diversification between households increases, and the region develops a more diversified economy (figure 6.4).

The RuralStruc survey data illustrate this evolution of diversification/specialization patterns between the household and regional levels. Additionally, the data enable a comparison of different stages of transition within the structural transformation process owing to the characteristics of the country sample.

Instead of using the average diversification index of a region presented in the previous section, it is possible to more closely investigate this process by using the share of household income from off-farm sources as a proxy for diversification. In the initial stage of the transformation process, the share of off-farm income is low, and both households and regions are specialized in farming. As the structural transformation begins, off-farm incomes grow. However, because "off-farm" is an aggregate, corresponding to different activities and incomes, an increasing off-farm share could imply that households are specializing in different off-farm activities, leading to diversification at the regional level.

One can use the average share of off-farm income to explore this distinction, because it can be calculated in two ways: once as a mean of household shares and once as a share of regional means (see box 6.2).

BOX 6.2

From Income Diversification Means to the Diversification Gap

Calculating average shares is a simple operation that can produce nuanced results, because there are two ways of performing it.

In the first way, each household's share of off-farm income to total income is computed, and these shares are averaged at the regional level: This is the mean of household shares (MoHS). In the second way, the average value of off-farm income is computed for an entire region, then divided by the average of regional households' total income: This is the share of regional means (SoRM). The distinction between these two variables is that the MoHS smoothes the effect of outliers while the SoRM does not.

The means correspond to the formulas below:

- Mean of Shares   • Share of Means

$$\frac{\sum_i^n \left(\frac{o_i}{y_i}\right)}{n} \qquad \frac{\left(\frac{\sum_i^n o_i}{n}\right)}{\left(\frac{\sum_i^n y_i}{n}\right)} = \frac{\sum_i^n o_i}{\sum_i^n y_i}$$

where:
o_i = off-farm income of HH i.
y_i = total income of HH i.
n = number of HH in region

In the RuralStruc surveys, the difference between these two means is strongly correlated with income (the Pearson correlation is relatively high: 0.60). The value of this difference is directly influenced by the distribution of households engaged in diversification along the income gradient. A negative sign typically means that the richest households diversify while the majority does not. A positive sign means the opposite: the poorest households diversify.

$$\frac{\sum_i^n \left(\frac{o_i}{y_i}\right)}{n} = \frac{\sum_i^n o_i}{\sum_i^n y_i}$$

The difference between the two means is the diversification gap.

Table 6.4 shows that significant differences can exist between the mean of household shares (MoHS) and the share of regional means (SoRM). The two different means refer to the two different patterns. Because the MoHS calculates the off-farm share at the household level, it refers to patterns within households. The SoRM indicator, as a regionwide aggregate, also takes into account patterns occurring between households and expresses the average regional pattern of change.

The difference between these two means says something about the diversification/specialization pattern in every surveyed region. This pattern can be captured and synthesized by computing a diversification gap, defined as the difference between MoHS and SoRM (box 6.2).

Table 6.4 Diversification Gap in the Surveyed Regions

		Specialization / Diversification pattern			
		Mean of HH off-farm shares (MoHS)	**Share of regional off-farm means (SoRM)**	**Diversification gap (MoHS − SoRM)**	**Average income $PPP per EqA**
Mali	Tominian	0.26	0.30	−0.04	235
	Diéma	0.35	0.51	−0.16	368
	Koutiala	0.12	0.12	0.00	368
	Macina	0.15	0.14	0.01	516
Senegal	Casamance	0.30	0.28	0.02	439
	Mekhé 1	0.64	0.67	−0.03	527
	Nioro	0.54	0.64	−0.10	484
	Haut Delta	0.41	0.49	−0.08	524
	Mekhé 2	0.54	0.51	0.03	769
	Bas Delta	0.55	0.54	0.01	1,205
Madagascar	Antsirabe 2	0.36	0.37	−0.01	409
	Alaotra 1	0.42	0.37	0.05	506
	Morondava	0.22	0.23	−0.01	597
	Itasy	0.35	0.31	0.04	622
	Antsirabe 1	0.22	0.18	0.04	744
	Alaotra 2	0.31	0.17	0.14	1,346
Kenya	Bungoma	0.37	0.49	−0.12	641
	Nyando	0.58	0.57	0.01	660
	Nakuru N.	0.55	0.65	−0.10	2,258
Morocco	Chaouia	0.55	0.40	0.15	2,280
	Saiss	0.16	0.11	0.05	3,419
	Souss	0.58	0.31	0.27	4,131
Nicaragua	Muy Muy	0.41	0.30	0.11	1,417
	Terrabona	0.35	0.40	−0.05	1,458
	El Viejo	0.50	0.31	0.19	2,575
	La Libertad	0.30	0.20	0.10	2,329
	El Cuá	0.09	0.05	0.04	3,610
Mexico	Sierra SM.	0.65	0.59	0.06	1,824
	T. Bajas	0.55	0.44	0.11	3,144
	Tequis.	0.93	0.89	0.04	2,879

Source: RuralStruc surveys.

The diversification gap illustrates a region's stage in the structural trans-formation process. A negative gap value corresponds to a stage of transition in which households are still deeply involved in on-farm activities. They are individually testing diversification without giving up their farming plots, and their share of off-farm income remains limited. Even if households are engaged in many off-farm activities, they tend to be low-return coping activities. The region as a whole remains specialized in farming, but a limited number of households (the richest) have already diversified,[13] pulling the regional mean to a higher value (which explains why MoHS < SoRM and why the gap value can be strongly negative).

On the other hand, a positive value in the diversification gap suggests that household shares of off-farm income are growing. Average incomes are increasing, many households are more fully engaged in off-farm activities, and the effect of the outliers is reduced (the value of the SoRM weakens). This process is strengthened by specialization in different activities corresponding to the inverted U: specialization in various off-farm activities for most households and in on-farm activities for a few. These "on-farm specializers" (the new outliers on this side of the inverted U) are captured more effectively by the SoRM, pulling down the mean and pulling up the positive value of the gap.

Thus, the diversification gap, as a single and composite indicator, reflects the complexities of rural income diversification and illustrates the process of rural transformation. It explicitly accounts for an inverted U shape, in which patterns of household diversification observed at early stages of economic transition give way to household-level specialization and emerging patterns of regional diversification.

Figure 6.5 shows the relationship between the diversification gap and incomes; it plots each region as a single data point on the income/diversification gap space.

Figure 6.5 Relationship between Income and the Diversification Gap

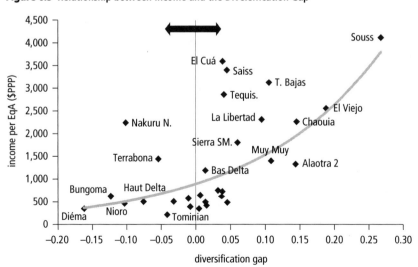

Source: RuralStruc surveys.

Figure 6.6 Income/Diversification Gap Relationship in SSA and Non-SSA Surveyed Regions

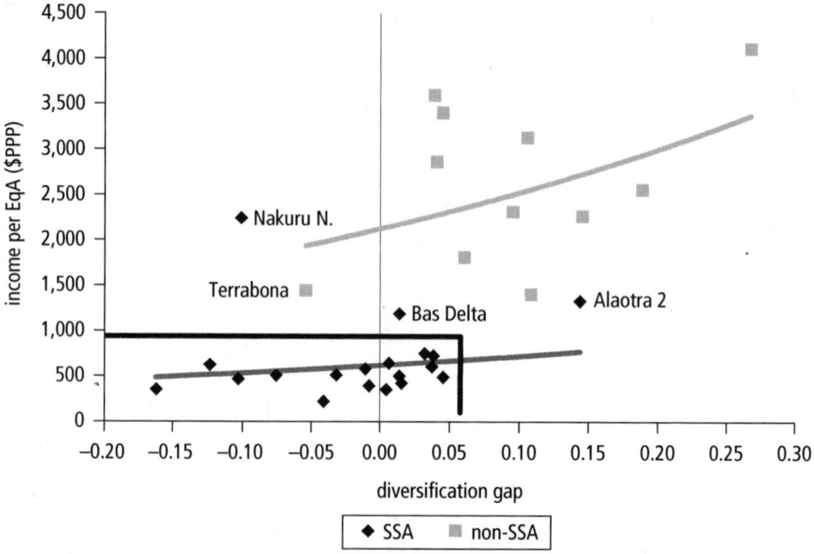

Source: RuralStruc surveys.

At low levels of income, the gap can take any number of negative values, but it is generally not until the gap is positive that incomes begin to grow substantially. The trend line in figure 6.5 slopes upward, confirming a strong positive relationship between income and the diversification gap. But there also appears to be an exponential component to this relationship: Until a certain level of the gap is reached, incomes do not generally rise; beyond that threshold value, incomes increase rapidly. Thus, every region that has a diversification gap above 0.05 has an average income above $1,000 PPP/EqA/year. On the other hand, of the regions with a negative value for the diversification gap, all but two have incomes below $1,000 PPP.

Beyond the general shape of the distribution, figure 6.6 illustrates the positions of the Sub-Saharan African countries. Every SSA region except Alaotra 2 has a diversification gap of less than 0.05, and all of these regions except Bas Delta and Nakuru North have an average income below $800 PPP/EqA—very close to the $2 PPP/day threshold. This means that 16 of the 19 SSA regions are characterized by very low incomes and limited regional diversification. In these 16 regions, the explanatory power of the diversification gap on income is very small. This suggests that households may be encountering a barrier: They may be unable to transition from patterns of household diversification to patterns of regional diversification (that is, household specialization) because

BOX 6.3

The Poverty Trap Pattern

Poverty traps are situations in which households are unable to accumulate assets over time and remain mired in poverty. They "can't get ahead for falling behind" (Barrett and Carter 2001). A vast literature describes the causes, symptoms, and mechanisms of poverty traps, the existence of which depends on "locally increasing returns to scale and exclusionary mechanisms that keep some people from enjoying higher return livelihoods or technologies" (Barrett and Carter 2004, 15). Locally increasing returns often appear when poor households make less-than-optimal allocation decisions because they have to deal with risks. Poverty traps are also accentuated by the existence of exclusionary measures, such as lack of credit access or lack of financial skills, which prevent households from finding any room to maneuver.

An example would be a household that spends all its resources on seeds and all its family labor on staple production, so it will have enough to feed itself. If the household were not so food insecure, it might invest in fertilizer, which would greatly increase the returns to overall expenditure. Without fertilizer, land degradation can occur rapidly, and declining fertility can result in increasingly lower returns each year, while at the same time the family might be growing. To try to make up for lost productivity on the farm, the household might send members to work in other sectors or areas, not always successfully.

This coping strategy is frequently observed in the RuralStruc data. Regions in which many rural households are struggling with poverty traps are often characterized by within-household diversification in low-returns activities. This situation is reflected in figure 6.6: The surveyed regions seem to be stuck, unable to specialize and unable to increase their incomes.

---

their incomes are too low and diversification opportunities are too limited. This indicates the possible presence of a poverty trap (box 6.3) and touches on the idea of transition impasses suggested in the program's third hypothesis.[14]

The surveyed regions outside Sub-Saharan Africa do not seem to encounter any such traps or barriers. With the exception of Terrabona, they are scattered generally well above and to the right of the SSA regions on the graph,[15] and they do not cluster around a specific value of the diversification gap. The trend line that emerges for the non-SSA regions is nearly twice as steep as that observed for SSA regions. So, not only are non-SSA regions richer and more diversified regionally, they also tend to respond more strongly to increasing regional diversification.

The probable underlying explanation for these observations is the returns to available economic activities. As discussed in chapter 4, in very poor regions of Sub-Saharan Africa, a household can be deeply diversified in many low-return activities—all EAP household members and often children work at least one and sometimes multiple jobs. In this situation, a household may still not earn enough to make its income sufficiently secure so it can begin to specialize. At this point, the household is trapped: It cannot earn more, and it consumes everything it earns—and sometimes even more if it consumes its assets. This is the definition of a poverty trap.

Outside of Sub-Saharan Africa, however, the poorest households in every region are engaged in activities that earn much higher incomes (see chapters 4 and 5). Consequently, diversification options provide enough security to eventually allow them to begin to specialize. As they begin to specialize, they become more productive—which means higher returns—and their incomes increase at a faster rate.

The RuralStruc survey's micro-level data on diversification/specialization patterns illustrate a country's stage in the structural transformation process. Most regions in a country follow the same pattern, which suggests that certain national characteristics determine the possible alternatives for diversification or specialization. These characteristics include assets, market functionality, business climate, institutional arrangements, overall governance, and political stability. The specific alternatives they enable reflect a country's stage in the economic transition process.

The trends and characteristics presented here are based on the survey data and correspond to the situations of the surveyed households in their respective regions. These trends are not deterministic; rather, they suggest where regions stand in the diversification/specialization process. They reflect changes that occurred in the past and suggest the causes of observed transition impasses. They do not predict future paths, which will depend on the idiosyncrasies of the local context and the nature of its interactions with the outside world.

Policy-Making Guidelines

From the previous analyses, it appears that if the determinants of rural household income and household diversification are mostly micro (household assets, portfolio characteristics, managerial skills), the determinants of returns to an activity refer broadly to meso and macro conditions. Markets are decisive, but the institutional environment is equally critical. The low returns to nonagricultural activities and the difficulty of on-farm diversification observed in Sub-Saharan Africa are clear reminders of the limitations of the overall context.

Designing adequate public policies to support the process of change is a challenge, and there is no silver bullet. The heterogeneity of local situations highlighted by the RuralStruc program's results reflects the need for a design targeted to regional specifics: There are no one-size-fits-all policies, and tailormade approaches must be the rule. It is, however, possible to suggest certain orientations for action, which refer to policy-making methodologies and possible building blocks, which are promising.

Methodological Considerations
The standardization of policy responses according to imported "recipes" has been a major obstacle to adequate policy design for a long time. A necessary first step is to reengage in development strategies as a way to identify and address major challenges, and then to define priorities and objectives for public and collective action.

Reengaging in Development Strategy Design. A review of the past two decades of development policies provides a well-known shopping list of policy measures that appear in every good publication related to economic development in general and rural development in particular. The main ingredients in the recipe for success are provision of public goods (infrastructure, research, information, and capacity building); improvement of imperfect markets (sourcing inputs, commercializing products, and cutting transaction costs); incentives for the development of missing markets (credit, technical support, assurance); and risk mitigation mechanisms. The hard part is to mix these ingredients in the policy bowl, to devise genuine policies and define their adequate sequencing on the basis of prioritization and targeting.

To identify priorities for action, the program's results suggest the need to reengage in development strategies to deal with the critical challenges faced by many developing countries. This is particularly the case for Sub-Saharan Africa, which must manage its demographic and economic transitions in the context of globalization and under the new constraints of global climate change (see chapter 2).

Many countries have neglected overall strategy design, most often since the end of the 1970s, a consequence of liberalization policies and state withdrawal, policy segmentation, and disinvestment in information systems—the latter being major obstacles today to adequate policy design.

A development strategy is more than the articulation of sector policies. It is the result of a process leading to a shared vision of the future, reflecting an agreement among stakeholders or constituents that allows a country to make choices and establish priorities. As described by Stiglitz (1998), a development strategy is a public good and deserves strong public support in its design.

Reengagement in development strategies implies, first and foremost, reinvestment in knowledge creation. As illustrated by the country reviews in Phase 1 of the program, information is missing in general, and necessary information about evolving rural economies is notably absent. The survey results show that heterogeneity leads to complex rural settings that cannot be understood without efficient information systems. Statistical systems must be reestablished and redefined to allow policy to account for the evolution of rural economies, the increasing mobility of people, and new family networks resulting from archipelago models (see chapter 4). Reengagement also implies reinvestment in processes. Here, consultation is the key word, because ownership is the determining factor of commitment. This approach takes time and must be carefully planned. Finally, reengagement in development strategies means an investment and a reinvestment in capacity building. Many countries do not have the skills to manage information systems, analyze results, monitor processes, and elaborate scenarios. The situation is particularly critical in Sub-Saharan Africa, where many central governments lost their technical skills in the aftermath of structural adjustment and state withdrawal in the 1980s; where new local government institutions created by decentralization are generally unprepared for this kind of approach; and where civil society organizations and think tanks are few.

Prioritizing and Targeting. Often, a critical issue for policy makers is the need to do everything at the same time. Of course, this is not possible because of limitations on financial and human resources. Choices must be made, and making them is difficult under the conditions in many developing countries, where the means for policy making are limited.

In this setting, prioritization and sequencing are required. They must be supported by adequate analyses for which general, sectoral, and regional diagnoses must be developed to identify existing "binding constraints." Using the program's perspective on rural transformation, a preliminary step would be to identify the regional constraints to agricultural growth—the necessary first stage for increasing rural demand and rural diversification.[16]

Then, priorities need to be discussed in terms of targets, which can be defined for groups of economic agents, sectors (types of products), and regions. The program does not aim to propose priorities and targets for the various countries and surveyed regions, but it is possible to provide an illustration of a first step of this kind of fine-tuning. This would help identify a set of priorities and facilitate the definition of possible building blocks that contribute to the design of policy instruments.

A rough identification of target groups, referring to levels of income, was tested using the survey results. (This approach is, of course, limited; a classification based on a more detailed typology—one using households' assets and their local opportunities and constraints—would be necessary.) This rough identification is useful in allowing one to consider general options based on the overall economic situation of the surveyed households.

Four groups of households were defined according to their levels of total income and on-farm income to assess their capacity for investment—a core indicator of room to maneuver at the household level, which must be understood to identify appropriate incentives and supports: *Better off* households

Table 6.5 Distribution of Households by Target Group in the RuralStruc Sample

Country	Target groups			
	Extremely poor	Poor	Capacity	Better off
Mali	69.8	19.7	7.7	2.8
Senegal	58.5	15.6	11.8	14.0
Madagascar	49.9	25.8	13.6	10.8
Kenya	45.7	12.5	12.8	29.0
Morocco	21.9	8.0	13.6	56.5
Nicaragua	24.6	13.8	14.4	47.3
Mexico	7.3	2.6	10.2	79.8
TOTAL	40.2	16.0	12.6	31.1
SSA	53.6	20.2	12.3	13.9
non-SSA	19.8	9.6	13.2	57.4

Source: RuralStruc surveys.

(>$4/day); *capacity* households (>$2/day); and *poor* and *extremely poor* house-holds (<$2/day). The poor group includes households that could exit poverty if they were able to double their current on-farm income. The extremely poor group refers to households that could not: Even if they were to double their on-farm income, they would still remain below $2 PPP. Even though the exercise is highly theoretical, one can assume that for households above $2 PPP per day, basic needs are covered and earnings are no longer fully allocated to consumption but can be used for investment and savings. Above $4 PPP, options for income allocation are obviously greater. The situation below $2 PPP is critical: All revenues are dedicated to basic needs, and they are still not enough.

Table 6.5 presents the share of the surveyed households that falls into each income group, and Figure 6.7 shows the breakdown at the regional level. Together, they show the very difficult situations faced by SSA regions, particularly those in Mali and Senegal, and illustrate the earlier discussion of poverty traps. They are a reminder of the stark reality faced by most rural households. The two "poor" groups—which include the vast majority of households surveyed in Sub-Saharan Africa—face huge challenges. The extremely poor group would remain poor even if its on-farm incomes were doubled, and the prospect of raising the poor group's farm revenues by 100 percent seems out of reach in most regional situations over the short to medium term.

The results presented in these figures can help in the consideration of possible policy orientations. It is unrealistic to expect households whose incomes are less than $2 PPP/EqA/day and that cannot satisfy their basic needs (the poor and extremely poor groups), to engage in any investment on their own. They will need local public goods in terms of infrastructure (transportation, water, and electricity), land rights, and research.

Figure 6.7 Distribution of Households by Target Group and Region

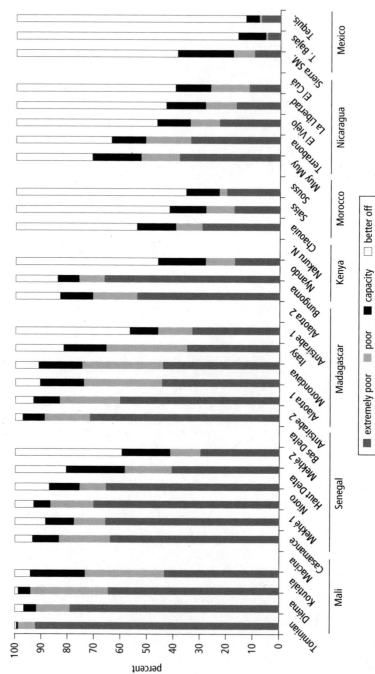

They will also need more direct support through smart subsidies,[17] especially to facilitate input access and extension services, as well as very low-interest-rate loans, which are the only way to improve the existing farming systems, facilitate innovation, and increase productivity.[18] Price risks are another major stumbling block. The increasing volatility of global markets and the well-known seasonal volatility of domestic food markets require actions that the private sector has little incentive to carry out. Public support is needed to implement information systems—a preliminary and indispensable step—and stabilization instruments must be adapted to local situations, depending on the type of instability (endogenous or imported).[19]

Any support related to provision of public goods and market improvement/ facilitation would benefit all farm households, including the "capacity" and "better-off" groups. These policies would not pit one income group against another; they could benefit all rural households while allowing the poor to catch up more rapidly.

However, the extremely poor group's prospects for escaping poverty by remaining completely within agriculture are severely restricted, and additional opportunities in terms of activities and incomes will be necessary. Options are limited in the short and medium terms, but improvement in skills and capacities will facilitate diversification. A critical objective for governments related to provision of public goods is education. The surveys show that the situation is heterogeneous among countries but improving: The next generation has achieved—at least formally—higher levels of schooling, although a huge push is still needed. A higher educational level facilitates mobility in the labor market and access to off-farm activities.

Again, strengthening educational levels will benefit all rural households. It will also help the "on-farm side." Higher skills mean possible access to new technical packages and cultivation practices that facilitate greater productivity and easier compliance with the stringent demands of modern agricultural markets.

Building Blocks for Rural Transformation

Although this section has focused so far on heterogeneity and the need to reengage in targeted development strategies on a national (or even subnational) level, certain trends emerge in the RuralStruc results and common themes appear. The program has distilled these results into building blocks for policy, keeping in mind the need to be selective. These building blocks are mainly targeted to Sub-Saharan Africa, which faces major transition challenges. They are not recommendations in and of themselves but rather frameworks to keep in mind in creating targeted development strategies.

Agriculture must remain a firm priority. In the agriculture-based countries of Sub-Saharan Africa, the major push for structural transformation, and for progressively unlocking the poverty traps, has to occur in agriculture. Even if public policies are also needed to facilitate the development of other sectors, transformation will depend first on increasing farm incomes and creating a more secure economic environment, changes that will foster rural demand and facilitate rural diversification.

The evidence gathered over the two phases of the RuralStruc program suggests three main building blocks: (1) supporting family agriculture, (2) promoting staple production and improving staple markets, and (3) strengthening rural-urban linkages.

Supporting Family Farms. The RuralStruc results contribute to the controversial (and often misleading) debate about the optimal size of farm structures, a topic of renewed discussion in recent years. This debate was reignited primarily as a result of the food price crisis of 2008 and the related trend of increased land grabbing (chapter 1); until now, it has been mostly couched in terms of food security. Part of the confusion was fostered by the publication of two essays by Paul Collier (2008, 2009) that focused on food supply. Some of his provocative arguments were used to feed the small versus large-scale debate.

This debate postulates a false dualism between smallholder and subsistence agriculture on one side and large-scale and commercial agriculture on the other. In fact, the reality is a continuum of situations shaped by local assets and the economic and institutional environment. Family agriculture is still the overwhelmingly dominant type of agriculture around the world. It covers a large spectrum of situations, from micro-farms to larger holdings (sometimes hundreds of hectares) that employ mechanization and wage labor, and are major suppliers to world food markets.[20] Family agriculture can be subsistence, commercial, or a combination. It has displayed, throughout history and in every region of the world, a remarkable capacity for adaptation and an ability to respond to growing demand. This is certainly the case in Sub-Saharan Africa, where it has done so despite extremely adverse conditions (Mortimer 2003; Toulmin and Guèye 2003).

Advocates of large-scale farming cite the wide and growing gap in output per hectare between land farmed by large-scale, mechanized operations and land worked by smallholders. They argue that developing countries (notably in SSA), by beginning to favor large-scale production and thereby producing more food from their own land, could control their growing trade deficits in food and reduce their vulnerability to swings in international food prices.

Proponents of smallholder agriculture also often frame their arguments in the language of food security. They point to the well-known lack of economies of scale in agriculture and the many failures of previous large-scale agricultural projects.[21] They argue that family labor has many benefits, such as no costs for worker supervision, very high effort levels by workers (who are directly interested in the farm's output), flexibility and adaptation (to varying labor needs over the year and to varying economic results depending on the crop season), and local knowledge that can make the smallholder model efficient.[22] The recent World Bank study *Awakening Africa's Sleeping Giant* (2009b) showed that African smallholder agriculture has competitive production costs compared with those of large-scale farms (in this case, those of the Cerrado region in the central-south of Brazil) and is competitive in its domestic markets but is disadvantaged in global markets owing to high logistics costs (which relate to a country's economic and institutional environment, not to farm size).[23]

Thus, the small versus large-scale debate is an example of the kind raised in chapter 1: A discussion about policies that will have long-term effects is being driven by a focus on short-term issues (in this case, the consequences of the food price crisis). By targeting food production only, the discussion fails to take into account the broader role agriculture plays in economic development and forgets its contribution to structural transformation.

In Sub-Saharan Africa, an incipient economic transition and an ongoing demographic transition ensure that agriculture will have a role to play over the medium term, notably for the absorption of a rapidly growing labor force. The 195 million rural youth who must be employed between now and 2025 will have to work in agriculture or in the rural nonfarm economy.

Because the majority of rural people are involved in family agriculture and because nonfarm activities are both directly and indirectly supported by farmers' incomes (and will develop with their improvement), the question for rural development is what kind of agricultural development model will offer the best outcomes in terms of overall revenues, employment, and poverty alleviation.

If governments were to encourage large managerial farms—which probably would mean new technical systems and mechanization—they would risk hampering the development of labor opportunities related to more labor-intensive family agriculture. In this light, the recent trend of large land purchases in Africa by foreign operators is troubling and paradoxical. As Karen Brooks said (2010, 9), "Large numbers of African young people with agricultural experience are joining the labor force, [while] the land that could secure their futures may pass under long-term rights to foreigners because of constraints on capital and property rights."

Policy choices must avoid radical positions. Investments in large-scale farming, including foreign investments, can offer opportunities for growth and employment, depending on the local context and the type of production. They can help the development of new value chains by facilitating the reach of minimum production thresholds, and they can facilitate agricultural development in sparsely populated regions. However, as noted in the *Sleeping Giant* study (World Bank 2009b), these investments could be better oriented toward segments of the value chain where capital is missing—input supply, marketing, transformation of products—where they would favor the use of the huge small-holder potential for production.

These arguments have important consequences in terms of policy design. Among the many policy ingredients related to public goods provision and market improvements, the priority should be to focus on land access and land rights. This conclusion was confirmed by the RuralStruc survey results, which show that land access is the most critical determinant of farm income (see the first section at the beginning of this chapter).

In countries that are deeply constrained in terms of land availability, the only solution to increase both farm income and farm employment is labor-intensive improvements in land productivity. Although input markets are a main stumbling block in terms of access and cost, the adoption of technical innovations at the farm level offers a wide range of sustainable answers.[24] These innovations must be coupled with necessary secure land tenure without which the economic risk level is unacceptable.

In countries in which increasing the amount of farmland under cultivation is an option, unlocking access to this resource through infrastructure provision, adequate regional planning, and land rights can be a powerful way to increase farm income and farm labor. This is the case in many parts of Africa, notably the Guinea savanna, where only 10 percent of 400 million hectares of potential farmland are currently cultivated (World Bank 2009b).[25] In these situations, a preliminary step is to catalog existing resources, critical information that does not exist in most SSA countries.

In addition, the difficult and rarely discussed question of land access for youth must be raised. Many young people are locked in agrarian systems in which land tenure and farm management are under the control of elders. In SSA, young household heads often remain dependent on their fathers or grand-fathers until the elders die, a situation that blocks initiatives and technical innovations that could more easily be adopted by young people. Facilitating access of young rural dwellers to farmland, the transmittal of farm assets to young family workers, and the standing down of elders are critical issues that must be tackled by public policies. Such policies will directly contribute to the economic insertion of youth and to agricultural growth.

A final recommendation relates to increasing the economies of scale of family farms, which are often hindered by the relatively limited production levels of individual farms. This obstacle can be overcome through effective producers' organizations, although adequate incentives and supports are required to develop these groups. Producers' organizations can facilitate the marketing of products through primary collection and can play a major role in investment in storage facilities and equipment for the transformation of products, and in organizing profitable input supply. Larger volumes of products can facilitate contractualization with downstream economic agents (wholesalers, agribusinesses, exporters), and the producers' organizations can use their increased bargaining power in contract negotiations.

Promoting Staple Crops. In the RuralStruc sample, staple production is over 50 percent of gross farm product in 18 of the 30 surveyed zones. In some cases, the number is as high as 80 percent. This result reflects a dual reality. First, it highlights the importance of self-consumption. The self-consumption share in a household's gross farm product reflects risk-management strategies (supply effect) that households employ to respond to a persistently insecure environment (incomplete and imperfect markets and sometimes unstable natural conditions that can affect the crop season). Second, it mirrors a potentially weak demand owing to poor access to and integration with markets (demand effects). The importance of staples reflects the lack of market opportunities in the surveyed zones, as well as regional situations in which new value chains and alternatives to traditional commodities are limited. Even though non-SSA regions display more on-farm diversification (with the exception of the Mexican regions), the importance of staple markets is a general pattern. It affects households at all income levels, as even households in richer quintiles can be heavily engaged in staple production and commercialization.

These results provide evidence-based justification for giving priority to policies that support staple production and the improvement of staple markets. This priority was the mainstay of the structural transformation of Asian economies, with the clear objectives of alleviating poverty, reducing food costs, and managing and slowing the exit from agriculture—it was a way to adjust to the pace of the overall structural transformation.

In general terms, the case for staples is supported by four broad arguments. The first argument refers to their inclusiveness, which results from their widespread development: Almost every farm household is engaged in staple production (98 percent and 76 percent of the surveyed households in SSA and non-SSA regions, respectively), while other agricultural products engage a more limited population. The oft-cited high-value exports frequently only affect tens of thousands of producers or fewer in a country, out of hundreds of thousands or even millions. Thus, targeted policies that promote and support staples can affect the overwhelming majority of rural households.

Generally, staple products are not very valuable compared with other farm products, such as horticulture or livestock. They offer a lower return, and it is clear that a production increase in staples cannot be the only solution for poverty alleviation. However, rising food prices are resulting in progressively better returns to staple farming, and the constraint of relatively low earnings is offset by the breadth of staple production, which offers major leverage in terms of labor, overall income, and growth linkages. By contributing strongly to farm incomes (and thus rural incomes) at the aggregated level, staples can play a major role in increasing rural demand and facilitating the emergence of other activities. This pro-staple option was a decisive component of the Asian Green Revolution, which facilitated the rural transformation of Asian countries (Delgado, Hopkins, and Kelly 1998). Also, it is easier for producers to access staple markets because they do not have the strict requirements found in the markets for higher value products, particularly when these high-value products are sold globally.

The second argument is related to the critical role played by staples in risk-management. Seventy-five percent and 30 percent of surveyed households in SSA and non-SSA regions, respectively, are in the two "poor" groups, in which the total income per adult equivalent is below $2 PPP a day. These households face severe risks, and food insecurity is present for a significant share of them.[26] In such situations, self-consumption and storage (when possible) are the rule, and any type of risk related to new crops, new production techniques, new marketing channels, or off-farm diversification is carefully avoided. Consequently, any increase in staple production can be a catalyst: It contributes to risk alleviation and can therefore help unlock the potential for innovation and diversification, both on-farm and off-farm.

The third argument in favor of staples is the huge growth potential of the sector. As a consequence of demographic growth—nationally, regionally, and globally—and increasing urbanization, demand for all types of staple products will rise steadily over the next decades. Progressive changes in diets related to rising incomes will result in the rapid development of meat, dairy, and horticulture products (Collomb 1999), but staples—especially cereals—will still account for the bulk of food demand for years to come.

In the case of Sub-Saharan Africa, staple production has been quite successful in growing to meet rising demand (Bricas, Zoungrana, and Thirion 2009), and this incentive will remain in place for some time owing to the demographic prospects of the region. The sector already represents three-quarters of total agricultural output.[27] Additionally, higher international food prices will reduce the competition from low-priced imports and will provide an incentive for increasing regional production. Domestic producers will be better positioned to capture some of the current $23 billion in food imports into Sub-Saharan Africa.[28]

The final argument for a pro-staples policy involves the huge potential for downstream activities related to processing. The initial transformation of staple products (typically, shelling and grinding) generally occurs either at the farm level for self-consumption or at the village level for local consumption. But most sales of staples, especially those directed to urban consumers in large cities, consist of raw products, and the value added is appropriated by urban economic agents.

Growth in staple production could easily result in more value added locally, strengthen the linkages between rural areas and their nearby small towns, and contribute to rural diversification. This evolution would require an improved investment climate, but investment needs are not necessarily high. Local transformation can be achieved with small equipment and labor-intensive transformation units, which can deal with initial processing and engage in secondary transformation of products and packaging for urban consumers.

On the basis of the survey results, it is easy to say that policies should focus on staples, but developing recommendations for specific policies to increase staple production risks re-creating the long shopping list related to productivity discussed earlier.[29] In Sub-Saharan Africa, two major issues must be addressed. The first relates to postharvest losses. This is an old theme, promoted after the 1970s food crises, that is still relevant because of the lack of storage equipment in most rural areas. Although estimates are difficult, particularly for roots and tubers, postharvest grain loss is generally agreed to be between 10 percent and 20 percent of total output.[30] Many actions can be promoted that would affect the postharvest process (sorting, drying, pest control, early processing), but good storage appears to be a major component and one that can be supported by adapted institutional arrangements, such as warehouse receipt systems, which can simultaneously ease the cash situation of producers and contribute to reducing their level of economic risk (World Bank 2010a).

The second issue relates to regional trade. Sub-Saharan Africa as a whole is a huge and rapidly growing market, but it is constrained by the political fragmentation of the continent and the large number of international borders, a situation highlighted in the WDR09. On average, in the 2000s, only 20 percent of SSA's agricultural exports were oriented toward other SSA countries (Lipchitz, Torre, and Chedanne 2010). Important progress occurred over the past two decades as a consequence of progressive regional integration and achievements of the regional economic communities (RECs). Generally, tariffs on goods were removed within regions, but this did not lead to an increase in regional trade (Faivre Dupaigre 2007). Difficulties are related to the nonenforcement of the RECs' rules; persistent nontariff barriers related to standards (on both products and inputs); and abnormal practices, mainly related to border crossing (bureaucratic hassle is often the rule).[31] Political commitment for effective harmonization and trade facilitation must be a key part of the solution, along with investment in transport infrastructure (Ndulu 2006; Foster and Briceño-Garmendia 2010), which is the target of one of NEPAD's major programs.

But although it is important to focus on staples, they should not be the only focus. Where other opportunities exist or when they arise, they should be supported. Traditional commodities or higher value products can offer important local alternatives. This is the case for livestock products, which are developed in many surveyed regions.[32] It is also the case in non-SSA regions, where more diversified agricultural sectors and better economic and institutional environments provide more room to maneuver for agricultural diversification, notably access to higher value markets—a conclusion that is consistent with the WDR08's policy recommendations regarding non-agriculture-based countries.

Strengthening Rural-Urban Linkages for Territorial Development. Rural transformation is all about the diversification/specialization relationship, in which regional economies evolve from on-farm specialization to rural diversification. This process occurs through risk alleviation and higher returns to on-farm activities (resulting from increased agricultural productivity and diminishing transaction costs), which translate into growing rural demand for nonagricultural goods and services. Rural demand generates new activities (processing of products, trade in and trade out, services) that concentrate in rural boroughs and small towns to benefit from economies of scale, while agriculture is, by nature, an activity scattered in multiple production units throughout the countryside.

The strengthening of linkages between small towns and their surroundings is critical for development and has contributed to economic transitions all over the world. These links create better local market opportunities, facilitate access to services, build community, and contribute to the weaving together of a region's economic and social fabric. The linkages progressively accelerate with increasing agricultural output and farm incomes, but changes occur slowly and are likely to develop over generations.

Thus, the question is how to strengthen these connections and reinforce the territorial (or regional) dimension of development, despite the fact that the growth of strong, localized rural-urban linkages has been challenged over the past few decades by the emergence in many developing countries of new urbanization patterns characterized by rapid metropolization. As discussed in chapter 2, better transportation networks in much of the world allow easier access to major cities, which offer more services and superior job prospects. This access often results in migration directly from rural to metropolitan areas (UNSRID 2010).

This urbanization pattern can inhibit the development of smaller towns, where dense rural-urban and on-farm–off-farm linkages might otherwise occur and offer multiplier effects for development. At the same time, it complicates urban management in large cities, which are burdened by an influx of poor and unskilled rural migrants who feed the spongelike informal urban sector. This growing population in metropolitan areas presents city planners with difficulties in terms of infrastructure, equipment, and services, because poor urban dwellers cannot contribute to their own maintenance (Paulais 2010 and forthcoming). It explains the growing problem of slums in the metropolitan areas of developing countries (UN-Habitat 2003).

New evidence on the significance of regional rural-urban dynamics strengthens arguments for the critical role of small and intermediate urban centers, and reinforces the need to focus development efforts at the local level. Christiaensen and Todo (2009) show that rural migration out of agriculture into what they call the "missing middle" (secondary towns and the associated rural nonfarm economy) has powerful effects in terms of poverty reduction, but that this is not the case with large-scale urbanization in mega-cities—a result that questions the benefits of concentration stressed in the WDR09. Using poverty data over a panel of 49 countries, Christiaensen and Todo show that if agglomeration in mega-cities translates into faster general growth, it also leads to higher inequality, while diversification into the missing middle smoothes the process and results in more inclusive development.

The question of how to support the linkage of small cities with their immediate surroundings is a major one, and it has drawn significant attention from academia and development practitioners over the past decades, although no definitive recipe has emerged.[33] As with general economic development and economic transition, there is no silver bullet for territorial development. However, policy makers can be guided by what is known about methodology, local institutions, and the strengthening of the economic functions of small cities, for which inclusive family farm development, staple markets, and local transformation of local products are key.

A territorial approach that strives to understand local strengths and weaknesses and binding constraints can help promote rural and local development.[34] It requires a careful diagnostic, created jointly by local stakeholders, that enables efficient prioritizing, sequencing, and targeting. Such a process parallels the development of local institutions and local governance. Decentralization and the strengthening of civil society organizations offer opportunities to make local policy choices; however, local governance bodies are often weak, and decentralization often precedes the development of the information systems and local analytical capacities necessary for effective governance—a clear field for external support.

Strengthening the economic functions of small cities has to do with their connection to markets and the type and level of services they provide. Although transportation infrastructure may be key (conventional wisdom in the development debate), it is not enough. An important result of the RuralStruc surveys is that well-connected rural areas with easy access to major urban centers are not necessarily better off than more remote areas, as exemplified by the situation of rural households in western Kenya or in the *bassin arachidier* in Senegal (see chapter 3). This discussion strengthens the debate about the missing middle, which is about the quality of urbanization, not just about avoiding excessive metropolization.

The characteristics of urbanization in West Africa are a clear reminder that metropolization does not necessarily prevent the development of small and medium-size cities, and that such cities are not necessarily the recipe for regional growth. As shown by the *Africapolis* study (Denis and Moriconi-Ebrard 2009), the number of urban centers with populations over 10,000 has grown rapidly in West Africa and has resulted in shorter distances to cities and a new geography of the region (Bossard 2009). However, the question here is the level of public goods provision and the quality of infrastructure and services. These are absolute necessities for a city to assume its economic role; without them, urban growth is characterized by an agglomeration of poor people. In many countries in Sub-Saharan Africa, public funds are exhausted in servicing a dominant capital city, preventing the wider provision of infrastructure and services that would facilitate a positive urbanization process (see box 3.2).

Thus, what appears to be critical at the regional level is the adequate provision of public goods (related to local administration, health, education, and communication infrastructure—not only roads) and of basic factors such as water and electricity, which cannot easily be provided by the private sector in the first stages of development. These public goods are indispensable to facilitate private investment and improve the living conditions of urban dwellers—a condition necessary to minimize rural depopulation toward metropolitan areas. They correspond to spatially targeted public interventions, which should more often be the rule rather than an individual response to a very specific situation.[35] Public goods provision can usefully be accompanied by fiscal incentives aimed at helping local service providers and entrepreneurs.

These kinds of public investments and supports have had positive effects on regional growth, the development of nonfarm employment, and the strengthening of rural-urban links (Fan 2008). They can directly contribute to promoting territorial development that makes use of local assets and resources, eases value addition to local products, and facilitates the provision of environmental services.[36] Agroclusters that take advantage of local knowledge, local networks, and specific geographical denominations of local products can be powerful engines.[37]

This perspective acknowledges the multifunctionality of agriculture and the fact that it can be a driving force for rural and regional development. It can serve as the foundation for a "new rural-urban compact" (Gutman 2007) based on a new type of regional governance, which would reconcile "urbanists" and "ruralists" and allow for an effective process of structural transformation that reconnects cities with their regional surroundings.

Notes

1. For a full explanation of the regression work and descriptions of the variables, see annex 5 in the appendix posted at http://www.worldbank.org/afr/ruralstruc.
2. Every effort was made to run the same regression in all 30 surveyed zones. This was not always possible, as certain pieces of information were available in some regions and not in others, and some variables were locally irrelevant (for example, irrigation). However, in general, the specification in each region is very similar.

3. The difficultly of capturing migrant incomes is addressed in chapter 4.
4. There also seem to be important level effects but not necessarily "certificate effects." The most significant difference in incomes is associated with the jump from having completed primary education to having some secondary education.
5. The survey did not conduct a detailed review of intensification practices. The technical package variable represents access to fertilizer and improved seeds only.
6. These five regions are Bas Delta (Senegal), the two Antsirabe zones (Madagascar), El Cuá (Nicaragua), and Tequisquiapan (Mexico). The results are not straightforward to interpret but make a point about the relative importance of physical distance to a city and quality of roads. Where the transportation quality variable is negatively significant, physical proximity to a city matters a lot; where it is positively significant, it is better to have a good road network than to be close to a city (see annex 5 in the appendix posted at http://www.worldbank.org/afr/ruralstruc).
7. The figure shows the shares of regional means by income sources and regional quintiles. The different types of average calculation are discussed later in this chapter.
8. The diversification index (1-HHi) is defined as the opposite of the Herfindahl-Hirschman Index (HHi).
   The definition of the index is the following:

$$1 - HHi = 1 - \frac{\sqrt{\sum_{i=1}^{n} P_i^2} - \sqrt{\frac{1}{n}}}{1 - \sqrt{\frac{1}{n}}}$$

   where i represents the different income sources (on-farm, agricultural wages, non-agricultural wages, self-employment, public transfers, private transfers, rents), n the number of income sources, and P the share of every income source in the total income. Because the HHi squares the shares, it strengthens the main pattern of the household.
9. As the diversification index is based on seven types of income (on-farm and six off-farm incomes), the presence or absence of one of these types can have a large effect on a household's overall score. One of the seven types is public transfers, which exist in every quintile in every region in Mexico and nowhere else in the survey. This significantly raises the diversification index in Mexico relative to other countries. Tequisquiapan's index is not raised in this way because although public transfers are present, only 27 percent of households have on-farm incomes, so the weight of subsidies related to agriculture (Procampo) is lower.
10. The following regions exhibit this pattern: Casamance, Mekhé 1 and 2, and Bas Delta in Senegal; Chaouia and Souss in Morocco; El Viejo, La Libertad, and El Cuá in Nicaragua; and Tierras Bajas and Sierra Santa Marta in Mexico.
11. This inverted U shape holds even when the households with the highest incomes are eliminated, those that heavily affect the 5th quintile's averages. The only exception is Saiss, Morocco, where excluding the five richest households leads to a different regression result and a U shape instead of an inverted U (see chapter 4 for a discussion of high incomes in Morocco related to rents).

12. For example, diversification is positively associated with income in Senegal and positively significant in five out of six regions in the regional level regression. The diversification variable is not significant in Haut Delta because of the high specialization in tomato production (see chapter 5).

13. Some of these households are engaged in services (health, education, local administration, or trade and transportation) that have higher returns.

14. The three SSA regional outliers—Nakuru North, Alaotra 2, and Bas Delta—have the highest regional average incomes in the SSA sample and are the richest regions in their countries. In Nakuru North, the negative gap value suggests that the regional income is pulled by a few richer households that are deeply engaged in off-farm activities. In Alaotra 2, the positive gap value illustrates a situation in which the richest households are deeply specialized in on-farm activities (rice), pulling down the off-farm regional average. The neutral position of Bas Delta, near the thresholds, reflects the higher returns to the activities of the richest households.

15. In Terrabona, one of the two poorest regions in Nicaragua, households are mainly engaged in on-farm activities with low-return off-farm diversification. The richest households have access to better paid jobs in *maquiladoras*.

16. The growth diagnostics method developed by Hausmann, Rodrik, and Velasco (2005) and its concept of "binding constraints" is a major reference and could be adapted to a regional approach.

17. The topic of subsidies is very sensitive, but positions have changed over the past few years (World Bank 2007). It is now acknowledged that smart subsidies can help unlock access to input markets for producers and provide incentives to providers. Voucher systems are a positive development that have been somewhat widely adopted, as they facilitate targeting of farmers' groups and regions. The major issue is the adequate management of this type of system and the ability to scale down.

18. On the basis of long-term review and modeling, Fuglie (2009) demonstrated that total factor productivity levels in Sub-Saharan Africa have grown at a very slow pace over the past 45 years, in contrast to other developing countries.

19. The price stabilization systems that developed worldwide between the two World Wars (and were implemented by the colonial powers in their former colonies) were all dismantled during the liberalization wave of the 1980s, with a few exceptions, such as the Ghana Cocoa Marketing Board. Many attempts have been made to implement market instruments (options, futures) and safety nets for the most vulnerable households, but the results have been very limited and uneven. The need for government involvement in market management is more widely accepted today, especially since the 2008 food price crisis. However, structural options for instability reduction and management are still highly debated. They include keeping high productivity growth through investment and maintaining coping instruments for crisis response (for example, individual country reserves, price bands). See Byerlee, Jayne, and Myers (2005), Poulton et al. (2006), World Bank (2007), Galtier (2009), and Timmer (2010). The dominant role played by global firms in agricultural markets since state withdrawal from supply management is a major issue. Many proposed solutions depend heavily on cooperation among firms; however, their willingness to cooperate is subject to some debate (Losch 2007).

20. As noted in chapter 4, family agriculture is defined by the strong link between household structure and farming activity in terms of assets and management. Its opposite is managerial or capitalist agriculture based entirely on a waged labor force and on shareholding. This type of agriculture targets returns to capital investment, while family agriculture mainly targets returns to labor (Lamarche 1991; Losch and Fréguin-Gresh forthcoming).

21. In the case of Africa, see Poulton et al. (2008), who also show that the few apparent successes in eastern and southern Africa were nurtured by strong public support.

22. See Hazell et al. (2007b), Wiggins (2009), and Binswanger-Mkhize, McCalla, and Patel (2009). There are few exceptions to the lack of economies of scale in agriculture, mostly related to the transformation and packaging of perishable products. Byerlee and Deninger (2010) also show that new computer-related technologies for farm management and technical operations could challenge this historical advantage of small farms.

23. The study confirmed economies of scale for some specific products (oil palm, horticulture) and noted the advantages of scale for meeting high quality requirements.

24. Most of these technical innovations are agro-ecological practices that have been fully endorsed by the International Assessment of Agricultural Knowledge, Science and Technology for Development (IAASTD 2009). They include improved cultivation practices and plot management, such as erosion control through terracing and ground cover, agroforestry, and integrated crop-livestock systems.

25. In the RuralStruc countries, this is the case in Mali (the broad savanna zone near the Guinean border in western Mali and the inland Niger delta), in Madagascar (the western and northeastern parts of the country), and in Nicaragua (the Caribbean coast). See RS 1 Country reports.

26. In 11 of the 19 SSA surveyed regions and in 2 regions in Nicaragua, more than 10 percent of households are food insecure (see chapter 3).

27. See World Bank (2008a). The overall value of staples also weights heavily compared with total agricultural exports: According to Diao et al. (2007), the estimated market value in 2003 was $50 billion, compared with $16.6 billion for exports.

28. WITS/Comtrade (SITC Revison 3), year 2008, product groups 0 (food and live animals) and 4 (animal and vegetable oils and fats). Imports of cereals (product group 04) represent 39 percent of total imports ($9 billion).

29. Irrigation, seeds, and fertilizer were the main ingredients of the Asian Green Revolution. They were complemented by massive government investments in infrastructure, research, and extension, and by strong price protection and support for both inputs and products.

30. In eastern and southern Africa only, the estimated value of these losses is nearly $2 billion a year (World Bank 2008b), compared with $9 billion in SSA cereal imports.

31. For a detailed analysis of prevailing trade policies and practices in West Africa (Economic Community of West African States and West African Economic and Monetary Union), see Rolland and Alpha 2010.

32. In 6 of 19 SSA regions, livestock product share is more than 20 percent of the gross farm product. All regions in Morocco and all but two in Nicaragua are above this threshold.

33. See, among others, Davis et al. (2002), Satterthwaite and Tacoli (2003), and De Ferrandi et al. (2005).

34. Regarding territorial development, a major international example is the European Union rural development policy and its flagship program, LEADER, which provides regional structural funding. A number of promising and successful territorial development initiatives have occurred or are under way in Latin America. See, for instance, the debates related to the *nueva ruralidad* (new rurality) and the Rural Territorial Dynamics Program managed by the Latin American Center for Rural Development (RIMISP). On *nueva ruralidad* see, among others, Pérez et al. (2008). For a comparison of *nueva ruralidad* and the European multifunctionality approach, see Bonnal et al. (2004).

35. The latter is a recommendation of the WDR09, which favors more spatially blind interventions and limits spatially targeted interventions to the most disadvantaged situations (see box 3.1).

36. Gutman (2007) says that supplying environmental services could boost rural development and inaugurate a new type of rural-urban relationship, which he calls a "new rural-urban compact." How to pay for these services is the major issue and will necessitate an evolution of the policy debate.

37. The agrocluster approach has been successfully developed in several Latin American countries and has facilitated the development of local agrifood systems based on the promotion of local assets. "Geographical indications," which refer to the unique geographical origins of a product (based on specific natural or human factors), are increasingly mentioned in the development debate and are now strongly challenged by trade liberalization policies. They are a major topic of WTO's TRIPS discussions (trade-related aspects of intellectual property rights). On local agrifood systems, see Muchnik et al. (2007). On geographical indications, see Giovannucci et al. (2009).

Appendix: Country Maps

For more information on the surveyed regions, see annex 3 in the appendix posted at http://www.worldbank.org/afr/ruralstruc

Mali

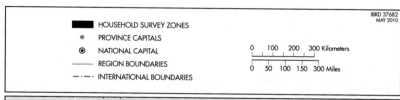

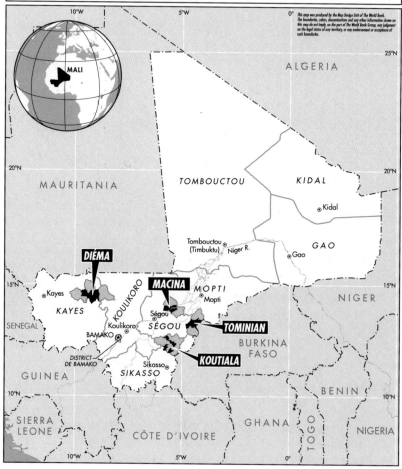

Senegal

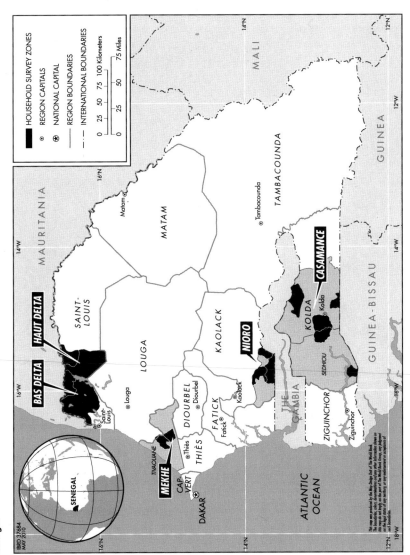

IBRD 37684
MAY 2010

Madagascar

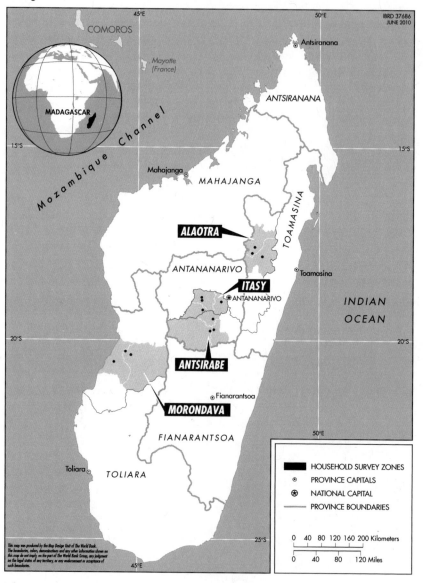

Kenya

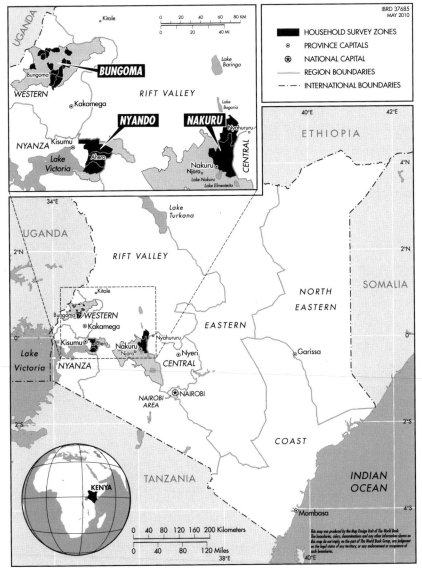

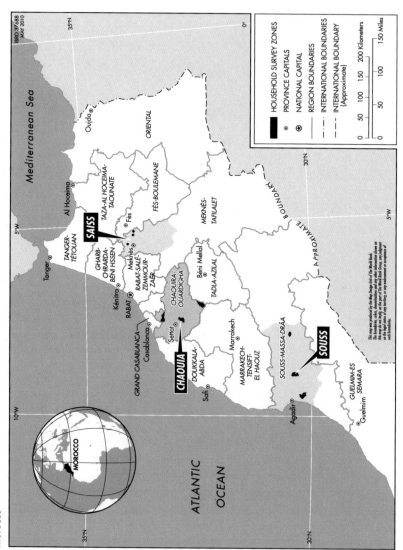

Morocco

Nicaragua

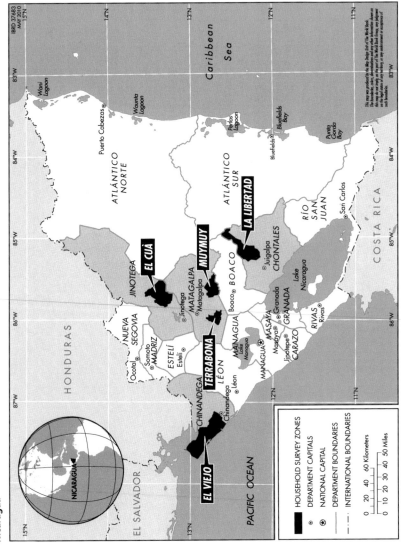

Mexico

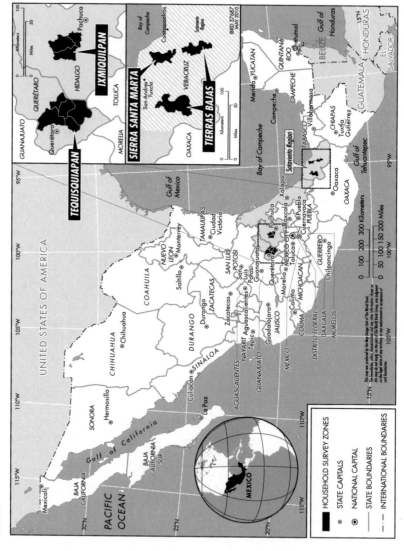

Bibliography

RuralStruc National Reports

Kenya

Gamba, P., and B. Kibaara. 2007. *Structural Implications of Economic Liberalization on Agriculture and Rural Development*. RuralStruc Program Kenya—Phase I. Nairobi: Tegemeo Institute, Egerton University, 145 p.

Kirimi, L., M. Mathengue, J. Olwande, P. Gamba, S. Onyuma, and J. Lagat. 2010. *Globalization and Structural Change in Rural Economies*. RuralStruc Program Kenya—Phase II. Nairobi: Tegemeo Institute, Egerton University, 153 p.

Madagascar

Pierre-Bernard, A., R. Ramboarison, L. Randrianarison, and L. Rondro-Harisoa. 2007. *Dimensions structurelles de la libéralisation pour l'agriculture et le développent rural*. Programme RuralStruc Madagascar—Phase 1. Antananarivo: APB Consulting, EPP-PADR, 267 p.

Rakotonarivo. A., Z. L. Ramialison, C. Martignac, and B. Gastineau. 2008. *Migrations internes et villes secondaires*. Programme RuralStruc Madagascar—Phase 2. Antananarivo: ICM-CIRAD-IRD, 25 p.

Randrianarison, L., N. Andrianirina, and R. Ramboarison. 2009. *Changements structurels des economies rurales dans la mondialisation*. Programme RuralStruc Madagascar—Phase 2. Antananarivo: APB Consulting, EPP-PADR, 285 p.

Mali

Samake, A., J.-F. Bélières, P.-M. Bosc, and O. Sanogo. 2007. *Dimensions structurelles de la libéralisation pour l'agriculture et le développent rural*. Programme RuralStruc Mali—Phase 1. Bamako: CEPIA, 278 p.

Samake, A., J.-F. Bélières, C. Corniaux, N. Dembele, V. Kelly, J. Marzin, O. Sanogo, and J. Staatz. 2008. *Changements structurels des économies rurales dans la mondialisation*. Programme RuralStruc Mali—Phase 2. Bamako: IER-CIRAD-MSU, 464 p.

Mexico

Brun V., E. Léonard, and R. Palma Grayeb. 2009. Inserción competitiva y trayectorias de las economías domésticas en el Sotavento de México. Entre integración agroindustrial y asistencia social. Programa RuralStruc Mexico—Fase II. Jalapa: CEMCA-IRD-Universidad Veracruzana—FLACSO, 33 p.

Rello, F., and F. Saavedra. 2007. *Dimensiones estructurales de la liberalización para la agricultura y desarrollo rural.* Programa RuralStruc Mexico—Fase I. Mexico, DF: FLACSO, 219 p.

Rello, F., F. Saavedra, V. Brun, E. Léonard, R. Palma Grayeb, H. Robles, C. Muñoz, and C. Gonzales. 2010. *Cambios Estructurales de las Economías Rurales en la Globalización.* Programa RuralStruc Mexico—Fase II. Mexico, DF: FLACSO, 340 p.

Morocco

Akesbi, N., D. Benatya, and N. El Aoufi. 2007. *Dimensions structurelles de la libéralisation pour l'agriculture et le développent rural.* Programme RuralStruc Maroc—Phase 1. Rabat: Institut Agronomique et Vétérinaire Hassan II, 181 p.

Icon2e. 2009. *Changements structurels des économies rurales dans la mondialisation.* Programme RuralStruc Maroc—Phase 2. Rabat: Icon2e, 234 p.

Nicaragua

Grigsby Vado, A. H., and F. J. Pérez. 2007. *Structural Implications of Economic Liberalization on Agriculture and Rural Development.* RuralStruc Program Nicaragua—Phase I. Managua: Nitlapán, Universidad Centroamericana, 128 p.

Grigsby Vado, A. H., F. J. Pérez, L. I. Gómez, E. S. García, M. A. Alemán, and Y. L. Marín. 2009. *Cambios Estructurales de las Economías Rurales en la Globalización.* Programa RuralStruc Nicaragua—Fase II. Managua: Nitlapán, Universidad Centroamericana, 191 p.

Senegal

Ba, C. O., B. Diagana, P. N. Dièye, I. Hathie, and M. Niang. 2009. *Changements structurels des économies rurales dans la mondialisation.* Programme RuralStruc Sénégal—Phase 2. Dakar: IPAR-ASPRODEB, 168 p.

Faye, J., C.O. Ba, P. N. Dièye, and M. Dansoko. 2007. *Dimensions structurelles de la libéralisation pour l'agriculture et le développent rural.* Programme RuralStruc Sénégal—Phase 1. Dakar: IPAR-ASPRODEB, 229 p.

Other References

Akram-Lodhi, A. 2008. "(Re)imagining Agrarian Relations? The World Development Report 2008: Agriculture for Development." *Development and Change* 39 (6): 1145–61.

Akram-Lodhi, A., and C. Kay. 2009a. "Surveying the Agrarian Question (Part 1): Unearthing Foundations, Exploring Diversity." *The Journal of Peasant Studies* 37 (1): 177–202.

_____. 2009b. "Surveying the Agrarian Question (Part 2): Current Debates and Beyond." *The Journal of Peasant Studies* 37 (2): 255–84.

_____, eds. 2009c. *Peasants and Globalization. Political Economy, Rural Transformation and the Agrarian Question*. New York: Routledge.

Akyiama, T., J. Baffes, D. F. Larson, and P. Varangis. 2003. "Commodity Markets Reform in Africa. Some Recent Experience." Policy Research Working Paper 2995, World Bank, Washington, DC.

Alexandratos, N. 2005. "Countries with Rapid Population Growth and Resource Constraints: Issues of Food, Agriculture, and Development." *Population and Development Review* 31 (2): 237–58.

Ali, S., and U. Dadush. 2010, "Is the African Renaissance for Real?" Carnegie Endowment for International Peace, *International Economic Bulletin*, September 30, 2010.

Amin, A., and N. Thrift. 1993. "Globalization, Institutional Thickness and Local Prospects." *Revue d'Économie Régionale et Urbaine* 3: 405–27.

Amsden, A. 2001. *The Rise of "The Rest": Challenges to the West from Late-Industrializing Economies*. New York: Oxford University Press.

Anderson, K. 2010. "Krueger/Schiff/Valdés Revisited. Agricultural Price and Trade Policy Reform in Developing Countries since 1960." Policy Research Working Paper 5165. World Bank, Washington, DC, 46 p.

Anderson, K., and W. Martin. 2005. *Agricultural Trade Reform and the Doha Development Agenda*. Washington, DC: World Bank.

Anderson, K., and W. Masters, eds. 2009. *Distortions to Agricultural Incentives in Africa*. Washington, DC: World Bank, 618 p.

Anderson, K., and A. Valdés, eds. 2008. *Distortions to Agricultural Incentives in Latin America*. Washington, DC: World Bank, 618 p.

Anseeuw, W., S. Fréguin-Gresh, and P. Gamba. 2008. "Une nouvelle politique agricole au Kenya: nécessaire mais suffisante?" In *Défis agricoles africains*, ed. J.-C. Devèze, 209–29. Paris: Karthala-AFD.

Appendini, K. 2001. *De la milpa a los tortibonos. La restructuración de la política alimentaria en México*. México, DF: El Colegio de México-UNRISD, 290 p.

_____. 2008. "Tracing the Maize-Tortilla Chain." *UN Chronicle* XLV: (3–4).

Appendini, K., and G. R. Gómez. Forthcoming. *La Paradoja de la Calidad. Los alimentos mexicanos en la región de América del Norte*. Mexico, DF: Pieran-El Colegio de México.

Arbache, J., and J. Page. 2007. "More Growth or Fewer Collapses? A New Look at Long Run Growth in Sub-Saharan Africa." Policy Research Working Paper 4384, World Bank, Washington, DC.

Arrighi, G., and L. Zhang. Forthcoming. "Beyond the Washington Consensus: A New Bandung?" In *Globalization and Beyond: New Examinations of Global Power and Its Alternatives*, ed. J. Shefner and P. Fernandez-Kelly. University Park: Pennsylvania State University Press.

Asfaw, S., D. Mithöfer, and H. Waibel. 2007. "What Impact Are EU Supermarket Standards Having on Developing Countries Export of High-Value Horticultural Products? Evidence from Kenya." Contributed paper at the 105th EAAE Seminar "International Marketing and International Trade of Quality Food Products," Bologna, Italy, March 8–10, 2007.

Augustins, G. 1989. *Comment se perpétuer? Devenir des lignées et destins des patrimoines dans les paysanneries européennes.* Paris: Société d'ethnologie, 434 p.

Bairoch, P. 1997. *Victoires et déboires. Histoire économique et sociale du monde du XVIè siècle à nos jours.* Paris: Gallimard-Folio.

Barrett, C. B., and M. R. Carter. 2001. "Can't Get Ahead for Falling Behind: New Directions for Development Policy to Escape Poverty and Relieve Traps." *Choices* 16: 35–38.

———. 2004. *The Economics of Poverty Traps and Persistent Poverty: An Asset-Based Approach.* Madison: BASIS-CRSP, University of Wisconsin.

Barrett, C. B., and E. Mutambatsere. 2005. "Agricultural Markets in Developing Countries." In *The New Palgrave Dictionary of Economics,* 2nd ed., ed. L. E. Blume and S. N. Durlauf. London: Palgrave Macmillan.

Barrett, C. B., and T. Reardon. 2000. *Asset, Activity, and Income Diversification among African Agriculturalists: Some Practical Issues.* Ithaca, NY: Cornell University.

Barrett, C. B., T. Reardon, and P. Webb. 2001. "Nonfarm Income Diversification and Household Livelihood Strategies in Rural Africa: Concepts, Dynamics, and Policy Implications." *Food Policy* 26: 315–31.

Barrett, C. B., and B. M. Swallow. 2005. "Dynamic Poverty Traps and Rural Livelihoods." In *Rural Livelihoods and Poverty Reduction Policies,* ed. F. Ellis and H. A. Freeman, 16–28. London: Routledge.

Barthélémy, D., H. Delorme, B. Losch, C. Moreddu, and M. Nieddu, eds. 2003. "La multifonctionnalité de l'activité agricole et sa reconnaissance par les politiques publiques." *Actes du colloque international de la Société française d'économie rurale,* March 21–22, 2002. Dijon: Educagri, 922 p.

Bates, R. H. 1981. *Markets and States in Tropical Africa. The Political Basis of Agricultural Policies.* Berkeley: University of California Press.

Bélières, J.-F., P.-M. Bosc, G. Faure, S. Fournier, and B. Losch. 2002. "What Future for West Africa's Family Farms in a World Market Economy?" Issue Paper No. 113. International Institute for Environment and Development, London, 42 p.

Berger, S. 2002. *Our First Globalization: Lessons from the French.* Cambridge, MA: MIT.

Berthelier, P., and A. Lipchitz. 2005. "Quel rôle joue l'agriculture dans la croissance et le développement?" *Revue Tiers Monde* XLVI (183): 603–20.

Bezemer, D., and D. Headey. 2008. "Agriculture, Development, and Urban Bias." *World Development* 36 (8): 1342–64.

Binswanger-Mkhize, H. P., A. F. McCalla, and P. Patel. 2009. "Structural Transformation and African Agriculture." Africa Emerging Markets Forum, Western Cape, South Africa, September 13–15.

Birdsall, N. 2006. "Stormy Days on an Open Field: Asymmetries in the Global Economy." Working Paper 81. Center for Global Development, Washington, DC.

Birdsall, N., D. Rodrik, and A. Subramanian. 2005. "How to Help Poor Countries." *Foreign Affairs* 84 (4): 136–52.

Black, R., C. Natali, and J. Skinner. 2005. "Migration and Inequality." World Development Report 2006, Background Papers. Development Research Centre on Migration, Globalisation and Poverty, University of Sussex.

Bloom, D., D. Canning, and J. Sevilla. 2001. "Economic Growth and the Demographic Transition." Working Paper No. 8665, National Bureau of Economic Research (NBER), Cambridge, MA.

Bonnal, P., P.-M. Bosc, J.M. Diaz, and B. Losch. 2004. "Multifincionalidad de la agricultura y Nueva Ruralidad ¿Reestructuración de las políticas públicas a la hora de la globalización?" In *Desarollo Rural y Nueva Ruralidad en América Latina y la Unión Europea*, comp. C. E. Pérez and M.A. Farah Q., 19–41.

Bossard, L., ed. 2009. "Atlas régional de l'Afrique de l'Ouest." *Cahiers de l'Afrique de l'Ouest.* Paris: OCDE—Club du Sahel et de l'Afrique de l'Ouest, 291 p.

Bouët, A., J.-C. Bureau, Y. Decreux, and S. Jean. 2005. "Multilateral Agricultural Trade Liberalisation: The Contrasting Fortunes of Developing Countries in the Doha Round." *World Economy* 28 (9): 1329–54.

Bourguignon, F., and C. Morrisson. 1998. "Inequality and Development: The Role of Dualism." *Journal of Development Economics* 57 (2): 233–57.

Boussard, J.-M., F. Gérard, and M.-G. Piketty. 2005. *Libéraliser l'agriculture mondiale? Théorie, modèles et réalités.* Montpelier, France: CIRAD.

Boussard, J.-M., F. Gérard, M.-G. Piketty, M. Ayouz, and T. Voituriez. 2006. "Endogenous Risks and Long Run Effects of Liberalization on a Global Analysis Framework." *Economic Modelling* 23 (3): 457–75.

Braudel, F. 1979. *Civilisation matérielle, Economie et Capitalisme. XVe-XVIIIe siècle.* 3 vols. Paris: Armand Colin.

Bricas, N., B. Zoungrana, and M.-C. Thirion. 2009. *Bassins de production et de consommation des cultures vivrières en Afrique de l'Ouest et du Centre.* Montpelier, France: CIRAD, CILSS, and AFD.

Brooks, K. 2010. "African Agriculture—What Do We Not Know? What Do We Need to Know?" AAEA Annual Meeting, Denver, July 26.

Brun, V. 2008. "Secteur privé et céréaliculture familiale dans le Mexique du libre-échange. Une étude dans les terres basses du sud-Veracruz. *Economie Rurale* (303-304-305): 90–107.

Bryceson, D. F. 1999. *African Rural Labour, Income Diversification and Livelihood Approaches: A Long-Term Development Perspective.* Leiden, Netherlands: Afrika-Studiecentrum.

———. 2002. "The Scramble in Africa: Reorienting Rural Livelihoods." *World Development* 30 (5): 725–39.

Bureau, J.-C., S. Jean, and A. Matthews. 2006 "The Consequences of Agricultural Trade Liberalization for Developing Countries: Distinguishing between Genuine Benefits and False Hopes" *World Trade Review* 5: 225–49.

Byerlee, D., and K. Deininger. 2010. "The Rise of Large Farms: Drivers and Development Outcomes." *WIDER Angle Newsletter,* November–December.

Byerlee, D., T. S. Jayne, and R. Myers. 2005. *Managing Food Price Risks and Instability in an Environment of Market Liberalization.* Washington, DC: World Bank.

Carletto, G., K. Covarrubias, B. Davis, M. Krausova, K. Stamoulis, P. Winters, and A. Zezza. 2007. "Rural Income Generating Activities in Developing Countries: Reassessing the Evidence." *Journal of Agricultural and Development Economics* 4 (1): 146–93.

Caron, P., and T. Le Cotty. 2006. *A Review of the Different Concepts of Multifunctionality and Their Evolution.* Multagri Project, European Series on Multifunctionality, no. 10. Anthony: CEMAGREF-INRA-CIRAD, 179 p.

Carton de Grammont, H. 2009. "La desagrarización del campo mexicano." *Convergencia* 50: 13–55.

Chang, H.-J. 2002. *Kicking Away the Ladder: Development Strategy in Historical Perspective.* London: Anthem Press.

Chenery, H., and M. Syrquin. 1975. *Patterns of Development: 1950–70.* New York: Oxford University Press.

Christiaensen, L., and L. Demery. 2007. *Down to Earth. Agriculture and Poverty Reduction in Africa.* Washington, DC: World Bank, 105 p.

Christiaensen, L., and Y. Todo. 2009. *Poverty Reduction during the Rural-Urban Transformation—The Role of the Missing Middle.* Washington, DC: World Bank.

Cline, W. R. 2007. *Global Warming and Agriculture: Impact Estimates by Country.* Washington, DC: Center for Global Development and Peterson Institute for International Economics.

Club du Sahel-OECD. 1998. *Preparing for the Future—A Vision of West Africa in the Year 2020.* West Africa Long-Term Perspective Study (WALTPS). Paris: Club du Sahel and OECD, 157 pp.

Codron, J.-M., Z. Bouhsina, F. Fort, E. Coudel, and A. Puech. 2004. "Supermarkets in Low-Income Mediterranean Countries: Impacts on Horticulture Systems." *Development Policy Review* 22 (5): 587–602.

Collier, D., and J. Mahoney. 1996. "Insights and Pitfalls: Selection Bias in Qualitative Research?" *World Politics* 49 (1): 56–91.

Collier, P. 2007. *The Bottom Billion: Why the Poorest Countries Are Failing and What Can Be Done about It.* Oxford, UK: Oxford University Press.

_____. 2008. "The Politics of Hunger: How Illusion and Greed Fan the Food Crisis." *Foreign Affairs* 87 (6).

_____. 2009. "Africa's Organic Peasantry. Beyond Romanticism." *Harvard International Review* 32 (2): 62–65.

Collomb, P. 1999. *Une voie étroite pour la sécurité alimentaire d'ici à 2050.* Rome: FAO; Paris: Economica.

Cook, J., O. Cylke, D. Larson, J. Nash, and P. Stedman-Edwards, eds. 2010. *Vulnerable Places, Vulnerable People. Trade Liberalization, Rural Poverty and the Environment.* Washington, DC: World Bank; Northampton and Cheltenham: Edward Elgar.

Corral, L., and T. Reardon. 2001. "Rural Nonfarm Incomes in Nicaragua." *World Development* 29 (3): 427–42.

Cortes, G. 2000. *Partir pour rester. Survie et mutation de sociétés paysannes andines (Bolivie).* Paris: IRD Éditions, 413 p.

Cotula, L., S. Vermeulen, R. Leonard, and J. Keeley. 2009. *Land Grab or Development Opportunity? Agricultural Investment and International Land Deals in Africa.* London and Rome: IIED, FAO, and IFAD.

Coulomb, P., H. Delorme, H. Hervieu, M. Jollivet, and P. Lacombe. 1990. *Les agriculteurs et la politique.* Paris: Presses de la Fondation Nationale des Sciences Politiques, 594 p.

Dabat, M. H., B. Gastineau, O. Jenn-Treyer, J.-P. Roland, C. Martignac, and A. Pierre-Bernard. 2008. "L'agriculture malgache peut-elle sortir de l'impasse démo-économique?" *Autrepart* 46: 189–202.

Daniels, R. 2003. *Guarding the Golden Door—American Immigration Policy and Immigrants since 1882.* New York: Hill and Wang, 328 p.

Davis, B., T. Reardon, K. G. Stamoulis, and P. Winters, eds. 2002. *Promoting Farm/Non-farm Linkages for Rural Development. Case Studies from Africa and Latin America.* Rome: FAO.

Davis, B., P. Winters, G. Carletto, K. Covarrubias, E. Quinones, A. Zezza, K. Stamoulis, G. Bonomi, and S. DiGiuseppe. 2007. "Rural Income Generating Activities: A Cross Country Comparison." Background Paper for the World Development Report 2008. World Bank and FAO, Washington, DC.

Davis, M. 2006. *The Planet of Slums.* New York and London: Verso.

Deaton, A., and S. Zaldi. 2002. "Guidelines for Constructing Consumption Aggregates for Welfare Analysis." LSMS Working Paper 135. World Bank, Washington, DC, 104 p.

De Ferrandi, D., E. P. Perry, W. Foster, D. Lederman, and A. Valdés. 2005. *Beyond the City. The Rural Contribution to Development.* Washington, DC: World Bank.

Deininger, K., and L. Squire. 1996. "A New Data Set Measuring Income Inequality." *The World Bank Economic Review* 10 (3): 565–91.

_____. 1998. "New Ways of Looking at Old Issues: Inequality and Growth." *Journal of Development Economics* 57 (2): 259–87.

De Ita, A. 2008. *Fourteen Years of NAFTA and the Tortilla Crisis.* Americas Program Special Report. Washington, DC: Center for International Policy.

De Janvry, A. 2009. "Agriculture for Development: New Paradigm and Options for Success." Elmhirst Lecture, IAAE Conference, Beijing, August 16–22.

De Janvry, A., and E. Sadoulet. 2001. "Income Strategies among Rural Households in Mexico: The Role of Off-farm Activities." *World Development* 29 (3): 467–80.

Delgado, C., J. Hopkins, and V. Kelly. 1998. *Agricultural Growth Linkages in Sub-Saharan Africa.* Research Report 107. Washington, DC: International Food Policy Research Institute (IFPRI).

Del Rey Poveda, A. 2008. "Determinants and Consequences of Internal and International Migration: The Case of Rural Populations in the South of Veracruz, Mexico." *Demographic Research* 16: 288–313.

Denis, E., and F. Moriconi-Ebrard, eds. 2009. *Africapolis. Urbanization Trends 1950–2020: A Geo-statistical Approach. West Africa.* Paris: Agence française de développement (AFD).

Dercon, S., and P. Krishnan. 1998. *Changes in Poverty in Rural Ethiopia 1989–1995: Measurement, Robustness Tests and Decomposition.* Discussion Paper Series DPS 98.19. Leuven, Belgium: Centre for the Study of African Economies—Katholieke Universiteit.

Devèze, J.-C., ed. 2010. *Challenges for African Agriculture.* Washington, DC: World Bank and Agence française de développement, 267 p.

Diao, X., P. Hazell, D. Resnick, and J. Thurlow. 2007. *The Role of Agriculture in Development: Implications for Sub-Saharan Africa.* Research Report 153. Washington, DC: IFPRI.

Djurfeldt, G., H. Holmén, M. Jirström, and R. Larsson, eds. 2005. *The African Food Crisis: Lessons from the Asian Green Revolution.* Oxfordshire, UK: CABI, 285 p.

DNSI (Direction Nationale de la Statistique et de l'Informatique). 2004. *Enquête malienne sur l'évaluation de la pauvreté (EMEP), 2001. Principaux résultats.* Bamako, Mali: Ministère du Plan et de l'aménagement du territoire and Banque mondiale.

Dolan, C., and J. Humphrey. 2000. "Governance and Trade in Fresh Vegetables: the Impact of UK Supermarkets on the African Horticulture Industry." *Journal of Development Studies* 37 (2): 147–76.

Dudwick, N., K. Hull, R. Katayama, F. Shilpi, and K. Simler. 2011. *From Farm to Firm. Rural-Urban Transition in Developing Countries.*Washington, DC: World Bank, 235 p.

Echanove, F., and C. Steffen. 2005. "Agribusiness and Farmers in Mexico: the Importance of Contractual Relations." *The Geographical Journal* 171 (2): 166–76.

e-Geopolis. *Population of Urban Areas of 10,000 Habitants or More.* http://e-geopolis.eu/.

El Hadad, F. 1995. "Enjeux et perspectives de la filière agrumes du Maroc." *Options Méditerranéennes* B 14: 249–64.

Ellis, F. 1998. "Household Strategies and Rural Livelihood Diversification." *The Journal of Development Studies* 35 (1): 1–38.

_____. 2000. *Rural Livelihoods and Diversity in Developing Countries.* Oxford, UK: Oxford University Press.

_____. 2004. *Occupational Diversification in Developing Countries and Implications for Agricultural Policy.* Programme of Advisory and Support Services to DFID (PASS). Project No. WB0207. London: Department of International Development (DFID).

English, P., S. Jaffee, and J. Okello. 2006. "Exporting Out of Africa. The Kenyan Horticulture Success Story." In *Attacking Africa's Poverty. Experience from the Ground,* ed. L. Fox and R. Liebenthal, 117–47. Washington, DC: World Bank.

Evans, P. 1995. *Embedded Autonomy. States and Industrial Transformation.* Princeton, NJ: Princeton University Press.

Fafchamps, M. 2004. *Market Institutions in Sub-Saharan Africa.* Cambridge, MA: MIT Press.

Faivre Dupaigre, B. 2007. *APE et dynamiques des flux régionaux : une application aux pays de la CEDEAO.* Coll. "Documents de travail." Paris: Agence française de développement (AFD).

_____. 2007. *The Roles of Agriculture in Development: The Policy Implications and Guidance. Research Programme Summary Report.* Rome: FAO, 27 p.

Fan, S., ed. 2008. *Public Expenditures, Growth, and Poverty: Lessons from Developing Countries.* Baltimore, MD: Johns Hopkins University Press and IFPRI.

Fay, M., and C. Opal. 2000. "Urbanization without Growth. A Not-So-Uncommon Phenomenon." Policy Research Working Paper No. 2412, World Bank, Washington, DC.

Ferry, B., eds. 2007. *L'Afrique face à ces défis démographiques*. Paris: Karthala, Centre Population et Développement (CEPED), and Agence française de développement (AFD).

Food and Agriculture Organization (FAO). 2001. *Food Balance Sheets. A Handbook*. Rome: FAO.

———. 2004. *The State of Food Insecurity in the World*. Rome: FAO.

Foster, V., and C. Briceño-Garmendia, eds. 2010. *Africa's Infrastructure: A Time for Transformation*. Washington, DC: World Bank and Agence française de développement, 355 p.

Fox, L., and R. Liebenthal, eds. 2006. *Attacking Africa's Poverty. Experience from the Ground*. Washington, DC: World Bank, 389 p.

Fréguin-Gresh, S., C. O. Ba, J.-F. Bélières, B. Losch, and L. Randrianarison. 2010. "Pauvreté, diversification rurale et transitions africaines : état des lieux et perspectives à partir d'analyses croisées de situations régionales dans quatre pays." Colloque international sur l'agriculture africaine, Centre d'Etudes, de Documentation et de Recherche Economiques et Sociales (CEDRES), Ouagadougou, December 6–8.

Friedmann, H., and P. McMichael. 1989. "Agriculture and the State System: the Rise and Fall of National Agricultures, 1870 to Present." *Sociologia Ruralis* 29 (2): 93–117.

Fuglie, K. O. 2009. "Agricultural Productivity in Sub-Saharan Africa." Symposium on The Food and Financial Crises and Their Impacts on the Achievement of the Millennium Development Goals, Cornell University, Ithaca, NY, May 1–2.

Gabas, J.-J., and B. Losch. 2008. "Fabrication and Illusions of Emergence." In *Emerging States: The Wellspring of a New World Order*, ed. Ch. Jaffrelot, 13–27.

Galtier, F. 2009. "How to Manage Food Price Instability in Developing Countries?" Working Paper Moisa No. 4. CIRAD, Montpelier, France.

Gastellu, J.-M., and J.-Y. Marchal, eds. 1997. *La ruralité dans les pays du Sud à la fin du XX° siècle*. Montpelier, France: Office de la Recherche Scientifique et Technique Outremer (ORSTOM).

Gazel, H., D. Harre, and F. Moriconi-Ebrard, eds. 2010. *Africapolis II, L'urbanisation en Afrique centrale et orientale*. Paris: Agence française de développement/e-Geopolis.

Gendreau, F. 2010. "The Demographic Challenges." In *Challenges for African Agriculture*, ed. J.-C. Devèze, 9–33.

Gibbon, P., and S. Ponte. 2005. *Trading down: Africa, Value Chains, and the Global Economy*. Philadelphia: Temple University Press, 251 p.

Giordano, T., and B. Losch. 2007. "Transition: Risques d'impasse?" *Courrier de la planète* (81–82): 22–26.

Giovannucci, D., T. Josling, W. Kerr, B. O'Connor, and M. T. Yeung. 2009. *Guide to Geographical Indications. Linking Products and Their Origins*. Geneva: International Trade Centre, 207 p.

Giraud, J.-N. 1996. *L'inégalité du monde. Économie du monde contemporain*. Paris: Gallimard.

Goody, J. 2006. *The Theft of History*. Cambridge: Cambridge University Press.

Gore, C. 2003. "Globalization, the International Poverty Trap and Chronic Poverty in the Least Develop Countries." CPRC Working Paper No 30. United Nations Conference on Trade and Development (UNCTAD), Geneva.

Groupe Polanyi. 2008. *La multifonctionnalité de l'agriculture—Une dialectique entre marché et identité.* Versailles: Editions Quae, 360 p.

Guengant, J.-P. 2007. "La démographie africaine entre convergence et divergence." In *L'Afrique face à ces défis démographiques,* ed. B. Ferry, 27–121.

Guengant, J.-P., and J. F. May. 2009. "Proximate Determinants of Fertility in Sub-Saharan Africa and Their Possible Use in Fertility Projection." United Nations Expert Group Meeting, Population Division, United Nations, New York, December 2–4.

Gutman, P. 2007. "Ecosystem Services: Foundations for a New Rural–Urban Compact." *Ecological Economics* 62: 382–87.

Haggblade, S. 2007. "Alternative Perceptions of the Rural Nonfarm Economy." In *Transforming the Rural Nonfarm Economy,* ed. S. Haggblade, P. Hazell, and T Reardon, 25–54.

Haggblade S., P. Hazell, and T. Reardon, eds. 2007. *Transforming the Rural Nonfarm Economy: Opportunities and Threats in the Developing World.* Washington, DC: IFPRI; Baltimore, MD: The Johns Hopkins University Press, 490 p.

_____. 2010. "The Rural Nonfarm Economy: Prospects for Growth and Poverty Reduction." *World Development* 38 (10): 1429–41.

Harre, D., F. Moriconi-Ebrard, and H. Gazel. 2010. "Fiche République du Kenya." In *Africapolis II, L'urbanisation en Afrique centrale et orientale,* ed. H. Gazel, D. Harre, and F. Moriconi-Ebrard. Paris: Agence française de développement/e-Geopolis.

Harris, S. 1992. *Kenya Horticultural Subsector Survey.* Nairobi: Kenya Export Development support project.

Hart, G. 2010. "Redrawing the Map of the World? Reflections on the World Development Report 2009." *Economic Geography* 86 (4): 341–50.

Hatton, T. J., and G. W. Williamson. 2005. *Global Migration and the World Economy. Two Centuries of Policy and Performance.* Cambridge, MA: MIT Press.

Hausmann, R., D. Rodrik, and A. Velasco. 2005. *Growth Diagnostics.* Cambridge, MA: John F. Kennedy School of Government, Harvard University, 35 p.

Hazell, P., S. Haggblade, and T. Reardon. 2007. "Structural Transformation of the Rural Nonfarm Economy." *Transforming the Rural Nonfarm Economy,* ed. S. Haggblade, P. Hazell, and T. Reardon, 83–98.

Hazell, P., C. Poulton, S. Wiggins, and A. Dorward. 2007. "The Future of Small Farms for Poverty Reduction and Growth." 2020 Discussion Paper 42. IFPRI, Washington, DC.

Headey, D., D. Bezemer, and P. Hazell. 2010. "Agricultural Employment Trends in Asia and Africa: Too Fast or Too Slow?" *The World Bank Research Observer* 25 (1): 57–89.

Hoekman, B., and L. A. Winters. 2005. "Trade and Employment: Stylized Facts and Research Findings." World Bank Policy Research Paper 3676, World Bank, Washington, DC, 36 p.

IAASTD (International Assessment of Agricultural Knowledge, Science and Technology for Development). 2009. *Agriculture at Crossroads. Synthesis Report.* Washington, DC: IAASTD, 95 p.

IFAD (International Fund for Agricultural Development). 2010. *Rural Poverty Report 2011. New Realities, New Challenges: New Opportunities for Tomorrow's Generation.* Rome: IFAD, 319 p.

ILC (International Land Coalition). 2009. *Increasing Commercial Pressure on Land: Building a Coordinated Response.* Rome: ILC.

INSTAT (Institut national de la statistique). 2009. *4ème recensement général de la population et de l'habitat du Mali.* Bamako, Mali: INSTAT.

Jaffee, S. 1994. "Contract Farming in the Shadow of Competitive Markets: The Experience of Kenyan Horticulture." In *Living under Contract: Contract Farming and Agrarian Transformation in Sub-Saharan Africa,* ed. P. Little and M. Watts, 97–139. Madison: University of Wisconsin Press.

_____. 1995. "The Many Faces of Success: The Development of Kenyan Horticultural Exports." In *Marketing Africa's High Value Foods,* ed. S. Jaffee and J. Morton. Washington, DC: World Bank.

_____. 2003. "From Challenge to Opportunity: The Transformation of the Kenyan Fresh Vegetable Trade in the Context of Emerging Food Safety and Other Standards." ARD Discussion Paper 1, World Bank, Washington, DC.

Jaffrelot, Ch., ed. 2008. *Emerging States: The Wellspring of a New World Order.* London: C. Hurst & Co.

Johnston, B. F., and P. Kilby. 1975. *Agriculture and Structural Transformation: Economic Strategies in Late-Developing Countries.* Oxford, UK: Oxford University Press.

Jütting, J., and J. R. De Laiglesia. 2009. *Is Informal Normal? Towards More and Better Jobs in Developing Countries.* Paris: OECD.

Kirsten, J., and K. Sartorius. 2002. "Linking Agribusiness and Small-Scale Farmers in Developing Countries: Is There a New Role for Contract Farming?" *Development Southern Africa* 17 (4): 503–29.

Kydd, J. 2002 "Agriculture and Rural Livelihoods: Is Globalization Opening or Blocking Paths out of Rural Poverty?" AgREN Network Paper, 121, Overseas Development Institute (ODI), London.

Lamarche, H. 1991. *L'agriculture familiale.* Vol. 1: *Une réalité polymorphe.* Paris: L'Harmattan.

Larson, D., and Y. Mundlak. 1997. "On the Intersectoral Migration of Agricultural Labor." *Economic Development and Cultural Change* 42 (2): 295–319.

Lederman, D., W. F. Maloney, and L. Servén. 2005. *Lessons from NAFTA for Latin America and the Caribbean.* Palo Alto, CA: Stanford University Press; Washington, DC: World Bank, 407 p.

Léonard, E. 2010. "Libéralisation et régulation privée du secteur agroalimentaire du maïs au Mexique au temps de l'ALENA. Note pour le RuralStruc Program." Washington, DC: processed, 8 p.

Léonard, E., and B. Losch. 2009. "La inserción de la agricultura mexicana en el mercado norteamericano: cambios estructurales, mutaciones de la acción pública y recomposición de la economía rural y regional." *Foro internacional* 49 (1): 5–46.

Léonard, E., and R. Palma. 2002. "Désagrarisation de l'économie paysanne et 'refonctionnalisation' de la localité rurale au Mexique." *Cahiers des Amériques Latines* (39): 155–73.

Léonard, E., A. Quesnel, and A. del Rey. 2004. "De la comunidad territorial al archipiélago familiar: Movilidad, contractualizacion de la relaciones intergeneracionales y desarrollo local en el sur del estado de Veracruz." *Estudios sociologicos* XXII (66): 557–89.

Lewis, A. W. 1954. "Economic Development with Unlimited Supplies of Labour." *The Manchester School* 28 (2): 139–91.

Lin, J. 2010. "New Structural Economics. A Framework for Rethinking Development." Policy Research Paper 5197, World Bank, Washington, DC.

Lin, J., and H-J. Chang. 2009. "DPR Debate: Should Industrial Policy in Developing Countries Conform to Comparative Advantage or Defy It? A Debate between Justin Lin and Ha-Joon Chang." *Development Policy Review* 27 (5): 483–502.

Lipchitz, A., C. Torre, and P. Chedanne. 2010, "Toward a Regional Food Market Priority." In *Challenges for African Agriculture*, ed. J.-C. Devèze. Washington, DC: World Bank— Agence française de développement, 153–178.

Lipton, M. 1977. *Why Poor People Stay Poor: A Study of Urban Bias in World Development*. London: Temple Smith.

Little, P., and M. Watts, eds. 1994. *Living under Contract: Contract Farming and Agrarian Transformation in Sub-Saharan Africa*. Madison: University of Wisconsin Press, 285 p.

Losch, B. 2004. "Debating the Multifunctionality of Agriculture: from Trade Negotiations to Development Policies by the South." *Journal of Agrarian Change* 4 (3): 336–60.

_____. 2006. "Les limites des discussions internationales sur la libéralisation de l'agriculture: les oublis du débat et les 'oubliés de l'histoire'." *OCL* 13 (4): 272–77.

_____. 2007. "Quel statut pour l'instabilité des prix dans les changements structurels des agricultures des Suds?" In *La régulation des marchés agricoles internationaux: un enjeu décisif pour le développement*, ed. J.-M. Boussard and H. Delorme, 113–131. Paris: L'Harmattan.

_____. 2008. "Migrations and the Challenge of Demographic and Economic Transitions in the New Globalization Era." Social Science Research Council, Migration and Development: Future for Research and Policy, New York, February 28–March 1, 15 p.

_____. 2010a. "The Need for Inclusive Agricultural Growth at the Heart of Africa's Economic Transition." In *Challenges for African Agriculture*, ed. J-C. Devèze, 35–58.

_____. 2010b. "Beyond Trade: Economic Transition in the Globalization Era and Prospects for Poverty and Environment." In *Vulnerable Places, Vulnerable People. Trade Liberalization, Rural Poverty and the Environment*, ed. J. Cook et al., 198–209.

_____. 2010c. "An Urgent Need for Structural Policies." *Spore* 146: 16.

Losch, B., and S. Fréguin-Gresh. Forthcoming. "Quels rôles pour quelles agricultures face aux défis des transitions africaines? Le *small-scale* versus *large-scale* en débat." *Cahiers Agricultures*.

Losch, B., S. Fréguin-Gresh, and T. Giordano. 2008. "Structural Dimensions of Liberalization on Agriculture and Rural Development. Background, Positioning and Results of the First Phase." Washington, DC: World Bank, processed, 187 p.

Losch, B., N. Laudié, F. Varlet, and F. Ruf. 1997. *Politiques publiques et agriculture: une mise en perspective des cas mexicains, camerounais et indonésien*. Montpelier, France: CIRAD, Coll. Repères.

Lucas, R. E. B. 2005. *International Migration and Economic Development: Lessons from Low-Income Countries.* Northampton and Cheltenham, UK: Edward Elgar.

_____. 2008. *International Labor Migration in a Globalizing Economy.* Carnegie Paper # 92. Washington, DC: Carnegie Endowment for International Peace.

Maertens, M., L. Dries, F. A. Dedehouanou, and J. F. M. Swinnen. 2006. "High-Value Supply Chains, Food Standards and Rural Households in Senegal." Working Paper no. 9, Interdisciplinary Research Group on International Agreements and Sustainable Development, Leuven, Belgium.

Maertens, M., and J. F. M. Swinnen. 2007. "Trade, Standards, and Poverty: Evidence from Senegal." Discussion Paper 177. University of Leuven, LICOS Centre for Institutions and Economic Performance & Department of Economics, Leuven, Belgium, 35 p.

Mahoney, J. 2001. "Path-Dependent Explanations of Regime Change: Central America in Comparative Perspective." *Studies in Comparative International Development* 36 (1): 111–41.

Maimbo, S. M., and D. Ratha. 2005. *Remittances. Development Impact and Future Prospects.* Washington, DC: World Bank, 378 p.

Mazoyer, M. 2001. *Protecting Small Farmers and the Rural Poor in the Context of Globalization.* Rome: FAO.

Mazoyer, M., and L. Roudart. 1997. *Histoire des agricultures du monde.* Paris: Le Seuil.

McCulloch, N., and M. Ota. 2002. "Export Horticulture and Poverty in Kenya." Working Paper 174. Institute of Development Studies (IDS), Brighton, UK, 40 p.

McKinsey Global Institute. 2010. *Lions on the Move: The Progress and Potential of African Economies.* San Francisco, CA: McKinsey & Co.

McMichael, P. 1996. *Development and Social Change. A Global Perspective.* Thousand Oaks, CA: Sage; New Delhi: Pine Forge Press.

_____. 2009. "A Food Regime Genealogy." *The Journal of Peasant Studies* 36 (1): 139–69.

Mesplé-Somps, S., A.-S. Robilliard, J. Gräb, D. Cogneau, and M. Grimm. 2008. *Impact de la culture du coton sur les conditions de vie des ménages. Etude sur le Mali et le Burkina Faso.* Paris: DIAL.

Mortimer, M. 2003. "The Future of Family Farms in West Africa. What Can We Learn from Long-Term Data?" Issue paper no. 119. International Institute for Environment and Development, London, 72 p.

Muchnik, J., D. Requier-Desjardins, D. Sautier, and J.-M. Touzard. 2007. "Les systèmes agro-alimentaires localisés (SYAL): Introduction." *Economies et Sociétés*, Série "Systèmes agroalimentaires," AG 29 (9): 1465–84.

Muendo, K. M., and D. Tschirley. 2004. "Improving Kenya's Domestic Horticultural Production and Marketing System: Current Competitiveness, Forces of Change, and Challenges for the Future." Working Paper No. 08C/2004, Tegemeo Institute of Agricultural Policy and Development, Egerton University, Nairobi, Kenya.

Ndulu, B. 2006. "Infrastructure, Regional Integration and Growth in Sub-Saharan Africa: Dealing with the Disadvantages of Geography and Sovereign Fragmentation." *Journal of African Economies* 15, SUPP/2: 212–44.

Neven, D., and T. Reardon. 2004. "The Rise of Kenyan Supermarkets and the Evolution of Their Horticulture Product Procurement Systems." *Development Policy Review* 22 (6): 669–99.

O'Rourke, K. H., and J. G. Williamson. 1999. *Globalization and History: The Evolution of the Nineteenth-Century Atlantic Economy.* Cambridge, MA: MIT Press.

Oudin, X. 2003. "Transition démographique et transformations sociales dans les pays en développement." *Economies et sociétés,* Série développement 5 (41).

Oya, C. 2009. "The World Development Report 2008: Inconsistencies, Silences, and the Myth of 'Win-Win' Scenarios." *The Journal of Peasant Studies* 36 (3): 593–601.

Pachauri, R. K., and A. Reisinger, eds. 2007. *Contribution of Working Groups I, II and III to the Fourth Assessment Report of the Intergovernmental Panel on Climate Change.* Geneva: Intergovernmental Panel on Climate Change, 104 p.

Paulais, T. 2010. "Financing African Cities: Changing Scale and Changing Paradigm." *Villes en développement* 88.

———. Forthcoming. *Financing Africa's Cities.* Washington, DC: World Bank–AFD–Cities Alliance.

Peréz, C. E., and M. A. Farah Q., eds. 2004. *Desarollo Rural y Nueva Ruralidad en América Latina y la Unión Europea.* Bogotá: Pontificia Universidad Javeriana; Paris: CIRAD.

Peréz, C. E., M. A. Farah Q., and H. Carton Grammont, eds. 2008. *La nueva ruralidad en América Latina: avances teóricos y evidencias empíricas.* Bogotá: Pontificia Universidad Javeriana, 380 p.

Peréz, M., S. Schlesinger, and T. Wise. 2008. *The Promise and Perils of Agricultural Trade Liberalization. Lessons from Latin America.* Washington, DC: WOLA (Washington Office on Latin America); Boston, MA: GDAE at Tufts University, 36 p.

Pierson, P. 2000. "Increasing Returns, Path Dependence, and the Study of Politics." *The American Political Science Review* 94 (2): 251–67.

Polaski, S. 2006. *Winners and Losers: Impact of the Doha Round on Developing Countries.* Washington, DC: Carnegie Endowment for International Peace.

Pomeranz, K. 2000. *The Great Divergence.* Princeton, NJ: Princeton University Press.

Poulton, C., J. Kydd, S. Wiggins, and A. Dorward. 2006. "State Intervention for Price Stabilization in Africa: Can It Work?" *Food Policy* 31: 342–56.

Poulton, C., G. Tyler, P. Hazell, A. Dorward, J. Kydd, and M. Stockbridge. 2008. "All-Africa Review of Experiences with Commercial Agriculture. Lessons from Success and Failure." Background paper for the Competitive Commercial Agriculture in SSA. World Bank, Washington, DC.

Pritchett, L. 2006. *Let Their People Come—Breaking the Gridlock on Global Labor Mobility.* Washington, DC: Center for Global Development.

Puricelli, S. 2010. *El movimiento El campo no aguanta más. Auge, contradicciones y declive (México 2002–2004).* México, DF: Plaza y Valdés, 248 p.

Quesnel, A., and A. del Rey. 2005. "La construcción de una economía familiar de archipiélago. Movilidad y recomposición de las relaciones intergeneracionales en el medio rural mexicano." *Estudios Demográficos y Urbanos* 20, 2 (59): 197–228.

Radelet, S. 2010. *Emerging Africa: How 17 Countries Are Leading the Way.* Washington, DC: Center for Global Development.

Ranis, G., and F. Stewart. 1999. "V-Goods and the Role of the Urban Informal Sector in Development." *Economic Development and Cultural Change* 47 (2): 259–88.

Ratha, D., and W. Shaw. 2007. *South-South Migration and Remittances.* Washington, DC: World Bank, Development Prospect Group, 38 p.

Ravallion, M., G. Datt, and D. van de Walle. 1991. "Quantifying Absolute Poverty in the Developing World." *Review of Income and Wealth* 37: 345–61.

Reardon, T., J. Berdegué, C. Barret, and K. Stamoulis. 2007. "Household Income Diversification into Rural Nonfarm Activities." In *Transforming the Rural Nonfarm Economy,* ed. S. Haggblade, P. Hazell, and T. Reardon, 115–140.

Reardon, T., J. Berdegue, and G. Escobar. 2001. "Rural Nonfarm Employment and Incomes in Latin America: Overview and Policy Implications." *World Development* 29 (3): 395–409.

Reardon, T., and J. Huang. 2008. "Keys to Inclusion of Small-Scale Producers in Dynamic Markets." Synthesis report—meso-study: Meso-Level Restructuring of the Food Industry in Developing Countries, Regoverning Markets Programme.

Reardon, T., and C. P. Timmer. 2007. "Transformation of Markets for Agricultural Output. In Developing Countries Since 1950: How Has Thinking Changed?" In *Handbook of Agricultural Economics,* ed. R. Evenson and P. Pingali, 2087–855. Amsterdam: Elsevier.

Rello F., and M. Morales. 2002, "The Rural Non-Farm Economy and Farm/Non-Farm Linkages in Querétaro, Mexico." In *Promoting Farm/Non-Farm Linkages for Rural Development. Case Studies from Africa and Latin America,* ed. B. Davis et al., 61–95.

Republic of Kenya. 2005. *Nakuru District Strategic Plan 2005–2010.* Nairobi: National Coordinating Agency for Population and Development.

Rist, G. 1996. *Le développement. Histoire d'une croyance occidentale.* Paris: Presses de Sciences Po.

Rolland, J.-P., and A. Alpha. 2010. *Etude sur la cohérence des politiques commerciales en Afrique de l'Ouest.* Paris: AFD–Nogent-sur-Marne–GRET.

Rygiel, P. 2007. *Le temps des migrations blanches. Migrer en Occident (1850–1950).* Paris: Aux Lieux d'être, 208 p.

Sadoulet, E., A. de Janvry, and B. Davis. 2001. "Cash Transfer Programs with Income Multipliers: PROCAMPO in Mexico." *World Development* 29 (6): 1043–56.

SAGARPA (Secretaría de Agricultura, Ganadería, Desarrollo Rural, Pesca y Alimentación). 2007. *Situación actual y perspectivas del maíz en México, 1996–2012.* SIAP. México, DF: SAGARPA, 208 p.

Sala-i-Martin, X., and M. Pinkovskiy. 2010. "African Poverty Is Falling . . . Much Faster Than You Think!" Working Paper 15775, National Bureau of Economic Research, Cambridge, MA.

Sánchez Albarrán, A. 2007. *El Campo no aguanta más.* México, DF: Universidad Autónoma Metropolitana, Unidad Azcapotzalco, 312 p.

Satterthwaite, D., and C. Tacoli. 2003. "The Urban Part of Rural Development: The Role of Small and Intermediate Urban Centres in Rural and Regional Development and Poverty Reduction." Human Settlements Working Paper Series No. 9, International Institute for Environment and Development, London.

Schwentesius, R., and M. A. Gomez. 2002. "Supermarkets in Mexico: Impacts on Horticulture Systems." Development Policy Review 20 (4): 487–502.

Simler, K., and N. Dudwick. 2010. "Urbanization and Rural-Urban Welfare Inequalities." Draft report, World Bank, Washington, DC.

Stern, N. 2007. The Stern Review on the Economics of Climate Change. New York: Cambridge University Press, 712 p.

Stiglitz, J. E. 1998. "Towards a New Paradigm for Development: Strategies, Policies and Process." 9th Raul Prebisch Lecture, UNCTAD, Geneva, October 19.

Timmer, C. P. 1988. "The Agricultural Transformation." In Handbook of Development Economics, ed. H. Chenery and T. N. Srinivasan. Vol. 1. Amsterdam: North Holland.

_____. 1989. "Food Price Policy: The Rationale for Government Intervention." Food Policy 14 (1): 17–42.

_____. 2009. A World without Agriculture: The Structural Transformation in Historical Perspective. Washington, DC: The American Enterprise Institute Press, 83 p.

_____. 2010. "Reflections on Food Crises Past." Food Policy (35): 1–11.

Timmer, C. P., and S. Akkus. 2008. "The Structural Transformation as a Pathway out of Poverty: Analytics, Empirics and Politics." Working Paper No. 150, Center for Global Development, Washington, DC.

Todaro, M. P. 1971. "Income Expectations, Rural-Urban Expectations and Employment in Africa." International Labour Review 104 (5): 387–413.

Toulmin, C., and B. Guèye. 2003. "Transformations in West African Agriculture and the Role of Family Farms." Issue Paper No. 123, International Institute for Environment and Development, London, 84 p.

UNCTAD (United Nations Conference on Trade and Development). 2006. Developing Productive Capacities. Report on the Least Developed Countries. New York and Geneva: UNCTAD.

UNECA (United Nations Economic Commission for Africa). 2011. Governing Development in Africa: The Role of the State in Economic Transformation. Economic Report on Africa 2011. Addis Ababa, Ethiopia: UNECA.

UN-Habitat (United Nations Human Settlements Programme). 2003. The Challenge of the Slums: Global Report on Human Settlements. Nairobi: UN-Habitat.

UNIDO (United Nations Industrial Development Organization). 2008. Breaking In and Moving UP: New Industrial Challenges for the Bottom Billion and the Middle-Income Countries. Industrial Development Report 2009. Vienna: UNIDO.

United Nations. 2010. The Global Partnership for Development at a Critical Juncture. MDG Gap Task Force Report 2010. New York: United Nations, 80 p.

UNRISD (United Nations Research Institute for Social Development). 2010. Combating Poverty and Inequality. Structural Change, Social Policy and Politics. Geneva: UNRISD, 360 p.

Van Buren, M. 1996. "Rethinking the Vertical Archipelago: Ethnicity, Exchange, and History in the South Central Andes." *American Anthropologist* 98 (2): 338–51.

Veltz, P. 1996. *Mondialisation, villes et territoires–L'économie d'archipel.* Paris: PUF, 288 p.

Viard, J. 1998. *La Société d'archipel ou les territoires du village global.* La Tour-d'Aigues: Editions de l'Aube, 126 p.

Vorley, B. 2003. *Food, Inc. Corporate Concentration from Farm to Consumer.* London: UK Food Group, 89 p.

Vorley, B., A. Fearne, and D. Ray. 2007. *Regoverning Markets: A Place for Small-Scale Producers in Modern Agrifood Chains?* Aldershot, UK: International Institute for Environment and Development—Gower, 220 p.

Wallerstein, I. 1989. *The Modern World-System.* 3 volumes. San Diego, CA: Academic Press.

Webber, C. M., and P. Labaste. 2010. *Building Competitiveness in Africa's Agriculture. A Guide to Value Chain Concepts and Applications.* Washington, DC: World Bank.

Wiggins, S. 2009. "Can the Smallholder Model Deliver Poverty Reduction and Food Security for a Rapidly Growing Population in Africa?" FAO Expert Meeting on How to Feed the World in 2050. ODI—FAO, Rome, June 24–26, 2009.

Wiggins, S., and J. R. Davis. 2003. *Types of RNFE activities and Their Returns: Framework and Findings.* NRI Report 2754. Natural Resources Institute; DFID; Washington, DC: World Bank.

Winters, L. A., N. McCulloch, and A. McKay. 2004. "Trade Liberalization and Poverty: The Evidence So Far?" *Journal of Economic Literature* XLII (March): 72–115.

Winters, L. A., T. L. Walmsley, W. Zhen Kun, and R. Grynberg. 2003. "Liberalising Temporary Movement of Natural Persons: An Agenda for the Development Round." *World Economy* (26): 1137–61.

Wise, T. A. 2009. "Agricultural Dumping under NAFTA: Estimating the Costs of U.S. Agricultural Policies to Mexican Producers." Global Development and Environment Institute, Working Paper 09-08, Tufts University, Medford, MA. 38 p.

Wodon, Q., V. Briand, P. Labaste, K. Nouve, and Y. Sangho. 2005. *Cotton and Poverty in Mali.* Washington, DC: World Bank.

World Bank. 2005. *Pro-poor Growth. Country Experiences in the 1990s.* Washington, DC: World Bank.

_____. 2007. *Agriculture for Development.* World Development Report 2008. Washington, DC: World Bank.

_____. 2008a. *Reshaping Economic Geography.* World Development Report 2009. Washington, DC: World Bank.

_____. 2008b. *Regional Trade in Food Staples: Prospects for Stimulating Agricultural Growth and Moderating Short-Term Food Security Crises in Eastern and Southern Africa.* Washington, DC: World Bank.

_____. 2009a. *Development and Climate Change.* World Development Report 2010. Washington, DC: World Bank.

_____. 2009b. *Awakening Africa's Sleeping Giant. Prospects for Commercial Agriculture in the Guinea Savannah Zone and Beyond.* Washington, DC: FAO and World Bank, 218 p.

_____. 2009c. *Youth and Employment in Africa: The Potential, the Problem, the Promise.* Africa Development Indicators 2008/09. Washington, DC: World Bank.

_____. 2010a. *Missing Food: The Case of Postharvest Grain Losses in Sub-Saharan Africa.* Washington, DC: NRI, FAO, and World Bank.

_____. 2010b. *Rising Global Interest in Farmland. Can it Yield Sustainable and Equitable Benefits?* Washington, DC: World Bank.

Yunes Naude, A. 2003. "The dismantling of CONASUPO, a Mexican State Trader in Agriculture." *The World Economy* 26: 97–122.

Zahniser, S., and W. Coyle. 2004. *U.S.-Mexico Corn Trade During the NAFTA Era: New Twists to an Old Story.* USDA Outlook, FDS-04D-01. Washington, DC: U.S. Department of Agriculture, 20 p.

Zepeda, E., M. Chemingui, F. Bchir, S. Karingui, C. Onynago, and B. Wanjala. 2009. *The Impact of the Doha Round in Kenya.* Washington, DC: Carnegie Endowment for International Peace, 83 p.

Ziébé R., E. Thys, and R. De Deken. 2005. "Analysis Method of an Animal Production System in Cameroon." *Revue d'Élevage et de Médecine vétérinaire des Pays tropicaux* 58 (3): 159–65.

Index

Boxes, figures, notes, and tables are indicated by b, f, n, and t following the page number.